DATE DUE

JAN 13 1994	
NOV 12 1997	
MAR 27 2004	

DEMCO, INC. 38-2931

Television Acting
and
Directing

A HANDBOOK

Walter K. Kingson

PROFESSOR, TELEVISION-RADIO DIVISION
DEPARTMENT OF THEATER ARTS
UNIVERSITY OF CALIFORNIA AT LOS ANGELES

and

Rome Cowgill

Holt, Rinehart and Winston, Inc.

NEW YORK · CHICAGO · SAN FRANCISCO · TORONTO · LONDON

The use of scripts and plays in this handbook is limited
to production in classroom and noncommercial educa-
tional broadcasts.

Preface

One of the chief problems in most television workshops and in production classes is a lack of scripts. The primary purpose of this book is to meet that need and, at the same time, provide instruction in the fundamentals of production, acting, and directing.

Because we believe that television acting and directing can only be learned by doing, each script is written to develop certain specific skills. The first is a complete shooting script designed to teach the basic elements of direction, camera, and picture composition. The last, an award-winning drama by Christopher Knopf, one of the best writers in television, involves every aspect of acting, directing, and technical skill. In between are scripts ranging from a newscast to an adaptation of a musical.

The last section of the book consists of specific production aids, such as a kit of production requisition forms, a sample of a marked script, instructions for preparing title cards, music, illustrations, plans suggesting four ways to design the set for one of the scripts, illustrations of studio hand signals, and other aids for the student-director.

We wish to thank William Bluem, Morton Miller, and Darrell Ross for their helpful comments; Jon Dahlstrom, Rachelle Dubin, and Robert Corrigan for their illustrations, and Serena Wade and Nancy Sammons for their clerical assistance above and beyond the call of duty.

W. K. K.
R. C. K.

Los Angeles, California
January 1965

Contents

PREFACE   iii

Part One
INTRODUCTION TO TELEVISION PRODUCTION

1	Studio and Control Room	3
2	Camera, Editing, and Composition	7
3	Lighting and Make-up	20

Part Two
SCRIPTS FOR NONDRAMATIC PROGRAMS

4	A First Production	29
5	The Interview	35
6	The Panel Discussion	41
7	The Newscast	47
8	A Choral Program	53

Part Three
ACTING IN AND DIRECTING TELEVISION DRAMA

9	Directing Television Drama	63
10	Elementary Exercises and Scripts	72

Part Four
ADVANCED ACTING AND DIRECTING

	NOTE ON ADVANCED ACTING AND DIRECTING	86
11	*The Frogs*—Aristophanes	87
12	*The Taming of the Shrew*—Shakespeare	101

13   *The Cherry Orchard*—Chekhov   117

14   *A Doll's House*—Ibsen   134

15   *The Molière Story*—Rome Cowgill   153

16   *The Beggar's Opera*—John Gay   177

17   *Interrogation*—Christopher Knopf   188

Part Five
PRODUCTION AIDS

A Production Kit   243

Audition Copy   259

Marking the Script   271

Timing the Program   276

Hand Signals for Television Floor Managers   277

Preparing Title Cards   281

Sets for *The Beggar's Opera*   282

Music for *The Beggar's Opera*   288

Glossary   293

INDEX   297

PART ONE

Introduction
to Television Production

Studio and Control Room

TELEVISION, like theater, motion pictures, and radio, is concerned with presenting a program to an audience. Each medium requires its own special equipment to project its story to the viewer or listener. All are similar in that the main factor in making a production artistically effective is not expensive equipment and elaborate facilities but creative imagination. However, in television, there are so many gadgets and pieces of electronic apparatus involved in merely getting the physical program before an audience, that frequently it is easy to lose sight of the fact that what is most important is the total impact of the idea behind the program. Without this motivating theme a production cannot succeed.

Nevertheless, every craft has its tools and the artist must learn to use his tools well for maximum effectiveness. Let us take various elements of television production and examine them one by one.

The Studio

The three desirable requirements for a television studio are area, height, and soundproofing. Ample area allows for more than one set, for camera mobility, special effects such as a rear projection screen, and for accessible storage and shop space. Adequate height[1] allows for good overhead lighting with lighting instruments mounted on pipe grids or tracks. A high studio also makes it possible to take dramatic overhead shots with cameras mounted on a crane or catwalk. As for soundproofing some kind of acoustical treatment is necessary to break up reflected sound waves and to prevent voices from sounding as if they are being spoken in a barn. Soundproofing also serves the obvious function of keeping extraneous noise from the studio during production. The floor of the studio, particularly, should be smooth, level, and stable, because cameras must move easily and operate undisturbed by any kind of floor vibration.

In Hollywood, television and motion picture sound stages occupy entire city blocks. On the Warner Brothers lot, for example, there are twenty-one vast stages; one measures 72 feet from floor level to rafters, and another extends over an area of 37,000 square feet. But few of you will have to be concerned about the special prob-

---

[1] CBS studios at Television City in Hollywood are 40 feet high, but half this height is very satisfactory for most television production. It is difficult to light a set effectively in a room less than 12 feet high.

lems involved with studios of these vast dimensions. You will probably be working in anything from a moderate-sized television studio (30 by 50 feet) to a converted barracks building.

This does not mean that your production need be any less exciting or dramatic than a Hollywood spectacular, but only that you will have to adjust the physical scope of your production to the space available. It also means that you must be resourceful beyond the requirements of many professional situations in which the director simply calls on the expert to provide the equipment or special effect required for a scene. You will have to devise your own special effects, and plan your production meticulously in advance on paper, in order to turn your studio limitations to advantage. No training could be better for you as an aspiring professional who someday will have a well-equipped studio to command. You will then appreciate the potential of this studio for telling a story with the fullest dramatic effectiveness, and realize that the size of your studio is not nearly as important as the significance of your story.

Whatever its size or shape, your studio is the theater in which you work. Many of the materials used for sets are the same as the materials employed in stage production; some have been borrowed from motion pictures, and many others were developed or modified to fit the specific needs of television.

A basic item is the cyclorama—made of ordinary butcher paper, cloth, plywood, or plasterboard—that extends around one end of the studio with generous wings on both sides Properly lighted, this can serve as a background for some of your scenes, and as an undefined backdrop for exterior sets. Equally handy is a floor-to-ceiling curtain hung from a track. Stretched tightly, it serves as a cyclorama; it also can be used as an additional drape background for many of your simple scenes.

When constructing television sets bear in mind the characteristics of the medium. First of all, since the audience sees only as much as you want it to see, you can build only portions of sets—single walls, corners, or partial façades—which

the audience will assume to be complete structures. Television is an intimate medium, and when sets are seen in close-up shots they must not destroy the illusion of reality. Color, too, must be considered; not for the way it appears to your eye, but with regard for the shade of gray it will register on the monochrome television screen.[2]

To make them look like the genuine article flats should be constructed of light, rigid composition material or plywood nailed to a frame made of 1– by 3–inch stock. Flats are usually built in units 2 to 4 feet wide, as standard stock comes in 4–foot widths. A desirable height is 10 feet, although 8 feet (the height of most rooms) will serve.

There are different methods for hanging flats in a television studio. Angle supports are attached to the flats by "C" clamps, but in most cases the supports cannot be nailed to the tile or concrete floor and must be secured by the use of lead weights. Sometimes additional supports are nailed to beams above the grid.

Whatever the height, or however you hang the flat, use regular lightweight doors securely mounted on sturdy hinges. A well-constructed door flat is as standard an item in a television studio as a sound-effects door in radio. Windows should be framed, as in regular house construction.

Considering that the studio is a fixed maximum area in which you will work with each production, you may want to have a basic floor plan stenciled or printed with lines ruled in $\frac{1}{2}$– or $\frac{1}{4}$–inch squares. If you use the scale of $\frac{1}{4}$–inch equals one foot, then the standard sheet of $8\frac{1}{2}$– by 11–inch paper will equal a playing area of 34 by 44 feet. Scale models of standard flats are also helpful in working out the arrangement of your set in a given studio area.

In addition to conventional sets and backdrops, photographic aids are frequently used in the television studio to supply background effects. A familiar piece of equipment is the rear

---

[2] The assumption is that most students will not be working with color cameras.

projector that projects an image onto the rear surface of a translucent screen. Viewed from the front, it provides a still or a moving background for a scene. If your studio is too small, you can reduce the distance required from the rear projector to the screen with properly placed mirrors.

You may do your production with minimal set construction, using impressionistic representations instead of realistic set detail, and substitute covered boxes for chairs and tables, or a single column for a temple. When actual furniture is used, however, you must take into account how it will appear on camera, and not how it looks to the eye. A faded secondhand sofa may be quite satisfactory on the television screen. Whatever props you use, remember that they must be in keeping with the spirit of your production. Above all, keep the set simple and uncluttered, and pleasing to the eye.

The Projection Room

Although it may or may not be physically adjacent to the studio the projection room is in effect an extension of the studio, because from it are fed motion pictures and video tape or slides which have already been produced and require only integration into the production. The film or slide is projected into a television camera which, in turn, sends the picture to a separate film monitor in the control room. A single camera can be used as a pickup for more than one projector. This is achieved with a multiplexer that uses mirrors set at an angle to direct the projected motion picture or slide into the pickup camera.

Some studios use several film projectors and achieve even greater flexibility by mounting their projectors on circular tracks. A projector can then be threaded with film, and moved on the tracks to its precise position in front of the camera where it is locked into place. The average college studio, however, does not have the luxury of too elaborate a projection setup. The complement of equipment probably consists of a 16–millimeter motion picture projector, a slide projector and, possibly, an opaque projector, with a vidicon film chain pickup.

The projection room should also include a 16–millimeter film splicer, film cement, a set of 16–millimeter rewinds, a few empty reels for emergencies, storage space for films and slides, a counter or a window through which a monitor may be seen, and a speaker to hear the audio portion of the production. The projection room, of course, should be connected with the control room on the intercom system for easy transmittal of your cues to the projectionist.

If there is no projection room you can project the film directly onto a screen placed in a darkened area of the studio, picking it up directly from the screen with the vidicon camera. Or, you can make your own portable darkened area in the studio by using a large rectangular box, open at one end to accommodate the film projector and the vidicon camera. The motion picture is projected from the open end of the box onto a beaded screen at the opposite end, and picked up by the vidicon camera placed adjacent to the projector. Even though the repetition rate of the image differs slightly for motion picture film (24 frames per second), and the television camera (30 frames per second), the result is satisfactory for nonbroadcast purposes.[3]

The Control Room

Control rooms differ as widely as studios in their size and arrangement of equipment; but regardless of its design, the purpose of the control room is the same. It is the center through which all elements of your production are channeled and co-ordinated. In it are located the camera control units with which the video engineer adjusts the cameras; camera monitors that allow the director to preview each picture on the cameras before he "takes" the shot; the switching unit with which the technical director switches the preview picture from the camera monitor to the

---

[3] If you are using an image orthicon camera, the black bars will be much more noticeable.

"on-the-air" screen—cutting, fading, or dissolving the picture as the director indicates; an audio console to manipulate the audio portion of the television production; turntables for sound effects and music; an audio monitor, and the tape recorder. A lighting control board may also be located on one side of the control room, although usually it is placed in the studio.

Because it is necessary to assign one person to operate each piece of equipment, the control room is a fairly well-populated place. Space is required for the video control engineer, audio engineer, audio assistant, and technical director —along with the director and assistant director. The control room for a college studio should be larger than the control room for the same size studio in a television station. It must accommodate not only the members of the regular control room crew, but student observers as well. There should be adequate ventilation; also ample counter area for scripts for the director and his assistant, for the technical director, and for the audio and video engineers.

The actual placement of the different units— video controls, sound console, picture and sound monitors—varies from studio to studio, because each director or engineer will have his favorite plan. All will probably agree, however, that it is important for the director and the technical director to work near each other, since the director calls shots that must be executed with split-second accuracy and timing by the technical director. It is equally important that the picture monitors are placed where they can be seen without too much strain on the part of the director, his assistant, and the technical director— ideally, on a line below their eye level. The audio monitor should be placed for comfortable monitoring of sound levels.

With all these separate operations involved in getting a television picture with sound on the air, it is obvious that good communication is of critical importance. This is achieved through the intercom with headsets that can be plugged into a community telephone system for two-way communication among the various members of the studio, the control room crew, and the director. In addition, the director has a "talkback" microphone through which he can address the studio cast and crew directly on the studio loud-speaker.

2

Camera, Editing, and Composition

THE CAMERA is your most important instrument for telling the story, and you must learn to operate it with understanding, skill, and imagination. After you have mastered the basic technical essentials of your camera, and know the potentials and limitations of the lenses, you will soon acquire the knack of thinking in pictures and imagining the story unfolding as action on camera. Of equal importance is that you learn how not to overuse camera shots, cutting frantically from one to the other without motivation or purpose.

The Camera

The conventional camera in most television stations in the United States is the image orthicon. The "IO" camera is a highly sensitive instrument, and has the advantage of delivering a clear picture with a minimum of lighting. It may be either a 3–inch or a 4½–inch tube, which is even more sensitive and delivers a remarkably sharp picture. For instructional purposes, however, its initial and maintenance costs are high. Most universities use vidicon cameras; these are much less expensive, and require greater light intensity for an adequate picture. Still other

classes use mock-up cameras. Although these may not provide the total production experience of the electronic camera, they are highly useful as a device in helping the student to understand the field of view and perspective of the various lenses. Even when live cameras are available, a mock-up camera is especially helpful to a novice in rehearsals. He can go through planning and production routines in a rehearsal room just as if he were working with electronic equipment, without tying up valuable studio space.

For easy maneuvering from one position to another in the studio, the television camera is placed on a camera mount. The mount may be a tripod on wheels, or a mobile pedestal, or a boom dolly. The tripod has the advantage of being inexpensive and light, and can be quickly transported for remote pickups. In the studio it does not have the stability of the heavier mobile pedestal which, because of its weight can be dollied forward and back more smoothly. The pedestal has the advantage of synchronous steering that allows all the wheels to turn as one. In addition, the camera mounted on a pedestal can be easily raised or lowered by means of pneumatic, or hand-operated mechanism. The boom dolly makes it possible to raise the camera for overhead shots, but takes up a good deal of studio space. And because of its high cost, the boom dolly is not usually standard equipment in a smaller studio.

The camera itself rests on a friction or "cradle" head. The friction head might be compared with the neck of the camera which enables it to look from side to side, or up and down. Together, the pedestal and the friction head are two elements of the television camera that make it an instrument of remarkable flexibility for telling your story.

CAMERA LENSES

While you are making an effort to learn and understand everything you can about the inner workings of the camera, as a director, you will be concerned specifically with camera lenses. Lenses are mounted on the lens turret in front of the camera and manipulated by rotating the turret. The lens that is in position directly in front of the camera pickup tube is known as the "take" lens. Most conventional turrets accommodate four lenses, and each serves a particular function. In a professional production the director merely calls for the kind of picture he wants, and the cameraman selects the lens best suited for the shot. However, in your production you will want to be thoroughly acquainted with the potential of each lens.

Lenses are described in terms of their focal length, and on vidicon cameras are measured in inches. Lenses on image orthicon cameras are described in millimeters, with all lenses over 135–millimeter usually labelled in inches.[1] Thus a typical vidicon camera turret with four lenses would probably include the following: a ½–inch lens, a 1–inch lens, a 2–inch lens, and a 3–inch lens.[2] These cannot be compared precisely with image orthicon lenses and are best described

in general terms as wide-angle, medium, and close-up lenses. Vidicon lenses are the same as those on a 16–millimeter motion picture camera. Image orthicon lenses, on the other hand, can be interchanged with those on a 35-millimeter motion picture camera.

Generally speaking, lenses are described as short, or wide-angle lenses, and long, or close-up lenses. Because of its scope, the wide-angle lens can serve to orient the viewer by relating a number of elements in a single picture. Therefore, you will usually use it for an "establishing" shot before reducing the picture field by dollying in, or by switching to a longer lens, for a medium or close-up shot of individual items in your picture.

The 1–inch lens on the vidicon camera is the basic lens, and the one you will use most frequently.[3] It is often used on simple one-camera productions in which there is no opportunity for lens changes. With this lens on such a show you can take reasonably wide-angle shots, as well as medium and close-up shots, merely by dollying forward and back. It has the further advantage of not distorting perspective as readily as the longer lenses, unless it is used in too close proximity to the subject.

The 2– and 3–inch lenses are close-up lenses used in showing intimate detail of an object even though the camera position is some distance away.[4] They are especially helpful when it is difficult to get near the object for a close-up with one of the other lenses. On the other hand, it is difficult to dolly when you are using a close-up lens as every minute movement of the camera is magnified.

There are additional lenses that can change their focal length without losing focus. The zoom lens is familiar in televising outdoor sports where it is important to move up to the action without the benefit of a dolly. In the studio, some programs are shot with a single camera using a

[1] All GPL (General Precision Laboratories) lenses are measured in inches. Lenses on vidicon cameras are described in inches.

[2] A typical image orthicon turret with four lenses would include a 50–millimeter (or 35–millimeter) lens, a 90–millimeter lens, a 135–millimeter lens, and an 8–inch lens.

[3] The 90–millimeter lens is the basic lens on the image orthicon camera.

[4] The 135–millimeter and 8–inch lenses are the close-up lenses on the image orthicon camera.

zoom lens, shooting the entire program with wide, medium, and close-up shots. The zoom also can provide shocking dramatic impact, zeroing in from wide-angle to close-up shots. It can be used effectively in *superimposing* titles, sometimes zooming in with a *spiral pan*[5] for a bizarre effect, and it is especially useful when employed with still pictures to give movement to a static scene. However, for a given adjustment of the zoom lens the distance between the subject and the camera must remain the same, plus or minus the depth of field. Good zoom lenses are expensive. But even if they are available to you, try to avoid the temptation of overusing them as a gimmick. They should be used with discretion, saved for special effects, and not regarded as a substitute for the conventional dolly shot.

DEPTH OF FIELD

Depth of field, in stage terms, is the area bounded by lines upstage and downstage beyond which the performer cannot walk without going out of focus. In other words, it is the distance between a point nearest to the lens and a point farthest from the lens that is in sharp focus. In blocking the movements of actors it is important to know the depth of field of each lens, and the various ways in which a lens can be extended and controlled. The depth of field is affected by three factors:

1. *The F–stop* (the iris or diaphragm) allows more or less light into the camera. Other factors being constant—the larger the F–stop, the smaller the depth of field.
2. *The distance between the camera and the subject.* Other factors being constant—the farther the camera is from the subject, the greater the depth of field.
3. *The focal length of the lens.* Other factors being constant—the shorter the focal length of the lens, the greater the depth of field.

For example, if you are taking a long shot of a scene (iris opening set at F2.8), using a 1–inch

lens on the vidicon camera, you will have considerable depth of field. If you open the F–stop to F1.9 you will decrease the depth of field, because the iris opening will be larger.[6] Similarly, if you dolly in for a medium shot with the same lens the depth of field will be decreased, because you will have decreased the distance between the camera and the subject. And if you use a 2–inch lens from the same position as you use the 1–inch lens, in addition to getting a tighter shot you will also decrease the depth of field, because a lens with a longer focal length reduces the depth of field.

CAMERA POSITION

You will tell the audience what is going on in your production through lens selection, stationary camera position, camera movement, and picture editing. We have already roughly discussed lenses and their characteristics. But the selection of your lens is closely tied in with the position of your camera. In general, stationary camera positions are divided into long shots, medium shots, and close-ups,[7] although these are flexible terms. The extent of detail in each type of shot naturally will vary, depending on the lens used. A 3–inch lens on a vidicon camera, for example, can take a close-up from the same position as a 1–inch lens used for a wide-angle shot that includes considerable detail of the set. The content of the picture depends on the shot the director calls. A ½–inch long shot might frame a wall of library books and a man reading a book at a desk. If the director calls for a waist shot of the man, the cameraman will change lenses and, without changing his camera position appreciably, frame only the man, excluding the surrounding detail.

Because of its small screen, television has been

---

[5] A pan shot executed as a combination tilt and pan.

[6] The student will note the inverse relationship between the size of the iris opening and the F–stop number. The larger the opening, the smaller the F–stop number. For normal studio lighting conditions vidicon lenses are usually set at F2.8.

[7] Script abbreviations are written as "LS," "MS," and "CU."

called the medium of the close-up. Close-ups, with their intimate reflections of a character's thoughts and emotions, are usually the most interesting shots in your story. However, wide-angle and medium shots have their important places too—particularly in orienting the viewer, and in advancing the action of the script.

The camera, approximating the eyes of the audience, is continually engaged in selecting and eliminating the detail of a picture as dictated by dialogue and action. Also, the close-up is a response to the natural curiosity of the audience, and we are familiar with the use of a close-up to satisfy the desire for a closer look at an object. The dramatic possibilities of close-ups, utilizing the values of pace and rhythm in cutting—perhaps noting an object hidden from the performer, but visible to the audience to create suspense—are the artistic uses inherent in the television camera for you, as a director, to explore.

The close-up, with its selective emphasis on detail, must be used with great care and only when the logic of the shot sequence demands it. This logic may not be long in coming before you sense the impulse to look more closely at a person, or an object, and understand that you are merely reflecting the same impulse that is experienced by the audience. Overuse of the close-up will result in irrelevant or intrusive details—as in a tight shot of a newscaster's face that calls the attention of the audience to the irregularity of his teeth, or the mole on his face. Furthermore, good close-ups do not happen by themselves. Always plan them carefully in advance for precise dimensions, effective lighting, and length of exposure.

CAMERA MOVEMENT

The long, medium, and close-up shots are general terms describing the stationary positions of the camera.[8] From these positions you can achieve various effects by moving the camera in a number of ways. You may *pan* to right or left; *tilt* up or down; *dolly* in or back; *truck* to right or left, or *follow* the action on the set.

Again, each of these camera movements has its own logic. For example, if a performer rises from a sitting position on a sofa, you may have to *tilt up* to keep his head from going out of the top of the frame. For more dramatic purposes you may tilt up to frame a performer, and create the impression of a dominant figure towering over others at a lower level in the picture, when you wish to achieve unusual effects.

The *pan* (derived from the word panorama) is used to scan a scene from right to left, or in reverse, with the idea of showing the audience the field of action or relate various elements of the scene to each other. Such a scanning movement also serves to guide the viewer's eye to a specific object, or to a person in a scene, much as a close-up does following a wide-angle or medium shot. Or, a pan shot might be used to follow a performer walking across the set. In a shot of this kind it is important to time the pan so that the camera does not seem to be following the performer in an effort to catch up with him. Direct your cameraman to anticipate the performer's movement and *lead with the camera*. Here, as in all on-camera movement, the television performer must move more slowly than he would on stage to *appear* to be moving at a normal rate, and allow for the execution of a good pan shot.

If, instead of panning with a performer as he crosses the stage, you move the camera pedestal laterally and parallel to him as he walks it is called a *trucking* shot. Thus you may instruct your cameraman to *truck* right, or *truck* left, to follow an officer reviewing a line of troops. On the other hand, if you wish to follow a circle of children playing games, the cameraman may have to *truck right*, then *arc* to follow the ac-

---

[8] Shots describing the proportion of the performer to be framed are conventionally labeled *full shot* (entire figure); *knee shot* (from knee to top of head); *waist shot* (from waist to top of head); *shoulder shot* (from shoulder to head); *big close-up* (close-up of head). To *tighten* a shot is to dolly in more closely. One person in a picture is a *one-shot*; two persons in a frame is a *two-shot*, and so on.

tion, describing a quarter-circle with the camera pedestal.

The *dolly* shot (dolly in) is most frequently used to follow a long, establishing wide-angle shot to take the audience in for a more intimate view of the picture. The procedure can be reversed (dolly back) in either nondramatic or dramatic sequences. A newscaster may have a guest seated near him but out of the close-up frame. He gives a general introduction, and turns his head to welcome the guest as the camera dollies back to include both in a two-shot. Like a slow pan, a good dolly shot can create suspense. For example, imagine a close-up of a hand dialing the combination of a safe, followed by a dolly back to a medium shot of a man opening the door of a safe in an office. You may dolly in straight up to an object, or performer, or you may dolly at an angle—tilting up or down as you execute the movement. But even with a heavy camera pedestal, or a crane mount with a dollyman, a dolly shot should be rehearsed for smoothness and accuracy. With a light camera mount, and vidicon cameras and dangling camera cables, even more care and practice are required before a dolly shot can be executed without distracting the viewer by a jiggling camera ending up with a badly framed picture. The cameraman must develop skill in keeping his lens in focus as he dollies forward and back, and in stopping precisely at the prearranged spot. Sometimes it is helpful to draw a chalk line, or use masking tape on the floor to indicate the exact distance of dolly movements.

Editing

Editing in television production is the process of relating one shot to another for narrative clarity or dramatic effect. Editing is an art, with a distinguished history in the older field of motion pictures, and the editor is often responsible for the success of a film. Brilliant editing, like any art, requires special talent; competent editing can be learned by any sensitive person.

In motion picture production the director usually "covers" every shot from many angles and camera positions, often shooting five to ten times as much footage as is needed, and the editor selects the most effective shots. In many instances the motion picture cutter cuts the film to conform to the script, and then the editor takes over. Ideally, the film is previewed by an audience. Then, guided by audience reaction to various scenes, the editor revises many of the shot sequences—shifting, juxtaposing, using film that has been discarded, substituting close-ups or long shots, or inserting titles—to achieve the audience reaction desired. Audience-testing before the major production is formally brought out is a familiar procedure in the theater when a play is first presented in a community, and then revised and doctored before it opens on Broadway.[9] This suggests that, ideally, a director should be able to preview his show with an audience before the final on-the-air production to see whether certain scenes are making the impression he intended. It is common practice with a number of comedy shows to present the dress rehearsal before an audience for a rough test of laugh lines, prior to going on the air.

In motion pictures, the editor has ample time for reflection in the editing room and a variety of film footage from which to choose the right shot. In live television the director must preplan every one of his shots before the production begins. His editing decisions must be made in advance.

Live television further differs from films in that the editing process is instantaneous. The preview screen of each camera allows the director to set the shot before "taking" it, but the decision he makes is final and cannot be corrected later in the editing room.

Good television editing calls for exacting preplanning of all shots and complete mastery of the production from the control room. All this

[9] An interesting account of this process is recorded in the correspondence between writer Archibald MacLeish, and Elia Kazan, in connection with the production of "J. B." in its journey from college production to Broadway. ("The Staging of a Play," *Esquire*, 51:144–158, May 1959.)

is not learned overnight. Only after considerable practice will you become skilled in the logic of camera positions and movements, and be able to use them as readily as another language. Remember, that just as you must clarify in your own mind what you want to say before you speak, you must be equally clear about a scene before you can portray it in pictures.

The disciplines of live television production are applicable to the production of programs on video tape. It is true that tape is unlike a live program in that it can be edited before the broadcast; but tape editing is tedious, and the director should try to hold down the need for such editing by taping a program with as few errors as possible. For the student it is bad practice to use tape as a crutch, taking advantage of the fact that production errors can always be corrected by editing or by repeating the entire production. The approach, "If it's a bad 'take' we can always do it over again," will hardly lead to effective production discipline. Besides, with such an attitude the cast tends to relax and let down on the opening-night tension that always gives a special edge to a performance. Good procedure suggests that a director should be limited to two "takes" of his show, and allowed to edit a minimum number of shots or sequences.

Tape offers other temptations which the director should avoid, and a principal one is the temptation to use tape as film—stopping the production at the end of each sequence, relighting the various segments of the drama, and repeating each unit until it is satisfactory. With an unlimited budget, this might be possible; but it is much better practice to use tape more nearly as a live production, capturing the spontaneity and immediacy of a program. Again, preplanning of all shots is the watchword.

Editing television pictures in a production is achieved by one or more of the following methods: the *cut,* the *fade,* the *dissolve,* the *superimposure.* And just as each lens and camera position serves its special function, each device for changing the picture also has its particular logic in telling your story.

The *cut* is the most familiar editing device in films and in television. At its best, it brings to your audience all the qualities that are a part of well-directed plays and motion pictures—clarity, variety, tempo and rhythm, contrast, climax. Precise cutting in a live production comes only with practice. There are, however, a few pointers that can be helpful to the novice.

1. If a performer is facing the camera with the intention of addressing the audience on cue from the floor manager, always cue the performer *before* cueing his camera—with the second cue following immediately on the heels of the first. The director says, "Cue talent, take one" in one breath. The floor manager points to the taking camera. On receiving his cue, the performer takes a natural breath before beginning. In this way, the camera can catch the performer just as he begins to speak.
2. Cut to action rather than to a still shot, with action beginning after the cut. This gives the impression that you are entering a scene where action is in progress and contributes to visual continuity.
3. In cutting to a reaction shot, cut just *before* the reaction to get the full impact of the shot.
4. Never cut to a reaction just before the first performer delivers a punch line or a phrase. This will kill the effect of the line.
5. Cut at suitable breaks in dialogue, but do not feel that it is necessary to cut every time a different performer speaks unless it is important to identify the new voice. In a dialogue scene, or in an interview where there are frequent exchanges between two persons, it is often more effective to get reaction shots with the second voice coming from off screen.
6. Do not overuse the cut without regard for the picture values involved. Indiscriminate cutting gives an over-all jumpy effect, and is irritating to the audience.

There are no rules about how long you should hold a shot before cutting to another. It depends on what the shot contains, and on what the performer is saying. For example, Jack Benny may come out on stage in a long shot and, as he begins to talk, the director will cut to a waist shot and hold it until Mr. Benny completes a joke and introduces a guest. The important thing to remember is not to cut to another shot unless it is motivated and provides good visual continuity.

The *fade* is the gradual transition from a black screen to a visible picture, and is achieved by moving the fader bar on the switcher up or down. The *fade in* is conventionally used at the beginning of a program to introduce the opening sequence, and "fade to black" is a familiar cue for the end of a production. Often, however, you may wish to *fade to black* after a sequence in the middle of a show, using the device to indicate a transition in time or location, and follow by a *fade in* after a passage of time into the new scene. Because it is easier to edit video tape on frames that have been faded to black, this device is frequently used in taped productions.

The *dissolve* is achieved by fading out the on-screen picture as the incoming picture is faded in. It can be used for a stream-of-consciousness narration that dissolves from a close-up of the actor's face to the scene being described. It is also commonly used as a traditional device for transition from one scene to another.

For example, two men are shown riding in a military supply truck; one is driving, the other is studying a map and following their route with his finger. The picture dissolves from a close-up of the finger to a hand holding a pencil and following a similar map, then widens to include a headquarters office with several officers watching their leader as he points out and describes the progress of the supply truck. The dissolve may also maintain an extended and varied action over a period of time to create the impression of continuous flow—as in a dance sequence, or in a musical presentation. When you use two identically shaped objects, dissolving from one to the other for magical or surprise effects, it is called a *matched dissolve*. A dissolve may be executed at different rates of speed, depending on its purpose. However, using a fast dissolve in place of a simple cut will only confuse the audience. As in other camera techniques, be guided by the logic and motivation of your shot sequence.

A *superimposure* is a device that requires the use of two cameras for additional picture information or special effect. You may wish merely to "super" a printed name below the image of a person who appears on the screen; or, you may run an entire list of credits at the opening or closing of your production over a pictorial or action sequence. For superimposing titles be sure to use dark cards with light lettering. If you use a light background, your picture will be lightened when the *super* is faded in. If you superimpose one image over another, take care to juxtapose the elements of each picture in such a way that they do not conflict with each other. The *super* may be cut into the picture sharply, or faded in, depending on the effect you wish to achieve.

Picture Composition

At its simplest, composition is the arrangement of objects in a picture. In good composition objects are so arranged that the picture is clear, pleasing to look at, and the viewer's eye is directed to the important elements of the scene—the center of interest. In bad composition the picture may be too cluttered for clarity, with performers and objects seemingly stuck in front of cameras rather than meaningfully positioned, and with nothing arranged to direct the viewer's eye.

FRAMING

The frame of a television shot is actually only the outer edges of the picture as it is seen on the home television screen. Therefore, it is essential for the director to remember that the picture he sees on the control room monitor must show a larger area than the picture that reaches the home screen. In a close-up, for example, if a performer's head almost touches the top edge of the studio monitor screen, it will appear to have been chopped off on the home screen. This is one reason why many directors prefer to avoid "tight" shots—shots which crowd the edges of the frame—and work for "loose" shots which leave ample space around the object or objects within the frame. As director, you will frequently ask your cameramen to tighten or loosen a shot. An exception to this is the deliberate use of the BCU—big close-up—in which attention is directed to a portion of the performer's face, usually to the eyes, nose, and mouth. The difference between this shot and a chopped off shot is that in the BCU there is a dramatic reason for closing in on the eyes, nose, and mouth: something is being said or reacted to with great emotional impact.

Big close-up

BALANCE

In a well-balanced composition, no one area seems to overbalance another. For example, a shot of a single performer usually has him cen-

Simple one-shot properly framed with adequate head room

tered within the frame looking toward the camera, with equal space on either side. However, balance is affected not only by objects within the picture, but also by objects implied as within the picture—but outside the viewer's vision. If a single performer is shown in profile looking at

Off-screen object balancing one-shot

something off-screen, it is better to frame him with less space behind his head, and more in the direction toward which he is looking; the unseen object is balancing the picture.

Again, if a single performer is holding an object in his hand up and away from his body, the picture will be better balanced if he is positioned slightly to one side of the screen. Or, if an object is prominent in the background on, say, the right side of the picture, a single performer should be positioned toward the left to achieve balance.

On-screen object balancing one-shot

Balance, in other words, is not a rigidly even distribution of objects. Two performers talking face to face, each with the same amount of space behind his head, are two equal, well-balanced units—but make an uninteresting picture. If they

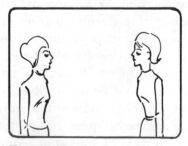

Too rigid and badly spaced

Over-shoulder shot

are angled, so that one is seen over the shoulder of the other, their figures blend into one unit with an interesting and pleasing form.

To achieve a satisfactory two-shot, it is sometimes necessary to "cheat." That is, figures are positioned in a manner which would not be normal but which looks natural. For example, two performers apparently face to face are actually profiled toward the camera.

Cheating

All group shots require careful positioning. Without being "arty" about it always remember the need for television scenes to look natural, and try to position performers and objects into one or two pleasing units. In grouping units, the various forms of the triangle are usually considered to be the simplest and most effective.

Conventional triangle shot

In all picture composition, light is a factor in balance. If you look at any good painting or drawing you will see how much the lighting of an object affects its importance in relation to other objects. In television production your lighting efforts have to be concentrated primarily on clarity of the picture and on your composition or arrangement of objects. Always remember that the viewer's eye is directed toward any object lighted more brilliantly than other objects.

Light in composition

COMPOSITION IN DEPTH

To create a feeling of depth in television picture composition, plan a definite foreground, middle ground, and background. First, of course, you must block your movement with depth-staging in mind. If you block lateral movement it will be far more difficult to compose a picture in depth without being tricky and, possibly, detracting from the impact of the scene. With movement blocked in depth, pictures can be quite easily composed in depth.

On the other hand, if there is no motivation for movement in depth, you can create a feeling of depth through set design. Suppose a segment of a scene shows a man sitting at a desk and writing a letter, his only movement that of his hand, while an off-screen voice tells us that the letter is a threat to someone. If there is a large lamp on the desk, on one side of the picture, it creates a foreground; the man seated at the desk becomes the middle ground, and a flat behind him is the background.

Any large object in the immediate foreground can give a sense of depth, even to a scene shot in a relatively shallow area. Similarly, a sense of in-

Large object creating foreground

creased depth in the background can be achieved through an open archway in a flat that apparently leads to a hall, or to another room suggested by a masking flat. A window, through which is seen a photo mural of sky, or trees, or city buildings, also gives an added sense of depth.

Illusion of depth through photo mural behind window, and open arch with masking flat

Remember too, that you are not composing a single picture seen from only one angle but a series of pictures—juxtaposed, each of which can be seen from several angles. In a chase, for example, a close shot of a terrified man running toward the camera, followed by a long shot of his pursuer, will give a sense of depth. Reverse angle shots also contribute to a sense of depth.

Unusual POV

UNUSUAL EFFECTS

With superimposition, split-screen techniques, and the image inverter, as well as other various technical devices, you can create many unusual effects; but you must always remember that they are effective rather than just tricky only if they are meaningful. For example, the inverted image, which turns the picture upside down, might have some usefulness or meaning in a comedy or in a horror story. But how could it in a panel discussion? Obviously, the latter is an exaggeration; but we hope that it emphasizes the point.

In addition, unusual effects must follow the basic principles of composition by being properly framed, balanced, and lighted. Thus, before you consider using an unusual effect in a shot, you must ask yourself whether the extra time required to produce it will add to the total impact of the program. Any unusual effect that draws attention to itself rather than to the purpose of the scene is self-defeating.

UNUSUAL ANGLES

In composing a picture for television, you have the advantage of being able to show a scene from a position that would not be on normal eye level for the viewer. Some of these shots have become almost cliches: the shot taken, apparently, from behind the dancing flames of the fireplace over which we see a couple seated on a couch; the shot taken from behind the sheriff's spread legs through which we see the slain villain; or, the bird's-eye view, overhead shot in which we see the performers as though we were somehow suspended above them.

Unconventional shot; not the viewers' ordinary POV

There is also the canted shot in which the view of the scene is tilted diagonally—an effect obtained either by tilting the camera, or by shooting the scene from an angled mirror.

Overhead angle shot

Canted shot

The use of unusual angles in composition must be both motivated and judicious. If the emotional impact of a scene can be intensified by an unusual composition of the picture, it is justified. But if an unusual composition is used for itself alone, it is not worth the time and effort involved. A canted shot of an unusual composition may give a scene a momentary jolt of excitement; but even if it is well motivated, it may have to be changed to a more conventional composition within seconds. For example, if you compose a picture in which two performers are seen as though reflected in a lake or in a stream, and then cut to a picture of the two performers seated on the bank of the lake or stream, there should be an emotional or psychological reason for showing them first reflected in the water.

WHAT TO AVOID

We have said it before but we shall say it again: your control room monitor has a larger scanning area than that which viewers receive on their home screens. Therefore, avoid composing a pic-

ture so tightly framed that it may be out of balance and unpleasing on the home screen.

Also, at all times keep your sense of proportion. A picture that seems quite harmonious in the studio may appear ridiculous on the screen. For example, from the control room window, a performer standing in front of the candlestick on the bookshelf may look like a performer standing in front of a candlestick on the bookshelf; but on the screen he may appear to be a performer with a candlestick growing out of his head.

Bad composition; object apparently growing out of performer's head

Space and composition

Never think of space as empty space. In a well-composed picture, space has significance. It can suggest or emphasize psychological relationships. Some are obvious: two shy people tend to keep their distance from each other, whereas two people deeply involved with each other may be—as in an angry quarrel—practically nose to nose. The space between or around people helps us to interpret and understand their relationship.

Similarly, the lonely figure on a deserted road looks lonely because of the space around him. Even though there may be some objects—a wind-blown tree, or a sagging barn—in the distance, they are not there merely to fill up space. Objects

Illusion of height

Cluttered picture

balance the picture, identify the locale or intensify the feeling of barrenness. But there should not be any more objects in the picture than are absolutely essential to create the mood.

The illusion of height is handled in the same way. A man apparently standing on top of a high bridge does not seem to be very high up unless you can see some of the space below him—into which he is probably staring as he ponders desperately whether or not to jump.

Space, then, is a positive factor in the composition of pictures. Use it!

Very much related to the concept of space are cluttered pictures. A cluttered picture has too many objects in it for any one object to be seen or defined clearly. This creates a special problem in television because we shoot pictures from many angles. A picture in which the composition seems excellent from one angle may be confusingly cluttered from another angle.

In television, each picture relates to the one preceding it, and the one which follows it. For example, in a dialogue scene between two people we often see one person as he speaks, then the other person as he speaks, and so on. However, if we see one person in a close shot and the other in a long shot, we assume that they are talking to each other from a great distance. If we see them framed in identical close shots, we assume that they are talking to each other face to face. This, obviously, is the simplest type of physical relationship. However, there can also be an emotional relationship of one picture to another. We see the nose of a revolver as though it were being pointed directly at us, then the body of a man toppling down to the street. We relate these two pictures. And even though all that they spell out is a cliche of violence and death, for the moment *we* faced that revolver, and then saw the result of its action. Television is primarily a close-shot medium, and you can make full use of the emotional impact of related and juxtaposed close shots.

COMPOSING IN ACTION

Although the basic principles of composition always apply in television, as a director, you will frequently be called on to compose on the run. Also, because television is a dynamic medium, you will often compose pictures as action develops. Whenever you have sufficient rehearsal time (which is seldom), you can preplan most of your shots in detail; but only with much practice can you acquire the judgment to make quick esthetic decisions and feel confident that your shots will be effective.

The preceding illustration pictures one possible set for the scene from *The Cherry Orchard,* in Part Four, and the entrance of the leading character, Madame Ranevsky. As an exercise in picture composition in action, cut out a rectangle 2¼ by 3 inches (a 3 by 4 aspect ratio), and frame the entrance of Madame Ranevsky. Then, after carefully reading the first page of the script, mentally frame the succeeding shots as other characters enter.

3

Lighting and Make-up

IN A HOLLYWOOD STUDIO, the director can depend on his lighting technician—a member of IATSE (International Alliance of Theatrical Stage Employees)—to solve all lighting problems in his production. You, on the other hand, must depend on your own knowledge and resourcefulness to light your show effectively. Although lighting alone can easily occupy the full time of a specialist, there are some general principles the novice should follow in order to do a competent lighting job. Your tools are lighting instruments of various types and light intensity which play an important part in helping to convey your mood and tell your story.

Lighting

Generally speaking, lights are of the fluorescent, incandescent, and quartz variety. Fluorescent tube lights were employed extensively in the beginning years of television, when early electronic cameras required more intense illumination than the current models. The fluorescent lights are cooler than the incandescents, and provide a large amount of light at extremely low cost. They are still occasionally used for general

illumination, but have the disadvantage of being impossible to focus.

The most common kind of studio light is the incandescent, and three are three types of incandescent lights: the floodlight, the spotlight or clear lens, and the ellipsoidal spotlight. Each type serves its particular purpose. The floodlight (sometimes called the "scoop") consists of a reflector and a large incandescent lamp ranging from 500 to 2000 watts. It is a soft, diffuse light used for general illumination. The spotlight (known as the "Fresnel") is the most commonly used studio lighting instrument and produces a soft-edged beam for specific area illumination. Fresnels are almost certain to be found in every television studio, and range from the 150–watt "inkie" through 250, 500, 750, 1000, 2000, and 5000 watts. The ellipsoidal spotlight (known as the "Leko" or "Kleig") is a spotlight with a "hard," well-defined edge, used to outline specific areas. For example, it can be trimmed by the use of its internal shutters (mattes) to frame a door precisely. It also can be used to project scenic light patterns on a setting or cyclorama. Quartz lights are a relatively new development in lighting. Watt for watt, they supply greater intensity than incandescents, but also generate considerably more heat. This involves special consideration for venting and heat dissipation. However, quartz lights are particularly effective in providing a soft, even light for cycloramas.

In the early days of television the lighting was flat and nondirectional. There were no shadows, few gradations, and little suggestion of depth or solidity. More recently, lighting for television has moved closer to lighting concepts in the theater and in motion pictures to provide more dimension and greater plasticity.

Skill in lighting, as in editing, is a matter of talent and practice; but you can easily learn the basic principles of using the lighting instruments in your studio. Essentially, there are four main types of light: *base* (or *general*) *light, key light, fill light,* and *back light.* The *base light* provides uniform diffuse illumination sufficient for a television picture of technical acceptability. The *key light* is your major source of illumination to the subject or area. The *fill light* is supplementary light to eliminate shadows and hollows where the base light is inadequate. The *back light* is a source of illumination coming from above and behind the subject (or object) toward which the camera is directed, and gives dimension and character to the subject.

You may design your scene for *high-key lighting* (a bright picture, with gray to white predominating), or for *low-key lighting* with middle grays to black predominating.

In lighting a particular set, your first consideration is to provide enough light to give a picture on the camera you are using. For example, a vidicon camera requires three to four times as much light as an image orthicon camera which can produce an acceptable picture with a minimum of 50 to 75 footcandles.[1] After you have provided this minimum illumination additional lighting will depend on the time of day represented, the mood you wish to create in your scene, and the special effects desired.

Basically, there are two ways of lighting your production. One method is to decide which por-

tions of the setting are most important, and what action should be modeled carefully to give shade and dimension. These should be lighted first. Then the remaining areas should be brought up to the level required by the camera without disturbing the central areas. The second method is the reverse procedure. Bring the base lighting up to the requisite level for the cameras, and then give special attention to the important areas of action. Either method is acceptable, although the writers have found that the second method works best for them.

Light readings should be taken from selected areas of your picture field rather than from the set as a whole. After you have decided on the lighting effect you wish to achieve, the simplest way to take a reading is to hold an incident light meter[2] in the specific areas to be lighted and point it directly toward the camera. Begin with the key light, then the fill light, then the back light. After you have lit several sets you will know the special characteristics of your studio, and the general proportions of the different kinds of light for various moods, as well as the various light intensities required to get a good range of gray scale values. Remember, the camera response to gray scale values is different from that of your eye, making it difficult to judge shades of gray without actually seeing them in the control room. Colors of objects that have contrasting values to the eye, may appear as almost identical shades of gray on the control room monitor.

For lighting on location work where a great deal of electricity is not available, portable step *transformer equipment* is recommended. This relatively inexpensive unit uses the 500–watt PAR64 lamp or the 1000–watt T24 bi-post inside-frost lamp. The transformer allows for increased voltage to the lamp, giving extremely high illumination at low cost. The PAR64 lamp comes in wide, medium, or spot beams for use as base and key light, and the T24 lamp with its reflector is good for fill light. The units are manufactured by either Color-Trans or Masterlite.

---

[1] A footcandle is the intensity of light a standardized light source will provide at a distance of one foot.

[2] The Norwood, Brockway, and Astra are examples of meters of this type.

Simplified Table of Incandescent Lighting Instruments

INSTRUMENT	SYMBOL

Fresnel Lens Spotlight

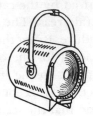

Instrument with 6–inch diameter lens and 500–watt T20 lamp.

Instrument with 8–inch diameter lens and 1000–watt G40 or G48 lamp. Basic and most frequently used lighting unit of lens variety.

Instrument with 12–inch lens and 2000–watt G48 lamp.

A spotlight with spherical reflector and provision for spot to flood focus. Utilizes a Fresnel lens for soft-edged light. Symbols indicate most common sizes, indicated either by wattage or by lens diameters. A color code is also helpful to designate wattage.

Ellipsoidal Spotlight

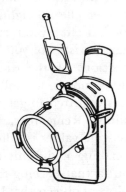

Instrument with 6–inch diameter lens and 750–watt T12 or T14 lamp.

Instrument with 8–inch diameter lens and 1000 to 2000–watt T24 or T30 lamp.

A spotlight with flatted ellipsoidal reflector giving a hard-edged light. Utilizes different lens system (stepped or plano-convex), depending on application of the unit. It can be used for projection effects with pattern drop-ins.

Beam Parabolic Spotlight

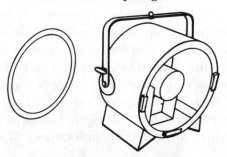

Instrument with 10–inch reflector and 750–watt T20 lamp.

Instrument with 15–inch reflector and 1500–watt G40 lamp.

A spotlight with a parabolic reflector and no lens, giving an intense soft-edged narrow beam of light. Excellent for sun and moonlight effects.

Ellipsoidal Floodlight

Instrument with 15–inch diameter and a 750–watt P5-52, I.F. lamp.

Instrument with 18–inch diameter and a 1000–watt PS-52, I.F. lamp. Basic and most commonly used floodlight.

A floodlight with a matte-finished ellipsoidal reflector. Uses general service inside frost lamp which, together with the matte reflector, gives a soft, diffuse and even illumination.

Striplights

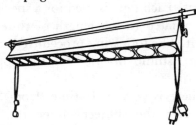

The standard unit is 6 feet long with 12 compartments wired in 3 circuits. It utilizes either R40 or PAR38 150–watt lamps, or R40 300–watt lamps.

The standard unit is 8 feet long with 12 compartments wired in 3 circuits. It uses either PAR56 300–watt or PAR64 500–watt lamps.

The striplight is fabricated in different lengths and for various lamp types and wattages. It is used primarily for top and bottom cyclorama lighting.

A 150 or 300–watt R40 lamp held by an alligator clip with porcelain receptacle.

A small supplementary lamp used to provide light for specific areas (such as "eye light" for actors, or extra light for title cards). Because of its small size, this lamp is useful in many emergency situations. It also can be mounted on the front of the camera, or on a light stand, or may be hand-held.

Make-up

Make-up is one more ingredient in a production that contributes to rendering the performer natural, believable, lifelike. Like good acting, good make-up presents the illusion of naturalness; but the moment it looks like make-up its basic purpose is defeated. Make-up should be there, but it should not call attention to itself. This is not to suggest that it must be applied every time you do a production in the classroom. But it should be understood that when you step before the television camera without the benefit of make-up you are accepting a compromise in your appearance as something less than natural.

To begin with, all colors on the monochrome

screen are reduced to shades of gray. In addition, studio lights illuminate your features with unnatural intensity. Your forehead, nose, and chin will catch more light than the rest of your face, and your eyes may seem shadowed. Some of this can be corrected by the engineer on the video controls, but he cannot compensate entirely for the artificial studio conditions. It is precisely to restore a natural, lifelike appearance to the features that make-up is used.

Many small independent stations do not require make-up for participants on some of their programs, being less concerned with the artistic effects of the participants' appearance than with the general impact of the program. From the management's point of view, make-up represents an extra chore and additional expense which they feel is not essential. However, in studying television as a form of art and a craft, you cannot take this casual view. You must learn all you can about the special functions of all elements that contribute to an effective and pleasing television picture. With this in mind, you should first become acquainted with some of the basic requirements of make-up for television in order to approach the problem of television performance as if you were in a professional situation.

As indicated above, make-up is most directly related to the factor of lighting, and make-up requirements for an individual performer depend on the lighting conditions under which he is working. Ideally a performer should be made up in the studio under the lights and in the exact place where he will stand. But as this is usually impractical, he is obliged to apply make-up in a dressing room where lighting conditions are different from those under which he appears when before the camera. You simply must make an educated guess as to the effect the studio lights will have on his particular features. However, as you become skilled in make-up, your guesses will progressively become more accurate. Often, you can give his face a supplementary touch-up after he has rehearsed under the studio lights and you have seen the deficiencies in the initial make-up application.

The general principle for natural make-up is to darken the areas of the face that are most prominent and reflect light, and lighten the shadowed or less prominent areas. Thus on most people the forehead, nose, chin, and the ears, tend to reflect more light than the eyes and the flat areas of the face. To give a person more nearly the appearance he has in ordinary daylight, apply a darker shade of make-up to the prominent areas, and a lighter shade to the shadowed areas.

In general, three types of make-up are used: powder, water-soluble, and grease-base. All three are manufactured by a number of companies, one of the largest of which is Max Factor of Hollywood whose trade names for the three varieties are: 1) Creme-Puff, 2) Pan-Cake, 3) Pan-Stik. Each type is used for a specific purpose, and is related to the length of time it takes to apply it. The following procedure is more or less standard studio practice for the application of make-up.

If there is very little time (from 3 to 5 minutes), give the subject either the "blue-plate special" or "quickie" make-up application with powder. As a general principle, use a powder that is one shade darker than the subject's complexion. If time allows, use three different shades of powder. Apply the lightest color around the recessed areas like the eyes, the medium shade on bases in the face, and the darkest shade for the ears, forehead, nose, and portions of the face you wish to tone down. In this way, you can correct minor facial irregularities that tend to reflect light and appear more prominent on the screen than they are in real life.

If there is more time (15 minutes), use Pan-Cake make-up, applying it with a natural sponge (make-up tends to "mud up" and cake on cellulose or rubber sponges). Again, use three shades of make-up, with the basic shade slightly darker than the subject's complexion, toning down the prominent areas that reflect light and highlighting the recessed areas. For better control, use a ½-inch camel's hair brush in working around the eyes and ears, and a 1-inch brush to dust and blend the make-up after it dries. On the set, it may be necessary to use a soft tissue to blot excessive perspiration or skin oils that seep through the make-up. Afterward, you can use a matching shade of powder to touch up the face. Pan-Cake covers better than powder, and allows for more control in subduing or highlighting parts of the face.

When you need heavier make-up to cover leathery skin or acne apply Pan-Stik. Again, use a natural sponge, first brushing it lightly over the Pan-Stik, and apply the make-up by stroking in light, upward movements over the face. (It is important to avoid grinding excessive make-up into the pores.) Follow the same principle when using lighter shades for areas you wish to highlight, and darker shades for areas like the forehead, nose, chin, and ears. After application, powder down the Pan-Stik with a translucent powder.

To remove powder or pancake make-up use mild soap and water. Ideally, one should get into a shower and let running water float off the make-up. Women usually follow the soap-and-water cleansing with cold cream or make-up remover. Grease-base make-up is removed with cold cream, or a similar commercial preparation. One of the best is "Unmask," which is sprayed on and then rinsed off with water.

The foregoing represents the standard procedure for applying (and removing) make-up when you want to achieve a natural effect and look like yourself on the television screen. It is not our intention here to discuss in detail the more complicated skills involved in character make-up. However, we must point out that since television is a close-up medium, all make-up should be applied with the tight camera shot in mind. This means that understatement rather than exaggeration should be the rule. If your make-up looks like make-up in a close-up, it will destroy the illusion of your character and make it appear synthetic and artificial. This is also true of excessive make-up, whether one is on the street or in the studio; but the impact of falseness is more dramatic in a television close-up in which every detail is magnified.

Basic minimal make-up stock should include the following items, specified with Max Factor types and numbers:

Powder (Creme-Puff)
- Translucent (to powder down Pan-Stik and for touch-up)
- Twilight Blush (for blondes)
- Gay Whisper (for light women and brunettes with fair complexions)
- Sun Frolic (for women with dark complexions, and men with light complexions)
- Bronze Tone (for darker complexions)
Pan-Cake and Pan-Stik
- 3N (for highlights)
- 5N (for women with light complexions)
- 6N (for women with darker complexions)
- 7N (for men with light complexions, and women with dark complexions)
- 8N (for men with darker complexions)
- 9N (for men and women with heavy summer tans)
- 11N (for ears)
- Dark Egyptian (for rims of ears)
Dry Rouge
- TV Light Tech. (for women)
- TV Dark Tech. (for men)
Moist Rouge (for lips)
- TV No. 2 or Brighter Red Lipstick (for women)
- TV T–3 (for men)
Eyebrow Pencil
- Brown (for women and men with light complexions)
- Brown or black (for women and men with medium or dark complexions)
Liner (eye shadow)
- 6 or 22 (for women)
- 22 (for men)

Your kit should also include:
- Powder puffs
- ½–inch camel's hair or red sable brush (for work around eyes)
- 1–inch brush (to dust and blend Pan-Cake make-up)
- 1 nylon powder brush (to dust off surplus Pan-Cake and Pan-Stik)
- Cosmetic cape (to place over shoulders for protection against spill)

In addition you should have several miscellaneous items such as cold cream, towels, tissue, hair spray, safety pins, bobby pins, straight pins, tweezers, and scissors.

PART TWO

Scripts for
Nondramatic Programs

4

A First Production

THE FIRST of these short, simple scripts will probably be used for your initial television production, and for that reason directions for it are far more detailed than those for later scripts. Here we put words in your mouth and call your shots. And although you need not follow these directions completely, the purpose is to give you experience in taking a program from preplanning through final performance. Everything you learn from directing this script will have application to all that you may do later.

At this point, we should say something about script form. Script form for various types of television programs differs among stations and networks. The most common practice on non-dramatic scripts, where the performers' lines are often read rather than memorized, is to leave a wide margin on the left-hand side of each sheet for video cues. On dramatic scripts, video cues may be marked on either the right or the left margin. However, since dramatic scripts are usually bound in a folder, limiting the use of the left margin, the authors have placed the video column on the more convenient right side for all dramatic exercises and scripts. Here, in your first production, the video cues are on the left margin.

As director, your first job is to read the script carefully. Your cast and crew will also have scripts which, you hope, they will read carefully. However, as director, when you read the script you must not only understand it but also develop an approach to it. You will also want to have a general idea as to how you are going to use your cameras and lights. Although this script requires no setting except your own television studio, you will want a rough set design. In other words, where in your studio will you position the various objects for most effective use of studio space? When you have made these decisions, you will be ready for your first rehearsal.

The Rehearsal

You begin your rehearsal by explaining to your cast and crew your own approach to the script. Then, with the studio monitor as a reference, you establish patterns of movement and cues for the cameraman, the floor manager, the boom operator, and the narrator. After that, you take your place in the control room at the director's desk, and run through the exercise for your allotted rehearsal time until all members of the crew perform their functions smoothly and confidently. To match his narration to the appropriate pictures, the narrator must watch for visual cues on the studio monitor. It is important that you "ready" all shots, so that your cameraman and floor manager are prepared when the "take" cue is given, and there should be a feeling of fluidity as you move through the various elements of the exercise.

The class will find the Production Assignment Sheet in the Production Kit helpful in rotating positions for each round of production.

The Broadcast

The following cues are listed as suggestions to be used *just before* the start of the exercise and while it *is in progress,* and are presented in detail for this first exercise to indicate the specific manner in which the director guides the members of his crew and cast.

BEFORE THE START OF THE EXERCISE

- "Let's have a voice level on the narrator."
- (To the audio engineer) "Kill audio."
- "One minute."
- "30 seconds—stand by!"
- "Open audio."
- "15 seconds."

- "Ready to fade in one (camera one); ready to cue narrator."

AFTER THE START OF THE EXERCISE

- "Camera one, start the pan."
- "Fade in one—continue pan slowly."
- "Cue narrator."
- "Dolly in on picture of camera. Hold." (Stop dolly at this point.)
- "Dolly back. Tilt up to microphone."
- "Pan to partial set."
- "Dolly in."
- "A little tighter." (Move in for slightly closer shot.)
- "Ready hand on lamp. Cue hand."
- "Frame up." (Frame picture so that it is in balance.)
- "Pan to Fresnel."
- "Pull back and pan to table."
- "Ready to cue student and prop man. . . . Cue!"
- "Pan to cameraman . . . to floor manager."
- "Dolly in . . . slowly."
- "Ready to fade to black."
- "Floor manager, ready with cut signal. . . . Cue!"
- "Fade to black."

AFTER THE EXERCISE IS OVER

- "Thank you, everybody."

Production Exercise I

VIDEO	AUDIO
	NARRATOR (VOICE OVER):
INTERIOR. YOUR STUDIO. FADE IN CAMERA 1. SLOW PAN.	This is our studio. Looks kind of barny, doesn't it? And a little messy? But that doesn't mean it's disorganized. There's not a thing here that doesn't have a purpose, that doesn't help us bring good television to you.
	(ON CUE)
DOLLY IN TO MS OF CAMERA AND FOLLOW ITS MOVEMENTS.	This is a camera. It's a highly complex piece of electronic equipment whose function is to bring you the video signal, or, to put it another way, to take pictures like the one you're seeing on your screen now. It's remarkably flexible and
	(AS CAMERA PANS, TILTS, ETC.)
	can pan right or left . . . . be raised or lowered on its pedestal . . . . and dolly in all directions.
	(AS BOOM IS REVEALED)
DOLLY BACK AND TILT TO SHOW BOOM MIKE.	The audio signal, or the sound, is carried by the microphone. This is called a boom mike. It's overhead, so it's out of sight of the audience.
	(BOOM MOVES IN VARIOUS DIRECTIONS.)
	It can be raised or lowered, or moved sideways, and dollied on its mount to follow performers around the studio. Now over . . . .
	(CAMERA REVEALS CURTAIN OR PARTIAL SET WITH TABLE AND CHAIR, A LAMP ON THE TABLE.)

TILT DOWN AND PAN TO MS OF PARTIAL SET.	This is one of our sets. From this angle it doesn't look like much, does it? But in television the director reveals only what he wants the viewer to see. Like this. (ON CUE)
DOLLY IN FOR TIGHTER SHOT OF SET. DOLLY IN FOR CU OF TABLE LAMP.	When you don't see it as part of the studio it looks pretty real, doesn't it? And, of course, part of it is real. The lamp on the table, for example. A real lamp . . . . (A HAND REACHES OUT TO TURN ON THE LAMP.) but the light it gives is hardly noticeable to the camera. Our studio illumination is provided by powerful lighting instruments suspended from a grid near the ceiling. We can't focus on them directly because the intensity of the light would damage the camera tube, but here is one mounted on a floor stand. It's called a Fresnel and contains a 1000-watt lamp.
DOLLY BACK AND PAN TO MS OF SET WITH PEOPLE.	(CAMERA RETURNS TO SET REVEALING STUDENT PERFORMER IN THE ACT OF SITTING AT TABLE. A PROP MAN WALKS INTO PICTURE, GIVES A BOOK TO THE ACTOR, AND ADJUSTS THE LAMP.) And one of the most important parts of our studio: people. People to perform in front of the camera . . . people to handle the props . . . people to operate the equipment . . .
PAN TO CAMERA-MAN, THEN TO	(FLOOR MANAGER HOLDS OUT FIST FOR 15 SECOND CUE. ON VERBAL CUE FROM THE DIRECTOR HE GIVES "CUT" SIGNAL.)

FLOOR MANAGER.

DOLLY IN FOR CU

AS HE "CUTS"

PROGRAM.

FADE TO BLACK.

and people to relay cues from the director in the control room to the studio.

Production Assignment Sheet

Student names are listed by number opposite positions on the production schedule. Assignments are rotated to give each member of the class an opportunity to fill each position. Thus the director on the first production becomes the assistant director on the second production, the technical director on the third, and so on.

1. (Name)

2.

3.

4.

5.

6.

7.

8.

9. (Name)

10.

11.

12.

13.

14.

15.

16.

Production Schedule

DIRECTOR
ASSISTANT DIRECTOR (A.D.)
TECHNICAL DIRECTOR (T.D.)
FLOOR MANAGER
CAMERA 1
CAMERA 2
VIDEO
AUDIO
BOOM
CABLEMAN 1
CABLEMAN 2
LIGHTING
TALENT A
TALENT B
CRITICS

5

The Interview

THERE IS NO ONE WAY of conducting a broadcast interview, but there are several ways how not to. One is the interview in which the interviewer does most of the talking:

"I understand that you are Jerry Jones, and you have just written an important book that has been received with great excitement by the critics. Is that right?"

"Yes, although . . ."

"And I understand that just prior to the publication of this book, you were in a desperate situation—illness in the family, your car smashed, and you lost your job. Pretty lucky thing for you that the book is such a success!"

"Yes."

And so on. Instead of asking questions that would allow us to hear the guest's story from his own lips, the interviewer tells the guest's story and permits him to add only a "yes" or "no." The first thing an interviewer should learn is that his guest, and not he, is the star of the show.

The second thing to learn is that even though an interview is apparently a series of questions and answers, it is most interesting only if it has development and organization which build up to some climax. Often a question asked at the beginning, but left unanswered until the end, provides an element of suspense and a direction for the line of questioning that leads to a climax.

Third, the interviewer should refrain from using verbal crutches like "Uh" or "Y'know." Phrase questions clearly and concisely and avoid indirect constructions and empty cliches like "Just how under the circumstances did you go about—I mean, when did you happen to decide to commence work on this literary enterprise?" Say simply, "When did you begin writing your book?"

The interviewer should avoid trapping himself by random questions he can answer only by saying "I see" or "Well." He also should refrain from repeating every answer his guest gives him:

"Where did you go to high school?"

"I went to Central High School."

"Oh, so you went to Central High School!"

Instead of meaningless repetition of the answer, or a rapid "I see," the interviewer should let each answer lead to the next question. That is, if each question follows naturally from the previous answer, and leads toward an eventual final question, an interview will have a sense of development and achieve the important feeling of mutual exchange.

Interviews can be scripted or unscripted. In either case, the questions are outlined first, after a preliminary talk to find out what is interesting about the guest and what subjects he can discuss most freely and enthusiastically. When the guest is enthusiastic, the interview has vitality. Sometimes a guest, who seemed spirited in prebroadcast preparation, freezes before the camera. It is important to have one or two leading questions in mind that will surprise and arouse him enough to give vigorous and emotional negative answers.

In addition to preparing the interview, it is wise to prepare the guest. Urge him to speak naturally and simply, and do your best to put him at ease by conveying your warm interest in what he has to say. As the interviewer, you should *back time* your closing remarks so that at the one-minute or 30–second sign from the floor manager you can adjust your questions, signal your guest, and have a comfortable margin of time in which to conclude. The best way to put yourself at ease is to have a well prepared introduction and closing. This gets you off to a good start, and guarantees an interview that, like old soldiers, will not simply fade away at the end.

An interview can be produced with one camera or two, presented in an elaborate setting or against a noncommittal drape, and have more or less movement. That is, during the entire interview two people may simply be seated comfortably close together, with the camera or cameras changing the visual picture through cutting, panning, and dollying in or back. You also can begin with a single shot of the interviewer, seated as he opens the program and then, as the camera draws back, rising to greet the guest who walks into the picture. After that both are seated. Or, the interview can be done dramatically, with the guest seated above upstage on an elevated platform in front of a black backdrop, and lights raised for a close-up as he is introduced. In this case, most of the questions may come from off-screen. It can even go so far as the one Steve Allen interview that was conducted while Steve played catch with the guest, who was a baseball player.

Again, the most important thing for the director to remember is that, from the video point of view, the guest is the star of the show. Sometimes there is a tendency to cut from interviewer to guest, question to answer, one-two, one-two. But it is often far better to hear the interviewer's question from off-screen and keep the camera on the guest, whose immediate reaction may prove to be much more interesting.

Although good picture composition is obviously a "must," fancy camera angles do not add to the interest of the program. There should be nothing in the picture to distract from the content of the program. For example, in one interview series the director wanted to achieve an effect of great informality. The set was a contemporary living room. The guest lounged in an easy chair, and the interviewer sat on the floor. The camera observed them both from high angle shots, close, medium, long, and over-the-shoulder. But the content of the program was diffused by too much visual distraction. In addition, the presumably informal effect of the interviewer sitting on the floor interfered with the sense of communication achieved when two people are sitting side by side. The interview was further complicated by the camera frequently dissolving instead of cutting from one shot to another. For the director, the best principle to remember is that people are interested in people.

Although the following scripted interview is cued for two cameras it can be done with one. An interesting variation of the exercise would be to try it with one camera, changing the cues accordingly. In either case, it is planned for the simplest type of setting, and a minimum of camera cues. Try this exercise in your first rehearsal as written, but feel free to make changes that can be adapted to the temperament of your guest, or of the interviewer. Later, if you wish, rewrite it completely, or substitute your own. Whether you use this exercise or your own version, prepare it with sufficient care to make it appear natural and spontaneous.

The interview is timed for 3 minutes. Title cards can be as simple as the sample form shown in the Production Kit, but if time and talent are available you may wish to illustrate them.

Interview

VIDEO	AUDIO
CAMERA 2 ON TITLE CARDS. DISSOLVE TO CAMERA 1.	**INTERVIEWER** (SEATED AT DESK OR ON SOFA AGAINST NEUTRAL FLAT OR DRAPE) Hello! I'm _____ back again with Hometown, a series of interviews with students from various parts of the state, nation, and the world. Today, our guest is John Wilson, whose hometown is . . . John?
CAMERA 2 - CU OF JOHN.	**JOHN** (GRINNING) The Athens of the Midwest!! It's Madison, Wisconsin.
CAMERA 1 - DOLLY BACK FOR TWO-SHOT.	**INTERVIEWER** And what makes Madison, Wisconsin the Athens of the Midwest? **JOHN** Oh, a lot of things. The University is there, and the State Capitol, and we have lots of good music and plays, and it's very beautiful. Four lakes you know. **INTERVIEWER** Four lakes, a good university . . . why did you come here?
CAMERA 2 - CU OF JOHN.	**JOHN** Why? Oh . . . well, I was looking for something, I guess.

INTERVIEWER

Maybe a better climate?

JOHN

Oh, the climate back there isn't really bad. Hot in the summer, sure, and cold in the winter, but there is so much to do . . . why, when I was a kid in the winter, I'd get snow in my galoshes and down my neck, and my nose would pinch up from the cold, but if I was on a sled going down a hill, I didn't even feel it. And, of course, in the summer there was always swimming and sailing. And spring and fall . . . . Boy! No, I never complained about the climate back there in Wisconsin.

CAMERA 1 - TWO-
SHOT.
CAMERA 2 - CUT
TO JOHN.

INTERVIEWER

What were you looking for, then?

JOHN

(VERY SERIOUS) Of course, obviously, I wanted to go to college, and in my field, English, this is one of the best. Mind you, I'm not saying that my home town university doesn't have a good department; but I suppose I just wanted to get away.

INTERVIEWER

Family problems?

JOHN

Oh, no. They'd have let me live in a dorm, anyway, if I'd gone to school there.

CAMERA 1 - TWO-
SHOT.

INTERVIEWER

Then maybe you just didn't like staying in your hometown.

JOHN

Maybe.

INTERVIEWER

Do you like it better here?

JOHN

Well, it's different. Madison has only 100,000 popu-
lation, so you do get to know a lot of people. And a lot
of people have been there a long time, like it was
settled in about 1850? And with all the lakes and
everything, it's a beautiful place, but I just . . . well,
I told you . . . I was looking for something.

INTERVIEWER

I wish you could tell us what.

CAMERA 2 - CU
OF JOHN.

JOHN

I haven't thought about it for a long time. And I don't
think I really understood it till I got here, but when I
was in high school, I read a thing by Carl Sandburg,
about the people going west?

INTERVIEWER

I'm not sure whether I remember.

JOHN

One guy drives up to the gas station in a jalopy and
asks the man, "What are the folks like in the next

town?" The gas station man says, "What were they like where you came from?" And the guy says, "Lousy." So the gas station man says, "You'll find them just about the same here." Then another car drives up and this guy asks the same question. Gets the same answer . . . "What were the folks like where you came from?" This guy says, "Oh, they were wonderful. I miss them already." And the gas station man says, "You'll find them just the same in the next town." Well, I thought that my hometown was a nice place to live in, but I thought I ought to get away . . . see new things, different things. I guess I was looking for adventure.

CAMERA 1 - TWO-SHOT.

INTERVIEWER

And you haven't found it?

CAMERA 2 - CU OF JOHN AFTER "NO."

JOHN

Yes and no. What I found was that adventure is how you feel about things. I sometimes think that until I went away I didn't even know my hometown.

CAMERA 1 - TWO-SHOT. DOLLY IN FOR SHOULDER SHOT OF INTERVIEWER.

INTERVIEWER

(TO JOHN) You know I think that you've found what you came here for. (TO US) And I think that we all want to thank John Wilson for his help in describing his hometown, which may very well be much the same as yours or mine. We'll find out next week! Good afternoon.

6

The Panel Discussion

IN A PANEL DISCUSSION the interest value is in what the various panel members have to say, what the reactions are to what is said, and generally in the conflict of opinions and ideas. Perhaps the dullest type of panel discussion is the one where nobody really seems to care what the other person's opinion is.

PANEL MEMBER 1: [*Reflectively*] I see your point, Sir Humphrey, but I can't say that I agree with it. At least, not totally.

PANEL MEMBER 2: [*Agreeably*] Well, I wouldn't expect anyone to agree with it totally!

PANEL MEMBER 3: [*Bored*] Perhaps it's a matter of phraseology. . . . However, although this polite tiptoeing about an issue is pallid, you don't want the fireworks which are so explosive that no real points are made.

PANEL MEMBER 1: You misunderstood me completely! What I was saying was . . .

PANEL MEMBER 2: I heard what you were saying, and I understood it very well. Hogwash, just hogwash! Besides . . .

PANEL MEMBER 3: If I could get a word in here . . .

PANEL MEMBER 1: Hogwash! Why, you . . .

PANEL MEMBER 2: Now, listen . . .

Somewhere between these two drastic examples lies the truly interesting panel where the conflicts are not between personalities, but in differences of ideas.

It is helpful to members of the television audience if they can identify a point of view with a particular face. For this reason it is usually wise not to include too many panel members, allowing the viewer time to become acquainted with the panelists and achieve a fuller vicarious participation in the discussion.

In planning your panel discussion ask yourself first, "Who is the intended audience?"—and keep this audience in mind as you prepare the program. Also, remember to select a topic about which students can speak easily and with authority. Do not underestimate the intrinsic value of youth in a discussion. The very fact that the viewer sees the faces of young people, and hears them expressing their own informed opinions on a topic vital to them, gives the discussion a refreshing appeal.

The success of your discussion will depend on its spontaneity. However, spontaneity in a discussion does not usually happen by itself. As in any art, good preparation conceals itself and appears to be effortless; but the expert recognizes the importance of meticulous preparation.

One of your most important responsibilities is

to make certain that you have a good moderator who can put the panel members at ease, and give them the feeling that each one is making a significant contribution. He will explore the opinions of the group in a prebroadcast conference, clarify issues, allocate areas of discussion, and try to bring the discussion to some kind of useful conclusion.

Although members of the panel should not memorize their lines, they may wish to make notes, or jot down cues or key phrases to remind them of points to bring up. With well-timed questions, the moderator can help create the feeling of extemporaneous give and take. It is his job to see that all points are covered, but this should not be done in mechanical fashion. The discussion should move easily from one point to another, each seeming to grow out of the one preceding it. The moderator usually writes his opening and closing remarks, and rehearses them carefully so that he can introduce and conclude the program with assurance and authority.

You will want to remind members of the panel that each of them is participating every moment. For, even though they actually may not be speaking at the time, the camera might be focussed on their reaction to what is being said by another panelist. At the same time, caution them to ignore the camera and behave as if it did not exist. The cardinal sin for a participant is to steal a sidelong glance at the camera when it is pointed at him, because it destroys the illusion of the viewer.

For you, as the director, the program poses a number of challenges. You have several participants who must be seated comfortably in a pattern that will present satisfactory pictures to the viewing audience. These pictures must range from establishing shots orienting the audience to the entire panel to individual shots of the panelists. Therefore, your camera strategy will depend on the number of cameras available to you. If you are working with only two cameras,

you must plan very carefully to achieve all the necessary shots.

You begin with the considerable advantage of looking at the panel through a television camera, not through a proscenium. The television camera is flexible, mobile, selective, telescopic. You can move it up and down and around on all sides for wide-angle shots, close-ups, pans, two-shots, and three-shots. An imaginative director will exploit these remarkable features of his instrument. One special note: After you have established the identity of your panelists, it is not necessary to cut to a person every time he speaks. Reaction shots are frequently much more effective.

In arranging members of the panel, make sure that they look well and feel comfortable. For example, an armchair that is too deep may make a person feel drowned. If you wish to use group shots in various combinations, seat appropriate panel members close together. This will enable you to frame them on the screen without leaving a gaping hole in the middle of the picture.

Let us suppose that your panel consists of four students and a moderator. The following are possible setups to consider; you may wish to suggest others.

1. Students seated horizontally behind a rectangular table with the moderator at the end.
2. Students and moderator seated in regular chairs around a circular table of normal height.
3. Students and moderator seated in small easy chairs around a circular coffee table.
4. Students and moderator seated behind a semicircular table.
5. Moderator seated in the foreground, with students seated in the background behind an elevated semicircular table. Moderator faces the audience for his opening remarks, then partially turns his back to the audience as he introduces members of the panel.
6. Students and moderator seated in chairs and on the floor in "bull-session" pattern.

Panel Discussion

VIDEO	AUDIO
	ANNOUNCER
FADE IN	
TITLE CARD:	"Campus World" . . . . A weekly visit with students
"Campus World."	at the University of _____ . Your moderator,
	_____ .
DISSOLVE TO	MODERATOR
MODERATOR.	Good afternoon. The world of the campus is a world in miniature. Each week on this program we select a different facet of life in the campus world to explore with representative students from all parts of the globe. Today we pose the question, "Should college students engage in political activity?" The views you will hear will have a distinctly international flavor, since our panel includes students from Ottumwa to
WIDE ANGLE OF	Tokyo. I'd like you to meet them . . . . Gerald Knox
PANEL MEMBERS	of England, Dapo Adeluba of Nigeria, Jeanne Mercier
CHATTING	of France, Junho Matsumara of Japan, and Katherine
INFORMALLY.	Schultz from the United States. First, may I present
	Gerald Knox.
CU OF KNOX	KNOX
SUPER NAME	How do you do. I'm from London. Actually I was born
UNDER PICTURE.	in Bristol, but I've lived in London for the past ten years.
	MODERATOR
(OFF SCREEN)	

	And Dapo Adeluba.
PAN TO DAPO	DAPO
SUPER NAME.	(IDENTIFIES HOMETOWN AND ADDS BRIEF COMMENT ON SIZE, POPULATION AND LOCATION OF NIGERIA.)
	MODERATOR
	(OFF SCREEN)
	Jeanne Mercier from Paris.
PAN TO JEANNE	JEANNE
SUPER NAME.	(IDENTIFIES HERSELF BRIEFLY.)
	MODERATOR
	(OFF SCREEN)
PAN TO JUNHO	Junho Matsumura.
SUPER NAME.	JUNHO
	(IDENTIFIES SELF.)
	MODERATOR
PAN TO	And Katherine Shultz from Ottuma, Iowa
KATHERINE	KATHERINE
SUPER NAME.	(IDENTIFIES HERSELF AS SORORITY MEMBER AND PRESIDENT OF STUDENT BOARD.)
CUT TO	MODERATOR
MODERATOR.	Thank you. Now let's have your opinions on the role of the student in politics. Should it be limited to the campus, or should it go beyond? Katherine, suppose you begin by telling us about politics in the campus world.

KATHERINE

(SPEAKS FOR ABOUT ONE MINUTE ON STUDENT

GOVERNMENT AND NAMES A FEW CAMPUS ISSUES.)

DAPO

(RELATES THESE ISSUES TO BROADER NATIONAL

AND INTERNATIONAL QUESTIONS. HE INDICATES

THAT THEY HAVE NO MEANING IF THEY REMAIN

PAROCHIAL ISSUES OF THE CAMPUS WORLD.)

GERALD

(SUGGESTS THAT UNTIL HE IS OF VOTING AGE

THE STUDENT ACTUALLY CAN DO LITTLE ABOUT

INFLUENCING DECISIONS BEYOND THE CAMPUS.

ETC.)

JUNHO

(TAKES ISSUE WITH THIS VIEW. TELLS OF STU-

DENT ATTITUDE AND ACTION GROUPS IN JAPAN-

ESE UNIVERSITIES.)

JEANNE

(TAKES A MIDDLE-OF-THE-ROAD COURSE. "THE

STUDENT," SHE SAYS, "HAS A GOOD OPPORTUNITY

TO BE OBJECTIVE, CAN RESEARCH AND DISCUSS

SOCIAL AND POLITICAL PROBLEMS AND DEVELOP

STANDARDS OF JUDGMENT." HE SHOULD, HOW-

EVER, PARTICIPATE IN CAMPUS POLITICAL

AFFAIRS WHERE HIS OPINION COUNTS.)

(DISCUSSION CONTINUES WITH PARTICIPANTS

CITING EXAMPLES FROM THEIR RESPECTIVE
COUNTRIES AND TRADITIONS. AT TWO MINUTES
BEFORE THE END OF THE PROGRAM THE MOD-
ERATOR SUMS UP THE ARGUMENTS BRIEFLY AND
THANKS THE PANEL MEMBERS. AT 30-SECOND
SIGNAL, HE TURNS TO THE CAMERA.)

MODERATOR

Views from the Campus World, ladies and gentlemen,

on students and politics. Next week students from

India, Denmark, Italy, Yugoslavia and our own coun-

try will exchange views on the subject, "The United

Nations—A Student Perspective" . . . from "Campus

World."

DISSOLVE TO   (PANEL MEMBERS CONTINUE THEIR DISCUSSION
                   WITH MIKES CUT.)
WIDE SHOT OF
                   ANNOUNCER
PANEL. SUPER
                   "Campus World" is a presentation of Station _____
TITLE CARD.
                   _____.
FADE TO BLACK.

7

The Newscast

THE FOLLOWING EXERCISE is not intended to provide experience in the essentials of gathering and preparing a television newscast. This is a specialized area in television and requires its own training and disciplines. But, if a newscast is poorly performed or directed, nothing less than a major disaster will interest the viewer.

What is a newscast? A man in front of a camera reading news stories? Sometimes it is not much more than that; but frequently it is a carefully directed program including slides, film clips, graphics, a rear projection screen, and different announcers for different parts of the news. The following exercise can be done in a number of ways. It is written as a newscast, with commercials read by an off-screen announcer, and includes various types of graphics. However, if you wish, you can omit the commercials, and most of the graphics, and concentrate on directing a single performer with a minimum of cuts to and from graphics.

The purpose of the exercise as written is to give you experience as a director in 1) cutting from performer to graphic and back to performer; 2) cutting from the performer to the film projection room and back to the performer; 3) following a moving performer, and 4) dollying in to a close shot. If your facilities do not include a film projector, you can omit the video on that news item and keep the announcer on-screen. Or, perhaps you can use a film and slide projector and a conventional beaded screen in the studio, or an appropriate still picture.

On the other hand, you may wish to add graphics to some of the news items even where graphics are not indicated. It is also possible that you might decide to use the script simply as a suggested outline for a newscast you prepare from newspapers and magazines, finding current stories and illustrating them with actual photographs. If you have the facilities, you may prefer to film your own footage with a 16–millimeter camera to illustrate some campus event you include in the news. And you also may wish to try your hand at making your own 35–millimeter slides, mounting them in 2 by 2 frames. In any event, here are a few principles that must be followed.

First, graphics. Choose simple, clear stills or charts, with a dull or matte rather than glossy finish. The main subject of interest on the photograph should be toward the center of the frame, not spread out to either side with an empty space in the middle. Keep in mind the 3 by 4 aspect ratio of the television screen when selecting photographs. Mount them on 11 by 14

47

or 14 by 22 cards. And, instead of placing a still in front of the camera, try tilting, panning, or dollying in for variety wherever possible.

Second, performance. Most news announcers on television obviously read from a script, but not with head apparently buried in the chest. As often as possible they look directly at the viewer via the camera. However, do not look up at regular intervals simply because you have heard that it is the right thing to do. Try to motivate the action. You may look up to emphasize a point, to stress a key word, or to conclude a thought and share its significance with the viewer. It will take practice to do this fluently. Your eye must keep a phrase ahead of your voice. Also, when you look up to underline a point, keep your finger on your place in the script so that you can return to your script with ease. Sometimes it is necessary to retard a phrase to gain time for making eye contact with your audience. Another important thing for the newscaster to remember is that he should achieve a sense of communication with the viewer, keeping an interested voice and an alert expression.

Third, direction. The content and meaning of the news are the most important parts of the broadcast. Too many graphics can be distracting; poorly chosen graphics can puzzle the viewer; and even though it was "taken at the scene of the crime," a blurry bit of film footage adds nothing to the newscast. As director, you must remember that unless graphics are meaningful they do not improve the broadcast, but only add to your directorial chores. The same is true of sets and lighting. A simple, well-lighted set is far more effective than one hung with flags and bunting, or dressed to resemble a newspaper office high up in a skyscraper overlooking an undefined section of town. Viewers are primarily interested in the news itself, which means, "What happened today—and how does it affect me?"

On the technical side, as director, you must direct the newscast cleanly. That means that all cues should be well rehearsed. Nothing is more confusing to the viewer than that moment when the announcer says, "And here is the scene of the fatal crash!" and on the screen comes the wrong still, or the announcer shuffling his script.

To direct this exercise cleanly, no matter how you alter it, you must continue to make decisions. Your first decision is whether your facilities are adequate for directing the exercise as written, or, even if they are adequate, whether that is the way you wish to direct the exercise.

Let us suppose that you decide to direct the exercise as written. What are your next decisions . . . because from here on it is going to be decisions, decisions, decisions!

To begin with, you will note that the initial audio cue is for "Music or Teletype BG." You must decide whether you want "news music," a teletype, or some other sound in the background, or whether you should start the broadcast with only the title card. The title card? Yes. You must choose a title card, or order it designed according to your specifications. Will it be simply white lettering against a black background, or will it have an identifying caricature or motif? You are the one who must judge and choose.

Your next decision concerns the choice of camera position and lens in relation to your newscaster. The script calls for a shot against a simple drape. Do you want a chest shot or a waist shot? If you choose a waist shot will it be that of a man standing, or of a man sitting behind a desk? You must decide.

Suppose the script calls for a slide of a Danish pastry. Is it in a store? On a plate? Is a hand reaching out toward it? Or is it, possibly, on the way to a mouth?

From here, according to the script, we cut to a wide-eyed boy. How old is he? How is he dressed? With or without freckles? Is he looking at us, or elsewhere? The same applies to the following slide of the grown man. In both cases, vitality is the cue for effective visuals. You may prefer to use existing photographs instead of making your own slides or graphics. If the still photograph you choose manages to capture an effect of appetite and enjoyment, it will be effective even if you cut it out of a magazine advertisement.

If you are directing this exercise according to the script, let us cut back to the newscaster. You have another decision to make. Is his position exactly as it was when we first saw him? It probably is, because his relation to us has not changed. If you decide to change the position of the camera, do it while camera two is on the graphic.

When, for example, the newscaster rises to walk to a wall map or a blackboard, you can practice cutting on an action. As he begins to rise, you can cut to a wider angle lens and follow him to the map. Similarly, as he moves his arm to point to the southern tip of Florida, you can cut to a close-up of the area. After that you will take the newscaster back to the table with a wide-angle lens, and cut to a chest shot as he resumes his original position. You will have to make many decisions, often depending as much on your facilities as on your esthetic judgment, but most of them will be closely related to the items described above.

If you use film footage, thread the film so that it is cued at No. 5 on the Academy Leader. There are 15 frames between each number on the leader, and 30 additional frames of black before the picture appears on the film. Since film is projected at a speed of 24 frames per second, about 4 seconds will elapse between the time you start the projector at No. 5 and the first frame of the picture. In order to cue the film precisely, you will find it necessary to time your announcer's last phrase preceding the film. The cueing procedure is as follows: First, "ready"

your projectionist in the film projection room; then, as the announcer speaks a particular word 4 seconds before the end of his copy, you give the "roll film" cue to the projectionist on the intercom line. As the announcer finishes his paragraph, you will give the switcher the signal to "take" film. If you have a film preview monitor, the problem of "taking" the film on its first frames will be simplified. If you do not have a monitor, you can still do a satisfactory job with the method described above.

"Coming out of film" presents the problem of cueing the studio program immediately at the conclusion of the film. For this cue, it is a good idea to use a scriber or ink dot to mark the upper right-hand corner of 11 frames at a point five seconds (120 frames) before the end of the film. At two seconds (48 frames) before the end, mark another 11 frames. When you see the 5–seconds mark roll by on the monitor "ready" the announcer's camera, and as the 2–seconds cue appears "take" your next camera shot. An alternate procedure is to have the projectionist count down from an arbitrary figure ("five" serves very well) over the intercom to alert the director. As the projectionist sees the end of the film coming off the reel, he adapts the speed of his countdown to match the movement of the film. The director gives his "ready" signal when he hears the projectionist say "five," and his "take" cue when he hears him say "one."

Newscast

VIDEO	AUDIO
TITLE CARD.	(MUSIC OR TELETYPE BG.)

ANNOUNCER I

Good evening. _____ here with the Six O'clock Report, brought to you by Danish, a famous name in pastry. First, the headlines: Revolt in South Feelah.

Train Robbers Captured. Jones Boy Found Unharmed.

We'll have the details on these and other late stories

for you in just a few moments.

CUT TO SLIDE OR

GRAPHIC OF A

DANISH PASTRY.

CUT TO WIDE-

EYED BOY. CUT

TO MAN, GRIN-

NING.

CUT TO

ANNOUNCER I.

ANNOUNCER II (VOICE OVER)

Danish pastry! Crisp, light, and chock full of fruits

and nuts! Warm in the oven and serve with milk,

coffee, or chocolate. Take one Danish and add it to

one hungry little boy . . . or to one happy husband . . .

and you'll know why Danish is a famous name in

pastry!

ANNOUNCER I

On the international scene today, the revolt in South

Feelah took a new turn. Protesting against President

Matchek's strongly nationalistic policy, rioters pick-

eted the Government Building and called for the

president's resignation. When police tried to dis-

perse them, a roaring mob of thousands drove the

police back. President Matchek issued an immediate

order for army troops and declared a curfew for the

entire city. With the arrival of the troops, both

pickets and mob left the scene quietly. But a spokes-

man for the revolt was quoted as saying, "This is

only the beginning." Nationally today, the big news

was the apprehension of the six-man gang that robbed

a mail train late last month. It was a robbery appar-

ently planned to the smallest detail, along the lines of

Britain's great train robbery some years back. FBI men refused to disclose the name of the informer who led them to the gang. But they said most of the money has been recovered and, equally important, the arrests may lead to a breakthrough on organized crime syndicates operating in the United States.

CUT TO FILM
CLIP OF A BOY
BEING CARRIED
IN A GROUP OF
SEVERAL MEN,
OR STILL OF BOY.
CUT TO
ANNOUNCER.

Locally, good news about a small lost boy. Little Craig Jones has been found.

(VOICE OVER) After a frantic 24-hour search, neighbors found five-year-old Craig, tired, hungry, but unharmed behind an abandoned warehouse a few blocks from his home.

Fears that he had been kidnapped appeared justified. Police now are looking for "the big man in a blue car" who, according to Craig, took him for an awfully long ride," and then let him out of the car at the warehouse, telling him to wait for his Mommy and Daddy. Police presume that after driving aimlessly for some hours, the kidnapper panicked and left Craig at the warehouse to give himself time to get out of the state. An all-points bulletin has been issued.

And for some more good news, Mayor Peter Fleming has announced that he will fight the council's proposed increase in property taxes. The Mayor stated that he believes a thoroughgoing overhaul of the municipal budget should come first.

Next, sports and the weather, after this word from

Danish.

CUT TO PICTURE   **ANNOUNCER II (VOICE OVER)**

OF WOMEN AT AN   If you're entertaining, you'll find nothing so easy, or

AFTERNOON   so delicious as Danish and coffee. Set out an assort-

PARTY, OR OF A   ment of tempting pastries, make the coffee, and you'll

SMILING WOMAN.   be praised as a hostess. Just be sure it's Danish, a

famous name in pastry!

CUT TO   **ANNOUNCER I**

ANNOUNCER I.   In football, it was Wee Willie Winkles' day again. The

five-foot-eight quarterback, whose real name is Dun-

can Winkle, threw three perfect passes to lead the

Oaks to a 21-20 victory over State. One of the passes

was for 19 yards, another for 31, but the shortest . . .

a mere 8 yards . . . was into the end zone for the win-

ning touchdown. Yardage gained on the other two

passes set up the running plays for the Oaks' first

two touchdowns. Elsewhere, Inland defeated Beaver

State, 14 to 3, Mountain College over Aspen, 7 to

nothing; and Stratham downed Foothill, 12 to 6.

Now let's look at the weather map for our local fore-

cast and a report on the hurricane in the East.

(ANNOUNCER RISES AND WALKS TO WALL MAP
POINTING TO BERMUDA ISLANDS, AND INDICATING
A PATH WHICH BY-PASSES FLORIDA, POINTS TO
TIP OF FLORIDA.)

Weathermen predict that Hurricane Florence, now

lashing the Bermudas, will bypass Florida. After

levelling hundreds of homes in Bermuda, the hurricane veered east, and the prediction is that it will blow itself out within 24 hours. Residents of southern Florida, however, are taking no chances. Houses are shuttered and small boats submerged.

For us, here at home, weather prospects are brighter. Tomorrow, the weatherman says, we should see clear skies, mild sun, and light to moderate winds. Tomorrow's high is expected to be 70 degrees; the low 58. That's the news to this hour. _____ inviting you to join us again tomorrow for the Six O'clock News.

CUT TO
PASTRY
GRAPHIC.
DISSOLVE TO
CLOSING
TITLE CARD
FADE TO BLACK.

ANNOUNCER II (VOICE OVER)

The Six O'clock News has been brought to you by Danish . . . a famous name in pastry!

(MUSIC OR TELETYPE BG.)

8

A Choral Program

FOR THE NOVICE, one of the most satisfactory types of broadcasts that provides television directorial experience in a nondramatic form is the choral program. In the first place, the talent for such a program is readily available, because every college or university has at least one choral group willing and eager to be seen by the television audience. Also, the local television station is usually pleased to provide air time for a program that carries the excitement of a live presentation without the elaborate preparation required for a drama. This is particularly true during the holiday seasons of the year, when a local station wishes to observe an occasion with a special presentation. The choral group fulfills this need admirably.

A program of this kind presents directorial challenges on many levels, depending on the qualifications of the director. For the novice, it provides a continuous performance that allows him to put to use the various lessons he has learned in basic direction. Even if he is inexperienced and has a minimum of imagination, he must still follow these conventional procedures:

1. Time the total program and its several segments.
2. Write the continuity for the various musical selections.
3. Prepare graphics for the opening and closing routines, with names of the singers and his production crew.
4. Place members of the choral group on risers so that they present a pleasing picture to the camera.
5. Light the group to make every member appear to good advantage.
6. Learn the music by score, or by ear, to help him motivate his camera shots.
7. Experiment with wide-angle shots, medium shots, close-ups, cuts, pans, dollies, and supers, as these are motivated by the lyrics and music, by the special qualities of members of the group, by the conductor, or by the announcer's copy.

The talented and imaginative director must do all of the above and, in addition, meet innumerable other challenges in making what is essentially a static and aural experience into an exciting visual experience as well.

The director may wish to check the following list of items, which should be kept in mind in a broadcast of this kind:

1. Remember that music is one of the most important things in the program. Everything that is done should add dimension to the experience of listening to the music, with the camera assisting the viewer in do-

ing what his eye would do normally if he were watching the group in a concert hall. In its simplest form, this means that when there is a solo passage, the camera will take a close-up of the soloist. When there is a duet, the camera will frame a two-shot. It does not necessarily mean that when the entire group is singing, the director must invariably call for a wide-angle shot of the group. He may prefer to do a slow pan with a close-up lens, giving the viewers an opportunity to see the fervor of individual singers as their voices blend into a full choral passage, and then follow by a dissolve to a shot of the entire group.

2. Avoid random and meaningless cutting and dissolving from one shot to another. Be sure that each shot is motivated, and key it to a musical phrase. If you cannot read a score, you should frequently listen to chorus rehearsals. Also, get acquainted with the individual members of the group. It is helpful, too, to make an advance audio tape of the program. Playing the program privately and committing the songs to memory will make it easier to plan valid shots for each selection.

3. Avoid the overuse of dissolves, as it makes for sameness and monotony. When a soloist or a section of the chorus begins a phrase of a song with a sharp attack, use the cut in favor of the dissolve.

4. Be sure that you do not waste the time of the entire choral group in your camera rehearsal. At best, you may require three camera rehearsals, each of 2 or 3 hours' duration, before all is ready for your final presentation. If you are not completely prepared before camera rehearsal, you will end up with a very tired group of performers for the final live presentation or video tape. This means that everything that is not of direct concern to the singers should be rehearsed thoroughly beforehand: production routines on the opening and closing graphics; placement and audio level of the narrator; general lighting plot for the group, and specific lighting for graphics and the narrator.

5. Since this is a musical program, the audio portion is of paramount importance. Pay special attention to the placement of microphones for audio pickup. A single microphone placed above and in front of a choral group usually gives a satisfactory pickup. However, if the bass section of the chorus is small, a single microphone will allow the sopranos to predominate. In that case, it might be advisable to hang another microphone above and in front of the bass section. For instrumental accompaniment by piano, strings, harp, harpsichord, or celesta, you may require an additional microphone. It is easy to permit your natural concern for the pictorial portion of the program to overshadow your awareness of the balance of the music. Try to avoid this, and be sure to watch the balance of the narrator's voice in relation to the chorus.

6. Place a program monitor in comfortable view of the narrator to help him integrate his off-camera announcements with the picture on the screen. Remember that voice and picture should be heard and seen simultaneously.

7. Make it absolutely clear to all members of the chorus that the effectiveness of the broadcast lies in their expressive faces as well as in their earnest and heartfelt singing. Warn them that they must keep their attention riveted on their conductor. Emphasize that under no circumstances must they steal sidelong glances at the camera, thereby shattering the illusion that they are not aware of the audience.

The following excerpt from a half-hour program was presented as a special television Christmas concert. It can serve as a format for your choral presentation. The Madrigal Singers in this case, consisted of eighteen voices and proved to be of a size desirable for television presentation. The group was not too large to embrace in a wide-angle shot, and small enough to allow the audience to become acquainted with individual faces in the course of the half-hour program. Camera shots of the singers are not indicated in the script. They can be marked on the actual musical score of each selection, or on separate pages with the lyrics typed out in regular split-sheet script form.

University Madrigal Singers Christmas Program

VIDEO	AUDIO
"UNIVERSITY"	NARRATOR:
CARD. DISSOLVE	The Television Division of _____ presents the
TO "MADRIGAL"	University Madrigal Singers in a special program of
CARD. DISSOLVE	Christmas music.
TO "CHRISTMAS"	
CARD.	NARRATOR:
WAIST SHOT IN	Welcome to our program of song and celebration of
FRONT OF BLACK	the Christmas time. The singers will present a var-
CURTAIN OR'	iety of selections on their concert—some from other
CHRISTMAS MOTIF.	centuries and other lands, some written more re-
	cently by contemporary composers. Some of the
	selections are not quite so well known as the familiar
	carols, but all are in the joyous spirit of the holiday
	season. To open, the University Madrigal Singers,
	under the direction of _____ have chosen a
	motet by the Sixteenth Century Dutch composer, Jan
	Sweelinck, "Venite, Exultemus Domino," "Come Let
	Us Glorify the Lord."
MADRIGAL	
SINGERS.	
CU NARRATOR.	NARRATOR:
	Orlando Gibbons, one of the greatest seventeenth cen-
	tury composers of England, is often called "The Father

of Anglican Music." The next selection, "O Thou the
Central Orb of Righteous Love," was written by Gibbons as an Advent Anthem. The text reads: "O Thou,
the central orb of righteous love; pure beam of the
Most High, eternal Light of this our wintry world.
Thy radiance bright awakes new joy in Faith, hope
soars above."

_____ plays the harpsichord accompaniment
and the opening solo is sung by _____.

MADRIGAL
SINGERS.
CU NARRATOR.

                              NARRATOR:

In contrast to this English anthem by Gibbons, we now
present a Latin hymn. It was written by Gibbons'
great contemporary, William Byrd, sometimes called
the Palestrina of England. His transcendent setting
of "Beata Es" is an offertory for the feast of the Virgin Mary. "Beata Es." ("Blessed Art Thou.")

MADRIGAL
SINGERS.
CU OF HANDS
PLUCKING HARP
STRINGS.

                    NARRATOR: (VOICE OVER)

"O Sing as thrushes in the winter
Lift their ecstacy aloft among black boughs
So that the dormouse stirs him in his drowse
And by the melting drift the newborn lamb
Bleats answer.

"Awake! For in the darkness of the byre

Above the manger, clapping with his wings

The cock of glory lifts his crest of fire.

Far among slumbering men his trumpet rings.

"O awake . . . awake and sing!"

The lines are by England's poet laureate, John Mase-

field; the musical setting by one of the great English

composers of this century, Gustav Holst.

"O Sing as Thrushes!"

MADRIGAL
SINGERS.
CU NARRATOR.   NARRATOR:

The text of "Nunc Dimittis" ("Now Let Us Depart") is

familiarly known as the Song of Simon from the Gospel

of Luke: "Now lettest Thou Thy Servant depart in

peace, for mine eyes have seen thy salvation." The

music is by Alexander Kastalsky. _____ is

the baritone soloist.

MADRIGAL
SINGERS.
CU NARRATOR.   NARRATOR:

We hope that you have enjoyed this special program of

Christmas music brought to you by the University

Madrigal Singers under the direction of _____

of the Department of Music.

WIDE SHOT OF   (MUSIC: SINGERS IN BG.)

GROUP.

SUPER ALL   This has been a presentation of the Television Divi-

CREDITS.   sion of the University of _____.

DISSOLVE TO

"UNIVERSITY"

CARD.

PART THREE

Acting in and Directing Television Drama

9

Directing Television Drama

THERE IS A PARODY on an old saying to the effect that if you can keep your head while others all about you are losing theirs, you simply don't understand the situation. We amend it by saying that if you can keep your head while others all about you seem to be losing theirs, you will make an efficient television director. However, if your qualifications are limited to the ability to keep calm under tension, you may be a director who turns out efficiently managed productions that lack imagination. On the other hand, if you can direct a drama containing subtle nuances and tense scenes with gripping climaxes but are unable to control the technical details, your productions may be lost on the home audience. To give you an over-all picture of this dual responsibility we will take you, step by step, through a complete production.

You begin with a script and a budget. In a professional production this budget would consist of above-the-line and below-the-line costs. Above-the-line costs include general talent items such as producer, director, actors, and musicians. Below-the-line costs include general production items: sets, music rights, special effects, technical personnel, art work, and studio costs. Let us assume that your budget is minimal and that your student talent, crew, rehearsal rooms, and studio are available without cost.[1] Much of the material for sets, props, and graphics will probably be available in the shop, prop room, and in general supplies for your university or college department. If you intend to use slides or motion picture film you may require additional funds for raw film stock and, later, money to pay for processing your film. If there are no additional funds, you must take this into account when you plan your production. "Keeping within the budget," is a lesson you cannot learn too soon.

You Study the Script

The budget may be inflexible, but the script is not. It is here that your most important work as a director begins, long before you have taken

---

[1] Nevertheless, it is a good idea to keep track of what your costs would be if you had to pay current rates for all these items. It also should help everyone to hold in solid respect the contributions each student makes to the production as a whole. Your producer (or your assistant, if you are serving as producer-director) can keep these records. You may wish to work out two budgets: one a mock-professional budget with cost estimates of all items, and a second one with your actual production costs over and above all items available to you free of charge.

any of the subsequent steps necessary in your production. Read the script carefully. Look first for its basic concept, the essential reason for its existence. What is the author trying to say? Are the characters clearly defined? Is their dialogue well motivated? Is the plot believable and well structured? Where does the climax occur? After you have scrutinized the script, and perhaps made some modifications (if the author is accessible you may wish to consult him), you must decide on your production approach. Will you treat the production as a sophisticated comedy—fast moving, bright, effervescent? Or, is it a serious drama to be paced slowly at the start, and built up to a shocking climax that involves strong emotional reaction rather than vigorous physical action? To determine the essential values of a script, and the production approach that will express them best, is not an easy matter. Correcting a deficient script is equally difficult. Both require sensitivity and experience, and you may wish to discuss your ideas with your instructor before making any firm decisions. Above all, if the author is available, consult with him.

You Confer with the Designer

When you are completely clear in your own mind how to approach your production, you will give a copy of the script to your designer with a written or verbal memo indicating your plan. After he has read the script, you will confer with him regarding the style of setting (realistic, stylized, cameo) that will best reflect the spirit of your approach. You will discuss such limiting factors as the size and shape of your audio; budgetary limitations; complexity of construction; the space necessary for camera movements, and also settle on the general floor plan for the production. This floor plan must be complete with precise detail by the time you are ready to begin blocking the rehearsals, so that from the start you can plan actors' movements and camera angles with reasonable exactness. The floor plan can be a simple top-view diagram showing the placement and dimensions of the set in the studio, and the location of various important props.

As the director, you will be concurrently engaged in a number of activities. While the designer is working on his set designs, a number of other preparations will need your attention before your production is ready for rehearsal.

You Reserve Studio Space

Along with the script, budget, and floor plan, you will at the outset want to be clear about your broadcast date and hour; the length of time you are allowed for camera rehearsal, and the availability of space for reading and dry-run rehearsals. Prepare a complete production schedule, indicating a detailed plan of rehearsal from the beginning to the end of the production. The schedule should include the following:

1. Scenes to be rehearsed.
2. Time and duration of rehearsal.
3. Place of rehearsal.
4. Actors and crew involved.

Although you might make some changes later on, this information should be ready immediately after the casting announcement has been posted.

You Select Your Production Crew

The members of your production crew will be assigned to you by your instructor, or you may select them from your knowledge of their skill and experience. In addition to the designer, you will have an assistant director, cameraman, floor manager, lighting supervisor, property man, costume, make-up, and graphics supervisors; grips (stagehands), microphone boom operator, camera cable pullers, technical director, audio engineer, video engineer, music supervisor, and film projectionist; and, possibly, a sound effects man, if you plan to use manual sound effects in the studio together with recorded effects played on turntables in the control room. Instruct your assistant to post all names on the bulletin board, with directions for each person to pick up his own script.

You may conduct your auditions without cameras, but it is a sound policy to both see and hear actors as they will appear on the screen during actual production. Use members of your crew to assist you with casting auditions. Have them report in advance of auditions to warm up the cameras and be assigned to staff the various studio and control room positions. Each member of the crew should function in the same position he will occupy during the production. Others can serve as assistants, handing out scripts and bringing audition forms to you in the control room. In addition, you may wish to assign someone to take photographs of the auditionees for your permanent records.

You Cast Your Show

The selection of a cast is crucial to your show. Mediocre acting can ruin a technically superior production and, conversely, superb acting can carry a show that is indifferent technically. Your responsibility in casting is to give a fair hearing to those who have troubled themselves to come to your audition. Remember that the actors have put themselves entirely at your mercy and, therefore, you should respond by treating them with consideration and respect. Never abuse your position of authority by ridiculing an actor's efforts, not even privately to a colleague in the control room. Particularly avoid laughter that may be heard through an inadequately soundproofed wall, or seen by an actor through the control room window. He will invariably interpret this as your reaction to his reading, although you may not have so intended it. This is not saying that the audition need be a grave affair, but rather that it should have an atmosphere of warmth, sympathy, and appreciation.

Make a script available to each actor in advance of his audition, giving him ample time to study it. Give every auditionee an opportunity to be heard even though you feel that, after he has read one line, you cannot use him. Be generous with the common words of courtesy. (Directions like "Thank you, Mr. Ballard. Now will you please read the second paragraph. Take it a little more slowly . . ." help to put the actor at ease.) Remember, too, that at the audition you set the tone for the production to follow, and that your colleagues will be quick to sense your lead. Be sure that you use this golden opportunity to establish your seriousness of purpose and show your appreciation of the sincere efforts of others.

Whenever possible, allow the actors to read together. You can then observe their ability to react to one another and judge their skill in interpreting lines. Where student talent is used exclusively, it is especially important to remember that, before the revealing eye of the camera, standard make-up will not camouflage a face as adequately as it does on the stage. An actor should look his age and his part as closely as possible.

You may not wish to make a final choice of cast at your first audition. If an actor seems at all promising, include his name on a list of auditionees to be called back for final auditions on the next afternoon or evening. Often, you will get better results when an actor has had time to think about the script after his first reading. You will also have a better perspective on the talent available. Be sure to keep a record of your evaluation of each auditionee, preferably on an audition form similar to the Audition Sheet in the Production Kit.

You Plan and Confer

Having selected your cast, your activities as director will run simultaneously along two lines that will converge as your production approaches completion. On the one hand, you will conduct rehearsals, blocking action, working with actors, and planning camera angles on paper. On the other hand, you will hold individual conferences with your set designer, costume designer, lighting, graphics, make-up, music supervisors, audio engineer, and technical director. You should be prepared for adjustments when the production moves into the studio for camera rehearsals; but if you plan well in advance with each supervisor, there may be only a minimum of such adjustments. It is much easier to change a plan on paper than it is to rebuild a flat or redesign a costume after it has been completed incorrectly because of a misunderstanding.

Just as you must plan in advance with all your supervisors you, as the director, must know precisely what you are going to do with the various scenes before rehearsals begin.

You may change your plan from time to time, but there must be an initial blueprint. You may work either with your floor plan or with a miniature set made of blocks cut to scale. Eventually, the blocking of each scene, choice of lenses and camera angles for each line of dialogue, placement of microphones, lighting diagrams, and cues for sound effects and music will all be incorporated in a production script. This script will serve as the master plan, and also represent a running account of the performance (which can be supplemented with still pictures) and the director's comments for a permanent file record of the production.

In planning your action and camera shots, keep in mind the special characteristics of the television medium. The variety of lenses and camera positions gives you an opportunity to view your dramatic action and settings from many angles and vantage points. Do not limit yourself to photographing a scene as it might look on a stage. Within the limitations of the depth of field of each lens, stage your action in depth as well as on a horizontal plane. As a rule, close-ups and medium shots are more effective than wide-angle shots with too much detail spread across the small rectangular home screen. At the same time, the wide-angle shot has its place in orienting the audience to a scene. But whatever shots you use—close-up, medium, long, overhead, low-angle, or eye-level—the important thing is to have a valid reason for your choice. Never change a shot or camera angle without

adequate motivation, and avoid the frantic cutting from one shot to another that succeeds only in disturbing the viewer. Remember the importance of reaction shots.

If you are employing two or three cameras in your production, it is a particularly good idea to have your cameramen use "shot cards." These are simply small cards clipped onto each camera, with numbered shots matching those on the director's script, briefly describing the nature of each shot. With such cards you can easily refer to all shots by number and, in addition, the notes will remind the cameraman precisely how you want the shot executed.

You will soon learn that certain cues and shots are more effective when executed in a particular way. For example, in tilting the camera up or down, and in a pan shot, always lead with the camera; do not follow the performer as if you are trying to catch up with him. Cut on an actor's movement, rather than from one static shot to another. When music, voice, or sound effects accompany a picture they should be faded or cut in simultaneously with the picture. It is very important to "ready" all shots so that your cameramen are prepared with their shots when you call them. ("Ready to cue talent; ready camera one. Cue talent, take one. Ready camera two. A little tighter on two. . . . Good. Take two.")

Time your production as soon as your cast is ready to run through it at approximately the tempo you have planned. Keep a running time; if the show is running long, note the places where you might conceivably make a deletion. For better or worse, broadcasting is a time-conscious medium, and you must begin and end your program "on the nose."

Pay particular attention to the composition of your picture. This is an esthetic matter that cannot be taught quickly, but it underlines the fact that television is a composite art, utilizing in its presentation the elements of many art forms. Sensitivity to line, form, texture, balance, and perspective, like sensitivity to different kinds of music, must be cultivated by study and exposure. This sensitivity can be developed through the study of outstanding examples of still photography, through formal courses in art appreciation, and informal observation of artistic presentations in the theater, ballet, motion pictures, and television itself.

Sound and Music

Although the emphasis will be on the visual aspects of your production, do not neglect the importance of the aural dimension. When blocking your camera action, keep in mind the fact that you will need space for the boom microphone. If possible, plan to so position the boom that it does not cut across the front of the cameras and lights at right angles, or cast the inevitable microphone shadow on your picture. Watch sound levels at all times, and caution your audio engineer to make this his special concern. Make sure that the boom mike is close enough to the action without dipping into the picture frame. Watch the perspective on your sound effects. A door closing, or a telephone ringing across the room, should not sound as if they are "on mike." As a rule, manual effects are preferable to sound records, and the use of recorded effects is usually limited to those that are hard to produce in the studio.

Do not overlook the impact of music for emphasis, mood, atmosphere, color, character identification, and dramatic or special effects. Music can either be taped or recorded. When transferring music to tape, always record more of the segment than is needed; you may want to use it for cover in case the visual sequence unexpectedly runs longer than you had planned. Leave about six feet of leader between your taped music bridges.

The First Reading

Before you meet your cast for the first reading, your production script will already be well on the way to its final form. Tentative decisions on all blocking and camera angles will be confirmed or slightly modified in later camera rehearsals in the studio, although with the use of a viewer lens you can predict with reasonable accuracy the coverage of each shot. Marking the script with pencils of different color to indicate the shots for each camera will help you to recognize instantly, by color as well as by number, which camera you are using. Music and sound can also be underlined in distinguishing colors (see Symbols for Television Script Marking in the Production Kit.)

Your call for the first reading should be posted on the bulletin board by your assistant, with directions for members of the cast to pick up their scripts in advance of the rehearsal. For this rehearsal only your cast and your assistant-director need be present.

You can begin by setting the approach to the total production as you wish it played, briefly describing your concept of all characters involved. None of this need be done in too great detail, but enough to give each actor an idea as to how you interpret his role. Since members of the cast have had their scripts in advance they should have read the play through before the first reading. However, an actor often tends to see his role as a separate performance rather than as a character with a particular function in the complete production. Therefore, as director, you can make his relationship in the story clear at the outset, but do not expect him to fully realize all the nuances of his role the first time around; it is too early to start fussing with details. However, the first reading should give you and the cast a chance to see how the story hangs together as a unit, as expressed by the men and women you have selected to interpret it. The first reading will probably take about two hours, and you may have a chance to read the script through twice.

After your first reading, most of the problems you envisioned with your cast will be clarified. For example, if an actor does not deliver the kind of performance you expected, you may have to schedule special sessions to give him individual assistance. Bear in mind that not everyone is a quick study, and often a student who is slow to develop a part eventually comes up with the best performance. As a rule, you can quickly discover whether an actor will prove satisfactory, and the fact that television drama allows minimal time for rehearsal makes it necessary to cast actors who do not take too long to mature in their roles. Try not to replace an actor except as a last resort, and only if you have made it clear at the outset that the assignment is tentative. Once you cast your show you have an informal contract with the students, who probably have to rearrange many activities to meet your rehearsal schedule. You should feel bound to honor this contract. Usually, any changes you make will not be enough of an improvement to justify the blow to the general cast morale involved in recasting a part.

Every director has his own way of working with his cast, but from the start you should exhibit a firmness of manner without being unfriendly or inflexible. Be sure the cast understands that you must make all decisions about any differences of opinion. If you are clear in your own mind as to what you want, the cast will sense that your authority stems from your understanding of the play rather than from your position as director and will respond with enthusiasm. In a professional situation, with experienced actors, you merely call for the interpretation you wish and expect the actor to respond. Working with amateurs, you may have to combine the job of directing with a certain amount of instruction and guidance for your weaker actors. In any case, allow the actors to be as creative as possible—accepting suggestions where they are helpful, and encouraging comments—so long as the results are not at variance with your essential plan of action.

Blocking the Production

The blocking rehearsals do not require a studio, but whatever space is required should be marked off with precise dimensions of the areas that eventually will be used in the studio. You can use masking tape or chalk to mark the exact boundaries on the floor, and whatever is available to substitute for regular props and furniture. If you plan to have a sofa in the final production, a chair or two or a piano bench will serve in rehearsal. But be sure to keep the spatial relationships the same. Do not be impatient if the blocking moves slowly at first, and maintain a critical attitude regarding every movement an actor makes. As you observe the rehearsal with live performers and props, you may find that what seemed satisfactory on your paper plan now looks static and uninteresting. Two people seated on the sofa, for example, may require more than their witty dialogue to hold the attention of the audience. You may have to invent some stage business to give the actors an opportunity to walk around the sofa and face each other standing, or have one actor rise while the other remains seated. Remember, stage business is not monkey business—every movement must be motivated by dialogue.

To inexperienced television actors the playing area often is confining; they might move too rapidly for you to change from one camera shot to another, or tend to stand too far apart for two-shots. You will have to explain that normal stage distances and movements are exaggerated on television the audience sees at home on a small viewing screen.

It is also important to explain to the actors the reasons for each piece of blocking you have planned. If you indicate the camera shots you are attempting to get at various points, it will help the cast to understand the logic of each movement. ("Jane, we'll open on an establishing shot of the room with you and John sitting on the sofa. On line five we cut to you for a close-up, then to a two-shot of both of you; so please don't move too far apart.") At times it may be necessary to remind an actor that every line he speaks and every action he performs must be motivated. ("Jane, on line 15 you look rather aimless as you walk across to the door. It might help if you remember that you're going into the hallway to make a telephone call.")

From this point until the dress rehearsal each prestudio rehearsal is an occasion for reinforcing all characterizations of the actors, and developing the mechanics of early blocking routines into easy-flowing action. Lines should be learned as quickly as possible. There is no rule about this, but urge your cast not to put it off too long. Give them deadlines, and tell them in advance the number of rehearsals you will need. Six rehearsals of 3 to 4 hours each should be sufficient for a 15-minute show, but more may have to be scheduled if the show is complicated. Camera rehearsals, of course, are additional.

Production Dynamics

During the first two or three rehearsals the actors usually are preoccupied with production mechanics and not fully conscious of the subtleties of the production. However, as they learn their lines and grow accustomed to their stage movements, and you can concentrate on the dynamics of the show as a whole, your skill as a director will reveal itself. Any competent person can put a production together and make it move neatly from one episode to another. But to give a production the dynamics of a living situation, to add to each scene a natural compelling quality, and to exploit minor peaks and build to a major climax, requires talent and experience which are as easy to recognize in the television director as in any other creative artist.

If a particular scene fails to jell because one actor is slow to respond to direction, do not hold up the entire group too long while you work with him. Limited detailed coaching of this kind may be good for the cast as a whole because of its transfer value for each individual role; but if it is too prolonged, it becomes boring. Make a separate appointment for a private rehearsal. You can probably get better results in such a conference if the situation calls for vigorous treatment; also, there will be less cause for embarrassment. ("John, you've been entirely too stiff in this scene. Tomorrow, why don't you go down to Miss Jeffers in the Creative Dance Department and get some help in limbering up your body. Meanwhile, let's run through the scene in caricature—playing it for comedy and exaggerating all movements. Maybe that will help you shake off some of your inhibitions.")

Rehearsals in the Studio

By the time you reach the date of your studio rehearsals with cameras and full studio facilities all problems of line interpretation should have been completed, and your production should be ready on paper. At this stage your major concern will be to integrate camera shots with technical factors of settings, props, lighting, graphics, film inserts, sound, and music. The blocking you have done outside may require minor changes now that complete settings are available. Take one scene at a time. Start your camera work from the floor of the studio, verifying and modifying your preplanned shots, and use masking tape on the floor to indicate the precise positions of the cameras. These shots can be viewed on the studio monitor. When the scene appears to be satisfactory on the floor, check it from the control room.

In blocking your camera shots you may find that, in order to get an eye-level shot of the actors, your cameras must be set too low on the pedestal for convenient manipulation by the cameramen. On the other hand, if you "ped up," your cameras may be constantly looking down on the actors. To rectify the problem you may wish to elevate the staging area by using platforms or individual blocks. Your lighting man will set his lights in accordance with your conference plan; and while you are working on camera shots, he can check on lighting problems from the control room. After the camera shots are set, you can review lighting problems by having the actors walk through their various positions to check against shots in which, for example, an actor's face is "washed out" as he rises from a sitting position on the sofa into the glare of a strong key light.

Warn your cameramen not to frame shots so tightly that the heads of actors are too close to the frame line. Remember that by the time the picture reaches the imperfectly-tuned home receiver it will probably be cut down in width and height, and the head may appear to be chopped off at the hair line. You can insure against this error by drawing a border around the view finder of each camera and keeping the picture within this border.[2]

Let your assistant-director help ease any tension you experience in calling shots and in checking elements of the production. For example, have him set up shots and "ready" cameras and other video sources, and leave yourself free to concentrate your attention on editing the action on the air. Your assistant will also be responsible for recording on the director's script all revisions made during rehearsals.

Depending on your experience, and the complexity of your production, the number of rehearsals required before the dress rehearsal will probably vary. Two 5–hour rehearsals may suffice, but it is possible that you may need more. In your first shows, it is better to have ample studio time until you have thoroughly learned the short cuts.

After you have ironed out the technical problems with your crew scene by scene, and have gone through the complete production for continuity on camera, work to give the show coherence, polish and, above all, dynamics. Coherence means that your production must hold together as a unit. Polish means that it must have a well-rehearsed, smooth-running look—especially in points of transition—and an authoritative opening and assured conclusion. Dynamics describes the living quality of the show—its pacing, surprises, peaks, and its climaxes. All these elements should be noted and checked before dress rehearsal.

The Dress Rehearsal

As you approach your dress rehearsal, a number of items may not be as ready as you would like. This is normal for television. Your job is to concentrate on the four or five essential weak points and not worry, let us say, about an actor whose performance will at this juncture not improve appreciably no matter how much more attention you give him.

Before beginning the dress rehearsal, run a check on the major technical elements of the production. Match cameras (that is, check the lighting to make sure that the light levels are the same when you switch from one camera to the other) by having actors walk through the various positions they will assume in the course of the show. Check sound levels for actors, sound effects, and music at key points in the production. If necessary, run a cue rehearsal of graphics, slides, and film inserts to insure smooth transitions. Then run through your dress rehearsal, having your assistant time the show. Also note items that may require correction with brief checks of a pencil, but do not let your concern with one error interfere with your over-all evaluation of the show.

After the dress rehearsal call the cast together in the studio and give them a brief critique, noting only those things that can be easily corrected, encouraging and praising wherever possible. ("John, that was so much better. Don't forget to work close to Jane in the opening routine; you're a little too far apart. Cameramen, get to your shots more quickly after your camera is free; you're still cutting off heads in some of the frames, but otherwise fine. Jim, sound levels are beautiful—keep them that way.") Don't kill the spirit of the show with too much criticism at this point. Preserve an air of expectation and encouragement.

And now you are ready for a live broadcast, closed circuit or video tape production, as the case may be. You know that all members of your cast will do their best. If you have prepared carefully for this moment, the show will undoubtedly go well. Things should move almost by themselves now. You need only to keep a calm, firm hand on the production, and let your crew feel your assurance. Your cast has no more contact with you; all their directions will be relayed through the floor manager. ("All right, this is it. Quiet everybody. Stand by! One minute . . . 30

---

[2] Similarly, allow ample margins on all graphics to prevent the printing from running out of the frame.

seconds. . . . Ready music, ready cameras one and two, ready announcer . . . 15 seconds. . . . Roll music. Take one. Cue announcer. Dissolve to two.") The show is on its way.

After the show is over be sure to thank members of the cast and crew, and everyone who had anything to do with your production. Later you may wish to have a critique, with or without a kinescope or tape; but at this point everyone is keyed up and excited. It is not a time for criticism, but for gratitude and praise. An objective critique can come later.

10

Elementary Exercises and Scripts

THE FUNDAMENTALS of acting and directing are the same in all media, but we cannot assume that everyone who studies television acting and directing has had experience in other media. Our approach here is to give some suggestions concerning acting and directing generally, with exercises relating to specific television techniques and problems of television production.

For example, in all acting and directing, certain controls are essential. They are usually described as self-discipline; the ability to cooperate, to work under pressure, and under difficult conditions. The difference in television is that the pressure is greater and the conditions are changed, but the fundamentals are the same.

Again, in all dramatic media the purpose is to create an illusion of reality, or, as some prefer to say, truth. Actors, with the help of directors, bring to life characters who are believable and whose emotions and actions are understood by the audience. In television the methods of revealing the emotions and showing the actions are different, but the fundamentals of bringing a character to life are the same.

In all media the director is responsible for the over-all effect of every line, light, movement, and the visual effect on the audience in relation to the story which he wants them to believe. In

television he shows movement and visual effects in ways that differ only in technique.

In the following exercises you will act in or direct short scenes which emphasize many of the fundamentals—but always in relation to television's small screen. Perhaps the most significant difference between acting and directing for television, and for other media, is the small screen. For example, motion picture and stage dramas can be presented with movement that is primarily horizontal. In television drama, the small screen requires movement in depth. In other words, a character does not enter from "stage right" and take a long horizontal walk to center stage; he may "enter" simply by having a camera pick him up in the background of a set, as a door opens. In television drama the camera becomes the eye of the viewer. For the director this means understanding what the viewers should see to make the story believable and the illusion true.

For actors this means two things. First, much of the time you are not certain whether you are on the screen or not. Your director is choosing the parts of each scene which he thinks the viewer should see; you may be in the scene, but not on the screen. Therefore, you should give total performance at all times. You may take a hasty glance at camera to see if it is on you just at the moment it is picking you up and, instead of Sir Alfred Teddlyby stoutly defying the mob, viewers see a worried actor peering at them.

Second, because most of your scenes will be staged in depth on a somewhat limited physical area, you may sometimes need to create an illusion of large spaces and movements in small sets with limited gestures. You may not have the facilities to recreate a chase across the rooftops of Paris, but you may have to create the effect of such a chase.

We begin with simple pantomimes primarily designed to give directors experience in staging and in composition, and actors experience in motivating movement and expression. Then we experiment with various ways of directing a long dialogue scene, and end with a scene that combines all we hope you will have learned about movement, staging, composition, and line reading.

Entering a Strange Place

Using any simple interior with a door, pantomime the following entrance situations:

1. You are frightened, running from someone, and are entering a room you have never seen before but hope to hide in.
2. You are timid, and have just been shown into an elegant room where you are to wait for an interview.
3. You are self-assured and entering a room you are thinking of renting if it pleases you, which it does not.
4. You are ill, entering a hospital room, and unsure as to where to put your belongings.
5. You are gay and happy, entering the living room.

FOR DIRECTORS

Assume, in each of these situations, that it is important to see the character's actual entrance. In each situation you will have to make several decisions. Is the door open when the character enters, or does he open it? In either case, when the door is open, does he walk directly onto the set, or stop to look around? When he does walk onto the set, where does he walk to and in what mood? Should you have a tape mark to show him where to stop? And, what lens, and which camera? The camera can show him in a close shot, a medium, or a long; it can show him to the viewers from various angles. Is it a stationary shot, an overhead, a pan, or tilt? Most important, why? What dramatic impact do you wish to achieve with this shot?

After you have made your decision you must plan your lighting in relation to your shots and your interpretation of the mood. Obviously, in a complete television play there would be other factors to consider: the relationship of this entrance to preceding or following scenes, shots, availability of technical equipment, and so on. In this exercise you simply assume that all entrances are extremely important.

FOR ACTORS

In each of these situations, the way you first look at the room will establish the idea that it is strange to you. For example, you might stop at the doorway and glance about quickly to size it up, or you may take a few steps into the room first. Whichever you do will be guided, if not dictated, by your director. Your job is to give a total performance. More accurately, you must give the total performance specifically because you may not know at what angle or distance you are being seen.

Entering a Familiar Place

Using the same or a similar set, pantomime the following:

1. You are cold, entering a familiar room, and you go straight to the fireplace to warm your hands.
2. You are late for work, and coming into your office eager to be at your desk before the boss sees you.

3. You are hurried, coming home laden with packages to find the telephone ringing.
4. You are sleepy, entering the kitchen early in the morning in order to start breakfast.

FOR DIRECTORS

In these exercises, assume that the actual entrance is not as important as the action that follows it—warming hands, sitting down at a desk, and so on, even though it is essential for the viewer to know that the character has just entered. Assume that the viewers have seen the character in the same room before, but in a different situation. In other words, it is not as necessary for the viewers to know where the character is so long as they know why he is there. And, because the viewers have seen the set before, you need not establish it as a kitchen or an office before you shoot the action. Your directorial problem is to show the action and its motivation. In each situation the character's motivation is clear and simple: to get warm, to answer a telephone, to look busy. However, as director, you will be concerned with staging. For example, does the character who enters, bearing packages, drop the packages on the floor before answering the telephone? Place them on a table? Carry them with him to the telephone? Where is the telephone?

For another example, how do you, as director, show us that the character entering the office is late? Do you show us a clock on the wall that says ten after nine? A roomful of people already busy at their desks? Or do you let the actor reveal it through his haste and fear? How do you show each entrance and action? How many cameras do you use?

FOR ACTORS

When you enter a familiar place, you do not have to look about you to see where things are. You know. You know, for example, that the coffee is on the bottom shelf of the left-hand cupboard, and the spoon in the drawer beneath; you can find both with your eyes half closed, then reach for the pot with one hand while you turn on the faucet with the other. It is what the viewers sense you do not have to look at that establishes your familiarity with the room. In the first set of situations it was important to establish the fact that you were not familiar with the room you were entering; but now we concentrate on why you are entering, and what that reason does to your movement.

For example, in the entrance where you go directly to the fireplace to warm your hands, do you move quickly or slowly? Are you rubbing your hands as you enter, to indicate that they are cold? Or, do you come in well-gloved and amble leisurely toward the fireplace, stripping off your gloves as you walk?

Because we are concentrating here on staging and movement, you and your director can assume that you have a neutral emotional character. That is, you are cold and eager to get warm, but not worried about anything else. Similarly, you are entering your house with an armful of packages and, for the moment, your only conflict is how to dispose of them and get to the ringing telephone.

A Long Dialogue Scene

VIDEO	AUDIO
	(INTERIOR OF A MODESTLY FURNISHED LIVING ROOM. PAUL AND NINA ARE SEATED ON A COUCH.)

PAUL

Let's go over it again, Nina. If your alibi doesn't hang together, we're sunk.

NINA

All right. I was coming out of the store . . .

PAUL

No! Start before that! Remember, it's the time element that's most important!

NINA

Oh, Paul! I'm so frightened I can't remember anything.

PAUL

That's why we have to go over it! You've got to remember! Start again!

NINA

It was about four o'clock in the afternoon. I'd gone to the store to look at some lamps that had been advertised in the paper.

PAUL

How did you know it was about four o'clock?

NINA

I had an appointment to meet a friend at five, and . . .

PAUL

Nina, we cut that out. You can't prove it. How did you know it was about four o'clock?

NINA

On my way to the store I stopped to mail a letter and
I checked to see if there was still time . . . I mean, I
wanted the letter to be picked up that afternoon, so I
looked at my watch . . .

PAUL

So you noted the time because you wanted to be sure
you mailed your letter in time for the last pickup?

NINA

Yes. So I saw it was only about quarter of four, so I
mailed the letter and went on to the store. That's how
I know what time it was.

PAUL

Go on!

NINA

I went on to the store and I looked and I looked, but I
couldn't find anything I liked. So I came home.

PAUL

Wait! Did anyone see you there, in the store?

NINA

No. I mean, yes!

PAUL

Nina! Get hold of yourself!

NINA

Paul, I'm trying, I'm sure that a great many people
saw me in the store, but I don't know whether any of

them would remember me. It was such a big sale and
there were so many people . . . .

PAUL

Good! A lot of people must have seen you.

NINA

A lot of people must have seen me.

PAUL

But you don't know if they'd remember you.

NINA

But I don't know if they'd remember me.

PAUL

And you were there for about half an hour.

NINA

And I was there for about half an hour.

PAUL

Don't just keep repeating what I say! Go on!

NINA

After I'd looked around awhile and couldn't find anything I liked, I decided I might just as well go home.

PAUL

And what time did you get home?

NINA

I'm not sure, but I think it was some time between
five-thirty and six.

PAUL

Five-thirty or six?

NINA

Yes. Just as I was leaving the store I realized that
one of my gloves was missing, so I went to the lamp
department and looked for it. When I couldn't find it
there, I thought maybe I'd left it in my car, so I went
back there . . . . Oh, Paul, they'll never believe it!

PAUL

Keep going!

NINA

I don't know how much time I spent looking for my
glove, but I know that I got home about . . . . Oh, Paul,
why can't I tell them the truth?

PAUL

Because I'll deny it. I'll swear that I never set eyes
on you that day.

NINA

But we weren't doing anything wrong! I know your
business deal is secret, but I wouldn't tell anything
about it, just that I was typing for you and . . .

PAUL

And I'll deny it. Start over.

NINA

DISSOLVE TO   It was about four o'clock . . . .

NINA ON WIT-

NESS STAND

FOR DIRECTORS

The most difficult part of directing a long dialogue scene is avoiding monotonous cuts from actor to actor and at the same time avoiding tricky shots, or unmotivated business that detracts from the dialogue.

A tricky shot is one that alters the viewer's picture of the scene without a purpose. For example, a close-up can be meaningful, even climactic; but if it doesn't reveal an important reaction, it is simply tricky. A high overhead or angle shot can change the viewer's perspective; but if it doesn't reveal anything dramatically fresh, it also is simply tricky.

A tricky shot is not only artistically inept, but often adds unnecessary extra work to the job of the director and crew. Consequently, it can interfere with the effective production of other, more valuable shots.

In the preceding long dialogue scene, motivation comes principally from the emotions of Nina and Paul. Both are frightened; but Paul is very firm, whereas Nina's mood changes. Each change of her mood can motivate a change of shot, just as each of Paul's reactions to her changes could motivate a shot. However, unless the change of shot helps us to understand the change of mood or reaction, it does not add to our understanding of the scene.

In motivating business, you face the same problem. You may feel a need for movement and action. But you cannot, for example, have Nina sweeping or dusting or putting her hair in curlers in this scene any more than you could have Paul doing push-ups during their conversation.

We have deliberately refrained from indicating specific action in this scene to let you experiment with different ways of motivating action that is meaningful in terms of your and your actors' concept of the scene.

FOR ACTORS

This is a scene in which line reading and facial expression will probably be most important, but you must remember that each character's emotions and changes of attitude will be apparent by his physical action. It is not necessary, as in old-time silent movies, to portray fear or tension by violent shaking of the body and eyes rolling wildly; your body will reveal your emotional state. It is suggested that Nina and Paul are sitting on a couch at the opening of the scene, although neither would be sitting in a relaxed position. Each is tense, and tension usually results in a stiffening of muscles; shoulders tend to be rigid, movements inhibited. In addition, most people have some specific bodily reaction to fear or tension. Some cough or clear their throats, some rub one finger against another or lick their lips nervously. Whatever your interpretation of the character you are playing in this scene, remember that you must give a total performance of a character who must be a total individual to your viewers.

A Scene with Movement, Dialogue, and a Special Effect

VIDEO	AUDIO
	(INTERIOR OF A SQUALID ROOM JOE IS
	STUDYING A ROAD MAP. A BRIEFCASE IS ON

THE FLOOR BESIDE HIM. LOUISE IS STAND-

ING AT THE WINDOW BUT TO ONE SIDE,

MAKING SURE SHE IS NOT SEEN.)

JOE

If we can make it to San Diego tonight, we'll be in

Mexico tomorrow!

LOUISE

San Diego! We can't even get out of this apartment!

JOE

(NOT LOOKING UP FROM THE MAP)

Why not? (HE POINTS TO THE BRIEFCASE) The

money is there.

(LOUISE SIDLES CLOSER TO THE WINDOW,

PARTS THE CURTAINS SLIGHTLY, LOOKS OUT

AND DOWN.)

CUT TO:

HIGH OVERHEAD

SHOT OF STREET

BELOW.

(IN THE DIM LIGHT OF A STREET LAMP WE

SEE A MAN LOUNGING AGAINST A BUILDING.)

CUT TO LOUISE,

BACKING AWAY

FROM THE WINDOW.

LOUISE

Bill's still there!

JOE

We'll just wait till he goes.

LOUISE

But what if he stays all night?

JOE

He won't.

LOUISE

How do you know?

JOE

(STILL LOOKING AT THE MAP)

In San Diego we can stay with Tony; he'll get us

across the border. We may take a plane from Tijuana

or . . .

LOUISE

(BREAKING IN)

Stop it! Can't you realize that we're not going any-

where? We're trapped . . . like mice in a cage. You

said we'd be rich . . . . One last job, you said, and we

could do anything we wanted. Sure! We can sit in this

lousy room and play with maps!

(LOUISE SEIZES THE MAP FROM JOE AND FLINGS

IT TO THE FLOOR. JOE SEEMS UNCONCERNED.

HE PICKS UP THE MAP.)

JOE

(AGAIN LOOKING AT THE MAP)

Of course, we could go to Ensenada. Actually, once

we're out of the country, we can go just about any-

where we want. . .Louise!

(LOUISE FURTIVELY PICKS UP THE BRIEF-

CASE. SHE BEGINS TO TIPTOE TOWARD THE

DOOR. JOE LOOKS UP AND SEES LOUISE

GOING TOWARD THE DOOR WITH THE BRIEF-

CASE. HE RISES AND RUSHES TO INTERCEPT

HER. SHE BACKS AWAY AND THE CHASE

BEGINS. AROUND THE CHAIR, TOWARD THE

DOOR, NEAR THE WINDOW, LOUISE TRYING

ALWAYS TO REACH THE DOOR. FINALLY, JOE

GRABS THE BRIEFCASE FROM HER. SHE GOES

TO THE WINDOW AND YANKS OPEN THE

CURTAINS.)

LOUISE

Bill! Bill!

(JOE, WITH THE BRIEFCASE, LEAVES THE

ROOM.)

LOUISE

Bill?

CUT TO SAME
HIGH OVERHEAD.
SHOT OF STREET
BELOW.

(BILL IS NO LONGER ON STREET BUT AS

WE WATCH, JOE STARTS ACROSS WITH

THE BRIEFCASE.)

LOUISE

Joe!

FOR DIRECTORS

In this exercise, as in the others, we are indicating only the most basic action. The chase, for example, can and probably should be much longer than suggested here. Joe intercepts Louise before she reaches the door, but it would be inadequate for them to play ring-around-the-rosy with the chair. You will not only have to use every inch of your set, but you will have an opportunity to work creatively with staging in depth and imaginative cutting. For example, the effect of a chase can be achieved with a long shot of Joe lunging toward the camera, with a cut to a close shot of a frightened Louise backing away. The effect of a chase can also be achieved by having both actors virtually motionless, watching each other for the first sign of movement. This can be done with a conventional two-shot, cuts from one over-the-shoulder shot to another, or with a variety of one-shots. In other words, instead of a lateral chase you will stage a chase in depth, quite possibly using more rapid cuts than in previous exercises.

Because the high overhead shot of the street has technical complications, the problem here is to decide first whether it is essential. A high overhead shot requires a separate and skillfully lighted set which, in a live production, virtually immobilizes one camera that would have to be placed on a catwalk or on a specially erected platform.

Let us assume that you have three cameras, and that this exercise is an excerpt from a drama which otherwise can be handled with two cameras. Your problem is to decide whether the effect of this high overhead shot justifies the use of the third camera and crew, in addition to other technical problems involved in staging and directing it.

Suppose you have only two cameras available. You will then have to decide whether the high overhead shot is, to put it simply, worth the trouble, and also whether the remainder of the scene will suffer if it must be shot with only one camera.

What is the purpose of the overhead shot of the street? What does it add to the scene? When Louise first looks out of the window, we see what she sees; we are not told what she sees. There is always some value in letting the audience become directly involved in any experience of a character, although it is not essential. In this scene—in addition to verifying Louise's assertion that Bill is still there—it intensifies the mood of fear, and offers both visual variety and an extension of the set. However, when the difficulties of production are too great, it might be better to hope that good acting will compensate for the lack of these values.

You can, for example, simply omit the overhead shots and depend on close-ups of Louise and Joe to help reveal all they see and feel. You can add dialogue to let them explain what they see and feel. Or, you can decide that they are not in a room on the second floor, but on the first floor, and use one camera for an out-of-the-window shot of Bill lounging against a building across the darkened street without immobilizing the camera's occasional additional use in the scene. In other words, if you cannot or prefer not to direct the scene as written, your job is to understand its purpose so well that you can achieve the same dramatic effects in a different way.

FOR ACTORS

The relationship between Joe and Louise is rather obvious at the beginning. Louise is fearful and hostile toward Joe, who is apparently unconcerned and unnaturally calm. Louise indicates her emotional state through activity; she is at the window, and we would assume that it is not the first time she has gone to it to look out and see whether Bill is still there. She is probably the kind of person who would keep glancing toward the window even when she was not near it.

Joe, on the other hand, is overcontrolled. He ignores not only the window, but also the reality of his situation. His exaggerated calm shows itself in his voice and in the deliberateness of each movement. However, at the moment when he realizes that Louise is trying to make off with the money in the briefcase, his control breaks and he becomes almost savage. Consequently, during the chase he is far more aggressive than she. All the fears he has been controlling are now released in the single fear of losing the money; all the hostility, which may have made him what he is, is now released against Louise. In other words, the emotional relationship between Louise and Joe is now completely reversed. To build up this change and make it believable is one of your two most important acting problems.

The second problem is to work with your director in order to create the effect of a chase. You may not become involved in anything remotely resembling an actual chase, but you will have to appear to be involved in one. If your director wants a shot of you advancing or retreating from any part of the set, you must be able to appear as though this movement is part of a continuous action—even though it is, in fact, an isolated shot. There is no dialogue in this chase, and this means that everything you portray must be done with the same sort of pantomime with which we began this series of exercises.

PART FOUR

Advanced
Acting and Directing

NOTE ON ADVANCED ACTING AND DIRECTING

POPULAR DRAMA has been in existence for centuries. By popular drama we mean neither good nor bad drama, but simply drama that appeals to a great many people. Much popular drama also includes universal and basic human qualities recognizable from generation to generation and from century to century. These we call classics.

Primarily, television today presents popular drama. A small percentage of it may survive and become classic, for the same reasons that the classic dramas of the stage have survived. However, the fundamentals of good showmanship have not changed since the Greeks first had a word for it. In the following section we present television adaptations of cuttings from popular dramas of the past, each of which is similar to entertainment currently found on television. If you can act in or direct these plays, you will have no difficulty with their contemporary counterparts on television.

For example, *The Frogs,* written by Aristophanes in 400 B.C., is broad comedy, almost farce. If you, either as actor or director, can bring out the comedic elements in this ancient Greek play then you can act in or direct any modern broad comedy.

Similarly, if you can act in or direct the adaptation of the cutting from Shakespeare's *The Taming of the Shrew,* you will be able to act in or direct any sharp drawing-room comedy. The cutting from *The Beggar's Opera* will give you experience in musical comedy; *The Doll's House* will help you understand good soap opera, and *The Cherry Orchard* provides a chance to experiment with the mood-and-method type of acting and directing. The section includes *The Molière Story,* which represents television's adaptation of the "bare-stage-and-stools" technique.

The script form of these plays is designed to give you maximum opportunity for creative directing. We have indicated rather than called the shots, leaving you ample room to mark the script for specific directions with regard to lens, angle, and staging.

Descriptions for opening titles and closing credits are also only suggestions. We have tried to keep them simple; but if your studio has the equipment, you may wish to experiment with more elaborate ways to establish the mood of each play when giving titles and credits. A word of caution, however: A tricky opening and closing may take time that would be far better used for polishing lines and improving action.

Directors and actors both would profit by reading the originals of each of the adaptations to get the full flavor of characters and action. It might be an interesting experiment to expand one or more to a full one-hour show, adapting second and third acts to television. In any event, working with some of the world's classic dramas will give you an insight into some of the fundamentals of good popular entertainment.

The section ends with a thirty-minute television script by Christopher Knopf. The script, *Interrogation,* was first produced on the Dick Powell-Zane Grey Theater, and represents television drama at its unique best—portraits of individuals in conflict as much with themselves as with others.

11

The Frogs Aristophanes

In 405 b.c., Aristophanes produced his play, *The Frogs*, and won the highest prize at the Lenaean festival in Greece. *The Frogs* is a classic example of satire—broad comedy with a serious point.

The serious point of the play is the question of whether Euripides or Aeschylus is the better playwright. Euripides is dead and Dionysus, known as the patron god of tragedy, wants to bring him back to earth again to prove his worth. To do so, however, he must go to Hades. Some time before, a friend of his, Heracles, brought back a man from Hades, and Dionysus decides to disguise himself as Heracles. When Heracles descended into Hades, he wore a lion's skin over his robe and carried a large club. Dionysus will do the same! And so, with Xanthias, his servant (what great Greek would travel without a servant?), Dionysus goes to Hades.

Obviously, even in 405 b.c., this was a comedic situation. For you now, as actor or director, the adapted scene requires the elements of slapstick comedy, and you will first have to decide how broadly you wish to play it. If you decide to play it as broadly as possible, your title cards and set should indicate this mood. On the other hand, you may wish to stage the scene on a set representing a Greek theater, or even against a cyclorama with a set piece indicating a house

and a door. In any event, you must keep the incongruities alive; Dionysus, the Greek God, must still act like a god, even though he looks ridiculous—dressed in his lion's skin, carrying a club—and feels woefully afraid. His slave, Xanthias, who carries a pole hung with lumpy bundles of luggage, must change from the meek servant to the blindly arrogant master with enough exaggeration to let us see the satire and understand the slave with his new-found power.

Because we wish you to use your own creative imagination as much as possible, we merely indicate here that title cards and credits are to be written in Greek letters with English subtitles— a rather obvious technique. Also, we suggest that you use several different types of sets. Undoubtedly you will improve on these suggestions, and we hope that you let your creativity have full sway. Our only caution is a reminder that skilled acting and directing are more important than the invention of technical tricks.

You may wish to consider whether the chorus is to be costumed in a Greek robe and sandals, or wear an ordinary suit like the narrator he actually is or whether the chorus should be male or female. In other words, you can act in or direct the script exactly as written, or change it to fit your own creative interpretation.

Scene from The Frogs*

ARISTOPHANES

Adapted by Rome Cowgill

CAST	SET
DIONYSUS	EXTERIOR: *Suggestion of a street in Hades, and a house with a huge door.*
XANTHIAS—his slave	
AECUS—the judge of the dead	
MAID OF PERSEPHONE	
THE CHORUS	

VIDEO	AUDIO
TITLE CARDS IN GREEK LETTER- ING WITH ENGLISH SUB-TITLES. CUT TO SET AND THE CHORUS.	
	THE CHORUS
	This is The Frogs, a play written by Aristophanes many centuries ago. In its way, it's a great debate. . . but it's way is most curious.
	(CHANGE ANGLE AS THE CHORUS MOVES TO THE

---

* Adapted from the Gilbert Murray translation of Aristophanes' *The Frogs*, with the permission of George Allen & Unwin, Ltd. (London).

SIDE AND POINTS DOWN THE "STREET." LONG

SHOT OF DIONYSUS AND XANTHIAS LOOKING

FEARFULLY ABOUT AS THEY WALK HESITANTLY

TOWARD THE CAMERA. PLAY FOR COMEDY.)

THE CHORUS

The god, Dionysus, coming up the street to your left,

wants to prove that Euripides was the greatest play-

wright of Greece. But Euripides is dead, and Diony-

sus has come here to Hades to bring him back.

He's frightened, no doubt of that, even though he has

his servant, Xanthias, with him, and is disguised as

the great Heracles. Heracles, wearing a lion's skin

and carrying a club, once brought a friend out of Hades.

Can Dionysus do less?

(THE CHORUS BACKS OUT OF THE PICTURE AS

DIONYSUS AND XANTHIAS REACH THE DOOR OF

THE HOUSE, LOOKING NERVOUSLY ABOUT.)

LEADER OF THE CHORUS (V.O.)

The luggage Xanthias carries on the pole contains the

regular garments of Dionysus.

MOVE IN TO WAIST

SHOT OF DIONYSUS   (DIONYSUS AND XANTHIAS APPROACH THE HOUSE.)

AND XANTHIUS

And now they're at the door of Pluto's house, planning

their strategy.

XANTHIAS

Dionysus, sir, shall I say one of the regular things

that people in a theater always laugh at?

DIONYSUS

Say what you like, except not "I'm over-loaded."

XANTHIAS

(DISAPPOINTED) Not anything funny?

DIONYSUS

No. (LOOKING AT THE DOOR) I ought, by rights, to

knock, but I don't know how they knock in this country.

XANTHIAS

Don't waste time. Do your best. Be like Heracles in

heart as well as dress.

CHANGE TO ONE-
SHOT

(DIONYSUS, EXAGGERATEDLY BRAVE, KNOCKS AT

THE DOOR.)

DIONYSUS

(VERY LOUDLY) Ho, there!

(DOOR OPENS.)

TWO-SHOT OF
AEACUS AND
DIONYSUS.

AEACUS

(POMPOUSLY) Who summons?

DIONYSUS

(FEARFULLY) Heracles the brave?

AEACUS

Thou rash, impure, and most abandoned man!

Foulest upon earth . . . now I have thee! May witches

adrip with blood surround these circling hounds and

the hundred-headed serpent . . . to whom (MENAC-

INGLY) I even now speed my course.

PULL BACK

(AEACUS SLAMS THE DOOR. DIONYSUS DROPS TO
HIS KNEES. XANTHIAS LETS THE POLE OF LUG-
GAGE FALL AND TRIES TO HELP DIONYSUS UP,
STRUGGLING AND PULLING.)

                    DIONYSUS

Please . . .

                    XANTHIAS

Quick, get up before they come and see you. You're

supposed to be Heracles the brave.

                    DIONYSUS

I feel faint. Put a cold, wet sponge against my heart.

(XANTHIAS FRANTICALLY SEARCHES THROUGH

THE LUGGAGE AND COMES UP WITH A COLD WET

SPONGE.)

                    XANTHIAS

(HANDING SPONGE TO DIONYSUS) Here.

                    DIONYSUS

(GRABBING BLINDLY FOR THE SPONGE) Thanks.

(DIONYSUS, STILL WITHOUT LOOKING UP, TAKES

THE SPONGE AND PUTS IT ON HIS STOMACH.)

                    XANTHIAS

Ye golden gods! Is that where you keep your heart?

                    DIONYSUS

The nervous shock made it go down and down.

                    XANTHIAS

You're the greatest coward I ever saw.

DIONYSUS

Weren't you frightened at that man's awful threats
and language?

XANTHIAS

I never cared a rap.

(DIONYSUS GETS UP ANGRILY AND STARTS TO
TAKE OFF THE LION'S SKIN. XANTHIAS MOVES
BACK A LITTLE.)

DIONYSUS

All right, you be me! Put on this lion's skin, and take
the club, and I'll be your luggage boy.

(FRANTICALLY, XANTHIAS PUTS ON THE LION'S
SKIN, WHILE DIONYSUS PICKS UP THE POLE AND
LUGGAGE. XANTHIAS IS STILL ADJUSTING THE
LION'S SKIN WHEN THE DOOR OPENS. THE MAID

CHANGE ANGLE.   WALKS UP TO XANTHIAS. MAID AND XANTHIAS IN

THREE-SHOT   FOREGROUND. DIONYSUS, NERVOUSLY HOISTING
THE POLE FROM SHOULDER TO SHOULDER, IN
THE BACKGROUND.)

MAID

(TO XANTHIAS) Dear Heracles, are you here again.
Come in! As soon as my mistress heard you were
here she sent her bread to bake, put pots of soup on
the stove, a whole ox on the coals, cakes in the oven
and big buns. Oh, do come in!

XANTHIAS

(IMPORTANTLY) She's very kind. Perhaps some other time.

MAID

I musn't let you go. There's also roast duck, spices and fruits, and gallons of wine.

XANTHIAS

(WAVERING) You are most kind!

MAID

(STRETCHING OUT HER ARMS TO HIM) And a flute player, and two or three sweet young dancing girls.

XANTHIAS

(DELIGHTED) Dancing girls? (TURNING TO DIONYSUS) Here boy, take the bags and follow me.

MOVE IN TO A
CLOSE SHOT OF
DIONYSUS, ANGRY.
THEN BACK TO
A TWO-SHOT OF
XANTHIAS AND
THE MAID.

XANTHIAS

(IMPERIOUSLY TO THE MAID) Tell those dancing girls that Heracles is coming.

CHANGE ANGLE   (MAID EXITS. DIONYSUS STARTS TO RIP THE

FOR A TWO-SHOT
OF DIONYSUS AND
XANTHIAS.

LION'S SKIN FROM XANTHIAS. XANTHIAS RESISTS.)

DIONYSUS

(FURIOUS) Did you take it seriously when I just
dressed you as Heracles for fun!

XANTHIAS

I leave it with the gods. (SCREAMING) Help! Help!
(XANTHIAS PULLS HIMSELF AWAY FROM
DIONYSUS. DIONYSUS KEEPS TUGGING AT THE
LION'S SKIN. HE STRUGGLES AND FALLS, AND
THE LION'S SKIN COMES OFF. XANTHIAS TURNS,
AND TRIES TO GRAB THE LION'S SKIN FROM
DIONYSUS. THEY TUSSLE. BUT DIONYSUS HOLDS
ON TO THE LION'S SKIN AND PUTS IT ON.)
Help! Help!

CHANGE ANGLE
FOR A THREE-
SHOT.

(DIONYSUS IS TRYING TO ADJUST THE LION'S SKIN
AS XANTHIAS TRIES TO GET IT BACK. BOTH ARE
STRUGGLING TOWARD THE DOOR. AEACUS
COMES OUT OF THE DOOR OF THE HOUSE. AS
AEACUS SPEAKS, XANTHIAS AND DIONYSUS COME
TO AN EMBARRASSED HALT JUST AT THE DOOR.)

AEACUS

What's going on?

XANTHIAS

(STILL FEELING LIKE HERACLES) My slave is
trying to rob me of my lion's skin.

AEACUS

He shall be put to torture. What tortures do you allow?

XANTHIAS

Use all you like, but nothing with onions.

CLOSE
SHOT OF
DIONYSUS.
CHANGE ANGLE
TO THREE-
SHOT.
CHANGE ANGLE
FOR A CLOSE
SHOT OF
DIONYSUS.

DIONYSUS

To torture me is an illegal act! I am immortal!

AEACUS

Immortal? Who do you think you are?

DIONYSUS

(PROUDLY) I am the immortal Dionysus, son of Zeus, (POINTING TO XANTHIAS WITH THE POLE) and this is my slave.

WIDEN TO
THREE-SHOT

AEACUS

(TO XANTHIAS) You hear what he says?

XANTHIAS

Yes . . . all the more reason for whipping him. If he's a real immortal, he won't feel it.

DIONYSUS

You claim to be immortal, too. They ought to give

you just the same as me.

XANTHIAS

(TRYING TO CARRY IT OFF) Fair enough.

AEACUS

(TO XANTHIAS) Sir, you behave like a true gentleman.

XANTHIAS

(NERVOUS) How are you going to test us?

AEACUS

You'll each take whack and whack about.

CUT TO A CLOSE   (AEACUS WHACKS XANTHIAS. XANTHIAS WINCES)

SHOT OF   XANTHIAS

XANTHIAS   (AS THOUGH HE HADN'T FELT THE BLOW) Well,

when are you going to begin?

CUT TO THREE-

SHOT.   AEACUS

(ASTONISHED) But I've already hit you!

XANTHIAS

(IMPERIOUSLY) I think not.

AEACUS

Upon my word! Now I'll whack the other.

(AEACUS WHACKS DIONYSUS. DIONYSUS WINCES

AGAIN.)

DIONYSUS

(AS THOUGH HE HAD NOT FELT THE BLOW)
When?

AEACUS

I've already done it!

DIONYSUS

Odd . . . it didn't even make me sneeze.

AEACUS

(PUZZLED) It is odd. I'll try the first again.

(AEACUS WHACKS XANTHIAS.)

MOVE IN TO A
CLOSE SHOT OF
XANTHIAS.

XANTHIAS

(OBVIOUSLY IN PAIN) Whew!

CUT TO THREE
SHOT.

AEACUS

Why did you say "whew"?

XANTHIAS

I was just thinking when my birthday was coming.

AEACUS

I'll try the other one again.

CLOSE-SHOT OF
DIONYSUS

(AEACUS WHACKS DIONYSUS.)

DIONYSUS

(OBVIOUSLY IN PAIN) Ow!

CUT TO THREE-

SHOT.

                              AEACUS

                    (SUSPICIOUSLY) What's that? And what makes your

                    eyes run?

                              DIONYSUS

                    There's a smell of onions.

                              AEACUS

                    You're sure it didn't hurt?

                              DIONYSUS

                    Not at all.

                              AEACUS

                    Then I'll have to try the other one.

CHANGE TO A   (AEACUS STRIKES XANTHIAS.)

CLOSE SHOT OF   XANTHIAS

XANTHIAS.   (HOWLING) Hi-yi---

CUT TO THREE-   AEACUS

SHOT.   Ah-ha!

                              XANTHIAS

                    (POINTING TO HIS FOOT) There's a thorn in my

                    foot.

                              AEACUS

                    (SHAKING HIS HEAD) Well, over we go again.

CUT TO CLOSE-   (AEACUS STRIKES DIONYSUS.)

UP OF DIONYSUS.   DIONYSUS

                    Oh, lord! (PRETENDING HE WAS QUOTING

                    POETRY) Lord of Delos or of Pythos Rock . . .

CUT TO CLOSE

SHOT OF

XANTHIAS.

XANTHIAS

(TRIUMPHANTLY) You see! It hurts!

CUT TO CLOSE

SHOT OF

DIONYSUS.

DIONYSUS

I was only saying a verse of old Hipponax to myself.

CUT TO THREE

SHOT

XANTHIAS

You're making nothing of it. (TO AEACUS) Hit him

harder, across the soft parts underneath the ribs.

AEACUS

A good idea!

(AEACUS HITS XANTHIAS UNDER THE RIBS.)

XANTHIAS

Oh lord!

DIONYSUS

(TRIUMPHANTLY) It hurt him!

XANTHIAS

(AS THOUGH CONTINUING) Oh, lord Poseidon of

cliffs Agean and the gray salt sea . . .

AEACUS

(BEWILDERED) Now, by Demeter, it's beyond my

powers to tell which one of you is the god. Come in!

We'll ask my master Pluto. He'll know, being a god

himself.

XANTHIAS

(HORRIFIED.) Pluto?

(XANTHIAS STARTS TO BACK AWAY.)

(DIONYSUS GRABS XANTHIAS AND PULLS HIM

TOWARD THE DOOR. XANTHIAS STRUGGLES.)

CHANGE TO CLOSE
SHOT OF DIONYSUS.

DIONYSUS

(GLEEFUL) Now we'll learn the truth, wretch!

(AEACUS HOLDS THE DOOR OPEN AS DIONYSUS

PULLS XANTHIAS THROUGH. AEACUS LOOKS AT

US AND, AFTER A SHRUG OF THE SHOULDERS,

FOLLOWS DIONYSUS AND XANTHIAS. AS THE DOOR

CLOSES, THE CHORUS WALKS INTO THE PICTURE.)

THE CHORUS

Now, by Zeus, the masquerade is over! Pluto will

know slave from master . . . (WRYLY) and Dionysus

from Heracles. But nothing ill befalls them and the

feasting continues through the night. Who wins the

debate? Forsooth . . . it hasn't ended yet!

FADE TO BLACK.
CLOSING TITLES
AND CREDITS.

12

Taming of the Shrew Shakespeare

THE CHIEF PROBLEM in acting in or directing *The Taming of the Shrew* is how to project the vital, bouncy quality of the two leading characters with the flavor of the Elizabethan drama. The tendency of many young actors is to take Shakespeare too seriously, intoning the lines and using stiff movements and gestures. In this adaptation we have used a teaser opening that sets up the situation in contemporary language—partly to give you a chance to experiment with a teaser-type opening, and partly to introduce the audience to the play without the barrier of unfamiliar language. After the teaser and the opening titles, we present the cutting in only slightly modified Elizabethan language. Some directors may wish to rephrase the lines of the teaser and give them the Elizabethan quality. Again, this is the privilege of the creative director.

Obviously, it is one of the first decisions which you, as director, will make. Your next decision, among many others, will probably be the degree of authenticity for sets and costuming. This adaptation is the only one of the advanced exercises that requires two sets. The street set of the teaser could be done by action taking place against black curtains with the actors spotlighted; or against a painted backdrop, or on a set depicting a reasonable representation of an Italian street of its period. The second set, the interior, could range from suggested realism, such as a pair of apparently ornately carved doors and a single large gilt-and-velvet chair, to a replica of a drawing room of its time. Except for the doors, which are necessary for entrances and exits, no furnishings or props are required for this scene.

In other words, you are quite free to decide what visual effects you wish to create within the limits of Shakespearian comedy.

The third, and possibly most difficult problem you face is directing the action. Because, superficially, the scene is primarily dialogue with a conflict of personalities rather than of physical actions, director and actors have a more subtle job of motivating action or movement than in, say, a play that includes a duel and a few episodes in which people leap from balconies or swing from chandeliers. There are possibilities for a great deal of motivated action and movement in this scene, but directors and actors alike need a thorough understanding of the scene and its purpose to achieve it. For example, in the final portion of the cutting, Petruchio and Kate spar with each other; both are belligerent, yet mutually attracted. Dialogue makes this utterly clear, but their physical movements should reinforce the dialogue.

Scene from The Taming of the Shrew

WILLIAM SHAKESPEARE

Adapted by Rome Cowgill

CAST

KATHARINA—Elder daughter of Baptista
PETRUCHIO—A gentleman of Verona in search of a wife
BIANCA—Sweet, younger daughter of Baptista
BAPTISTA—A rich gentleman of Padua
TRANIO—A suitor of Bianca
HORTENSIO—Another suitor of Bianca
A SERVANT

SETS

EXTERIOR, DAY: *Suggestion of an Italian street.*
INTERIOR, DAY: *Elegantly furnished Italian parlor.*

VIDEO	AUDIO
THE STREET. DAY.	
(PETRUCHIO WALKS INTO THE PICTURE, JAUNTILY AND GRINNING. HE STOPS AT ABOUT A WAIST SHOT AND TOSSES A COIN. HE CATCHES IT AND IS LOOKING AT IT WHEN HORTENSIO	

WALKS INTO THE
PICTURE FROM
THE OTHER SIDE.)

HORTENSIO

(TO PETRUCHIO) Sir?

PETRUCHIO

My name is Petruchio, sir.

HORTENSIO

And mine is Hortensio.

(THEY BOTH BOW, FORMALLY.)

HORTENSIO

Can you tell me, sir Petruchio, which is the way to

the house of Signor Baptista Minola?

PETRUCHIO

I'm a stranger here myself, sir.

HORTENSIO

Looking for work?

PETRUCHIO

Looking for a wife.

HORTENSIO

Aren't there any girls where you come from?

PETRUCHIO

None that I'd marry!

NEW ANGLE,
HORTENSIO.

HORTENSIO

(HE IS LOOKING ALMOST PITEOUSLY AT PETRU-

CHIO.) Oh, sir, I can find you a wife! If we can find

Signor Minola! He has two daughters! I am courting

his daughter Bianca, but he won't let her marry until

her sister Kate is married. If you could marry

Kate . . .

NEW ANGLE,
PETRUCHIO.

PETRUCHIO

(HE LOOKS DUBIOUS.) What's the matter with Kate?

Bowlegged? Squint-eyed? Fat?

NEW ANGLE,
HORTENSIO.

HORTENSIO

Nothing like that . . . but . . . well, Kate, they say,

has a temper. And a great dowry! (HIS FACE

LIGHTING UP.)

PETRUCHIO

(IGNORING THE DOWRY) A temper! I like a gal with

a temper!

NEW ANGLE,
PETRUCHIO AND
HORTENSIO.

HORTENSIO

(APPREHENSIVELY) They say it's a very bad temper?

PETRUCHIO

Sounds better and better. I'll tell you. . .my father

used to know Signor Minola and I was wondering

whether to go first to his house or another's.

(ANOTHER LOOK AT THE COIN) Now . . . if we can

find Signor Minola's house . . . (HE LOOKS OFF)

There's a man who looks like he's not a stranger in

town! (CALLING) Sir! (TRANIO WALKS INTO THE

NEW ANGLE.

PICTURE. HE HAS A LUTE ON HIS BACK AND A

PACKET OF BOOKS IN HIS HAND.)

TRANIO

You called me?

PETRUCHIO

Do you know the way to the house of Signor Baptista

Minola?

TRANIO

(MODESTLY) I was just on my way there myself. I am

am going to woo his daughter, Bianca!

HORTENSIO

Bianca!

PETRUCHIO

(LAUGHING) Two suitors for Bianca and none for

Kate!

THREE SHOT.

PETRUCHIO

Come, gentlemen, we'll all go together! Bianca can't

marry either one of you until Kate is married. And I

like the sound of Kate. Maybe I can tame the shrew!

CUT TO:

TITLES AND

SOUND UNDER

LUTE, RECORDER

AND OR OTHER

ELIZABETHAN

TYPE MUSIC,

ENDING WITH AN

EFFECT OF

CLASHING AS WE

CUT TO:

(INTERIOR. DAY. ELEGANTLY FURNISHED

ITALIAN PARLOR. KATE IS SLAPPING

BIANCA, WHO COWERS AND RETREATS, IS

CAUGHT AND SLAPPED AGAIN. BIANCA

STEPS BACK, WEEPING.)

BIANCA

Good sister, Kate! Please?

(BAPTISTA WALKS INTO THE PICTURE.)

BAPTISTA

Whence grows this insolence? Why dost thou wrong

Kate, who did ne'er wrong thee?

KATE

Her silence angers me and I'll be revenged.

(KATE STARTS FOR BIANCA AGAIN.)

BAPTISTA

(STEPPING BETWEEN THE TWO) What! In my sight?

Bianca, get thee in.

(BIANCA RUNS OUT OF THE PICTURE AS KATE,

FURIOUS, WALKS UP TO HER FATHER.

KATE

(FURIOUS) Bianca is your treasure. She must have a

husband, but I must dance barefoot on her wedding

day.

BAPTISTA

But . . .

KATE

Talk not to me. I will go sit and weep till I can find

occasion for revenge.

(KATE RUNS OUT OF PICTURE IN OPPOSITE

DIRECTION FROM BIANCA.)

MOVE IN TO A
CLOSE SINGLE
SHOT OF
BAPTISTA.

BAPTISTA

(LOOKING AT US) Was ever any gentleman thus

grieved as I? (LOOKING OFF) But who comes here?

CHANGE ANGLE
TO BAPTISTA'S
POV.

(HORTENSIO, PETRUCHIO ARE COMING INTO THE

ROOM.)

PETRUCHIO

Signor Minola? I am Petruchio, a gentleman of

Verona. You know my father well, and in him me.

BAPTISTA

I knew your father?

PETRUCHIO

Signor Antonio was his name.

BAPTISTA

I did know him, and if only for his sake, you are

welcome.

PETRUCHIO

Pray sir, have you not a daughter called Katherine,
fair and virtuous?

BAPTISTA

(DRY) I have a daughter, sir, called Katherine.

PETRUCHIO

Hearing of Katherine's beauty and her wit, her
bashful modesty and mild behavior, I am bold to show
myself a forward guest in your house to make mine
eye the witness of that report which I have so oft
heard. (POINTING TO HORTENSIO) I present you
with a man, Hortensio, cunning in music and math, to
teach her those sciences.

BAPTISTA

He is welcome for your good sake. (TO TRANIO) And
you, good sir?

TRANIO

I am Tranio, come to make myself a suitor to your
daughter, Bianca. Your firm resolve is known to me
in the preferment of the eldest sister. This liberty is
all that I request, that, upon knowledge of my parent-
age, I may have welcome amongst the rest that woo.

BAPTISTA

You are welcome, sir. (POINTING TO HORTENSIO)
Go with this man, and you shall see your pupils
presently. Holla!

PULL BACK TO
WIDE ANGLE
SHOT.

(A SERVANT ENTERS.)

Sirrah, lead these gentlemen to my two daughters and
tell them both these are their tutors. And now, you
sir?

(HORTENSIO AND TRANIO FOLLOW THE SERVANT
THROUGH THE DOOR.)

MOVE IN TO TWO-
SHOT OF BAPTISTA
AND PETRUCHIO.

PETRUCHIO

I am sole heir to all my father's lands and goods. So
tell me, if I get your daughter's love, what dowry shall
I have with her as a wife?

BAPTISTA

After my death, one half of my lands and twenty
thousand crowns.

PETRUCHIO

And for that dowry, I'll assure her of her widowhood,
should she survive me, in all my lands and leases
whatsoever.

BAPTISTA

(FIRST A BLANK LOOK. DUBIOUS) Ay? . . . Ay.
Ay! But only when the special thing is well obtained . . .
that is . . . her love.

PETRUCHIO

Why, that is nothing! I tell you, father, I'm as
peremptory as she is proud-minded; and where two

raging fires meet together, they do consume the thing

that feeds their fury.

BAPTISTA

Yet, be thou armed for some unhappy words!

PETRUCHIO

I am, indeed. . . . But what is this?

CHANGE ANGLE   HORTENSIO ENTERS HOLDING HIS BLEEDING

TO THREE-SHOT.   HEAD.

BAPTISTA

(GOING TO HIM) How now, my friend! Why dost thou

look so pale?

HORTENSIO

For fear, I promise you, if I look pale.

(REACTIONS FROM PETRUCHIO.)

BAPTISTA

Will my daughter prove to be a good musician?

HORTENSIO

I think she'll sooner prove a soldier.

BAPTISTA

Why, then, can'st thou break the lute to her?

MOVE IN ON

HORTENSIO FOR

ONE-SHOT.

HORTENSIO

(RUBBING HIS HEAD.) She hath broke the lute to me.

I did but tell her she mistook her frets, and bowed

her hand to teach her fingering, when, with a most

impatient devilish spirit, she said, "You call these

frets!" And with that, she struck me on the head.

PULL BACK FOR

THREE-SHOT.

(PETRUCHIO IS GRINNING, AND IN CENTER FOCUS.
BAPTISTA IS CONCERNED. HORTENSIO, STILL
RUBBING HIS HEAD, GIVES PETRUCHIO A LOOK
OF DISBELIEF.)

PETRUCHIO

Well, now, she is a lusty wench. I love her ten times

more than e're I did. Oh, how I long to have some

chat with her!

BAPTISTA

(RATHER UNCOMFORTABLE) I'll send my daughter

to you at once! (TO HORTENSIO) Good sir, come

with me!

(BAPTISTA AND HORTENSIO LEAVE.)

PETRUCHIO

Pray you do! And shall I woo her (TO THEIR RE-

TREATING BACKS, IMPISHLY) with some spirit

when she comes.

CLOSE IN TO

CLOSE SHOT OF

PETRUCHIO.

(STILL IMPISH. AS HE SPEAKS, MOVES ABOUT,
PANTOMIMING HIS WORDS.)

Say that she rail ... why then I'll tell her plain she

sings as sweetly as a nightingale. Say that she

frown ... I'll say she looks as clear as morning

roses newly washed with dew. Say she be mute and

will not speak a word . . . then I'll commend her
volubility. If she do bid me pack, I'll give her thanks
as though she bid me stay by her a week. If she deny
to wed, I'll crave the day when I shall ask the banns,
and when be married. But here she comes . . . and
now, Petruchio . . . speak!

(PETRUCHIO WHIRLS ABOUT AS KATHARINE
COMES THROUGH THE DOOR IMPERIOUSLY.)

Good morrow, Kate, for that's your name, I hear!

CHANGE TO TWO-
SHOT.

KATE

(IMPERIOUSLY) Well have you heard, but something
hard of hearing. They that talk of me call me
Katherine.

(KATE TURNS HER BACK ON PETRUCHIO AND
WALKS AWAY. PETRUCHIO FOLLOWS.)

PETRUCHIO

You lie, in faith . . . for you are called plain Kate and
Bonny Kate and sometimes Kate the curst . . . but
always the prettiest Kate in Christendom. (BEAT)
Myself am moved to woo thee for a wife.

(KATE MOVES UP TO HIM.)

KATE

Moved! Let him that moved you hither, move thee
hence!

PETRUCHIO

Come, come, you wasp! In faith you are too angry.

KATE

If I be waspish, best beware my sting!

PETRUCHIO

My remedy is, then, to pluck it out.

KATE

Ay, if the fool could find where it lies!

(TURNING HER BACK ON HIM) And so farewell.

PETRUCHIO

(SPINNING HER ABOUT TO FACE HIM) Good Kate,

I am a gentleman.

KATE

(FURIOUS) That I'll try. (SHE STRIKES HIM AND

THEN STANDS, ARMS AKIMBO, DARING PETRUCHIO

TO STRIKE BACK.)

PETRUCHIO

(CONTROLLING HIMSELF) I swear I'll cuff you if

you strike again.

KATE

If you strike me you are no gentleman.

PETRUCHIO

Come, Kate . . . you must not look so sour.

KATE

(BELLIGERENT) It's my fashion when I see a crab.

PETRUCHIO

Why, here's no crab, and therefore look not sour.

KATE

There is, there is!

PETRUCHIO

Then show it me!

KATE

Had I a glass I would.

PETRUCHIO

You mean my face?

KATE

Well aimed of such a young one.

PETRUCHIO

Now, by Saint George, I'm too young for you!

KATE

Yet you are withered.

PETRUCHIO

(SMIRK) 'Tis with cares.

(KATE STARTS FOR THE DOOR. PETRUCHIO
GRABS HER.)

KATE

I care not.

PETRUCHIO

In sooth, you 'scape not so!

KATE

(STRUGGLING) I chafe you if I tarry . . . let me go.

PETRUCHIO

No! Not a whit! I find you passing gentle.

(KATE BREAKS AWAY. PETRUCHIO BARS HER WAY
TO THE DOOR. SHE MOVES IN ANOTHER
DIRECTION.)

'Twas told me you were rough and coy and sullen, and
now I find report a very liar. Thou art pleasant,
gamesome, passing courteous . . . but slow in speech,
yet sweet in springtime flowers. Thou can'st not
frown nor bite the lip, as angry wenches will. Nor
hast thou pleasure to be cross in talk. Thou with
mildness entertain thy wooers with gentle conferences. Why dost the world report that Kate dost limp?
O slanderous world!

(HE CIRCLES, BARRING HER WAY AGAIN, AND
TALKING ALL THE WHILE. KATE HAS BEEN
WALKING ABOUT AND COMES TO A HALT, NOSE
TO NOSE WITH PETRUCHIO.)

KATE

Where did you study all this goodly speech?

PETRUCHIO

It is extempore, from my mother-wit.

(KATE BACKS UP, WHIRLS ON PETRUCHIO.)

KATE

A witty mother! Witless, her son.

(PETRUCHIO GOES UP TO KATE AND TRIES TO
HOLD HER IN HIS ARMS. SHE STRUGGLES, BUT NOT
TOO HARD.)

PETRUCHIO

Sweet Kate! In plain terms . . . your father hath consented that you shall be my wife, and will you, nill you, I will marry you.

(KATE STARTS TO STRIKE HIM AGAIN.

PETRUCHIO CONTROLS HER.)

Kate, I am a husband for you. By this light I can see thy beauty . . . thy beauty that doth make me like thee well. (KATE STRUGGLES.) Thou must be married to no man but to me. For I am he am born to tame you. Kate! I must and will have Katharina for my wife! Kiss me Kate!

(SHE DOES, PASSIONATELY.)

FADE TO BLACK.
CLOSING TITLES.
ELIZABETHAN
MUSIC.

13

The Cherry Orchard Chekhov

IN THIS CUTTING from Act I of *The Cherry Orchard,* you are directing or acting in a play in which mood and overtones are as important as action and dialogue. Madam Ranevsky arrives home after six years in Paris, where she went after the death of her husband. She is both impoverished and improvident; but if she sells her old mansion and the useless cherry orchard for a housing project, she will have money enough to live comfortably. However, she is an aristocrat of a past era, and a sensitive woman. To her, the idea of selling what was her childhood home and the home of her marriage is impossible. In addition, to turn this property over to the rising middle classes seems like a desecration. She feels that if only someone in the family could marry a rich man, their fortune would be made. But the only rich men available are members of this same rising middle class, and Madam Ranevsky cannot think of bringing them into her aristocratic circle. She is caught in the conflict of a changing society and cannot adjust to a new milieu—which coincidentally commenced at the time of her husband's death.

In playing and directing this episode you have many opportunities for experimentation, ranging from conservative realism with authentic sets and costumes to an abstract set dominated by exaggerated symbols. For example, the window looking out on the cherry orchard, and the cupboard to which Madam Ranevsky's brother makes his impassioned speech, could be distorted either through size or shape or both. The dialogue switches abruptly from passionate speeches to commonplace remarks, indicating the inability of the group to grasp the seriousness of the situation, and provides excellent opportunities for humor—especially in the character of old Firs, the manservant, with his irrelevant mumblings.

One of your problems will be the handling of a large group of performers, particularly in the opening portion of the scene. The nine people who follow Madam Ranevsky into the room cannot be left standing stiffly like statues in a row. Although they are all watching Madam Ranevsky and sharing in her big moment of homecoming they, themselves, experience various emotional reactions. Therefore, you may wish to give them some bits of business which, however, must be well motivated and never detract from the essential dramatic action.

Scene from The Cherry Orchard

ANTON CHEKHOV

Adapted by Rome Cowgill

CAST	SET

CAST

MADAM RANEVSKY—an attractive, middle-aged woman
ANYA—her daughter, aged 17
LEONID—brother of Madam Ranevsky
VARYA—Madam Ranevsky's adopted daughter, aged 27
LOPAKHIN—a merchant
SEMYONOV-PISHTCHIK—a landowner
CHARLOTTA—a governess
EPIHODOV—a clerk
DUNYASHA—a housemaid
FIRS—manservant, aged 87

SET

INTERIOR, NIGHT: *Madam Ranevsky's old nursery, dominated by a huge, ornate chest, and a large window. A sense of decadent elegance.*

VIDEO	AUDIO
UNDER TITLES WE SLOWLY PAN THE NURSERY, AND THEN DOLLY IN TO DOORWAY FOR MEDIUM CU OF MADAM RANEVSKY IN TRAVELING CLOTHES LOOKING	

ABOUT THE ROOM

TEARFULLY.

MADAM RANEVSKY

My old nursery! All those years I was in Paris,

I never dreamed that I'd see it again!

DOLLY BACK.

WIDEN ANGLE TO

LET US SEE THAT

SHE IS FOLLOWED.

(MADAM RANEVSKY WALKS INTO THE ROOM.)

ANYA, OLD FIRS, CHARLOTTA, EPIHODOV,

LEONID, DUNYASHA, AND PISHTCHICK ENTER.

THERE IS A SENSE OF A GRAND PROCESSION.

MADAM RANEVSKY SWEEPS TO THE WINDOW

AND LOOKS OUT.)

MADAM RANEVSKY

And my cherry orchard . . . . My orchard. . .my

nursery. . .where I lived when I was a girl. (WEEPING)

I am the little girl, Lyuba, still.

MEDIUM CU OF

MADAM RANEVSKY

AS SHE TURNS

FROM THE

WINDOW. WIDEN

ANGLE TO SHOW

THE WHOLE

GROUP.

(MADAM RANEVSKY GOES TO LEONID AND KISSES

HIM.)

MADAM RANEVSKY

Leonid! My dear brother. . .!

(THEN GOES TO VARYA AND KISSES HER) Varya!

My sweet adopted daughter!

(AND THEN BACK TO LEONID. SHE MAKES AN

EXPANSIVE GESTURE) I love you all! (THEN

MADAM RANEVSKY GOES TO DUNYASHA AND

KISSES HER) I knew you at once, Dunyasha!

LEONID

Your train was two hours late, dear sister. It's already three o'clock in the morning.

(NOBODY PAYS ANY ATTENTION TO HIM.)

CHARLOTTA

(BRIGHTLY, TO PISHTCHIK) My little dog eats nuts.

PISHTCHIK

(ASTONISHED) You don't say so!

CHARLOTTA

(STARTLED) My little dog! Where is my little dog?

(MOURNFUL) He's with the luggage.

EPIHODOV

The luggage! I must be going!

(HE STARTS TO RUN OUT THE DOOR AND KNOCKS AGAINST A CHAIR, WHICH FALLS TO THE GROUND. THE OTHERS FOLLOW HIM, CHARLOTTA RIGHTING THE CHAIR BEFORE SHE LEAVES.)

MADAM RANEVSKY

The luggage! (TURNING TO DUNYASHA) Dunyasha! Make tea or something for poor Anya!

(MADAM RANEVSKY RUSHES OUT THE DOOR. ONLY DUNYASHA AND ANYA REMAIN IN THE ROOM.

ANYA

I haven't slept for four nights. I'm frozen to death.

DUNYASHA

It was Lent when you went away. There was snow on the ground. Oh, how I've longed to see you. I must tell you something at once. . .I can't wait another minute.

ANYA

(WITHOUT INTEREST) What, again?

DUNYASHA

Epihodov, the clerk, proposed to me.

ANYA

Same old story

(ANYA STRAIGHTENS HER HAIR AND YAWNS.)

A DIFFERENT
AND WIDER SHOT,
REVEALING THE
DOOR BEHIND
THE TWO WOMEN.

ANYA

All my hairpins have dropped out.

DUNYASHA

I hardly know what to think of it. . .he loves me!

ANYA

(LOOKING ABOUT) My room, my windows, just as if I had never gone away! (YAWNING) I want some coffee.

DUNYASHA

Right away.

(DUNYASHA DASHES OUT, ALMOST RUNNING INTO VARYA, WHO COMES INTO THE ROOM WITH A BUNCH OF KEYS HANGING FROM HER BELT. VARYA GOES TO ANYA AND HUGS HER.

DIFFERENT TWO-
SHOT OF VARYA
AND ANYA.

VARYA

Thank Heaven, you're home!

ANYA

What I've had to go through! When we got to Paris, it was so cold! And I can't talk French a bit. Mama was on the fifth floor of a big house. When I arrived there, there were a lot of Frenchmen with her, and ladies, and a priest with a book, and it was very un-comfortable, and full of tobacco smoke. I suddenly felt so sorry for Mama. I took her head in my arms and couldn't let it go and Mama kept kissing me and crying.

VARYA

(CRYING) Don't go on. . .don't go on. . .

ANYA

She's sold her villa already. She has nothing left, absolutely nothing. And I haven't got a penny either.
(ANYA WALKS TO THE WINDOW AND LOOKS OUT.)

SINGLE CLOSE
SHOT OF ANYA.

ANYA

But Mama won't understand. We get out at a station

to have some dinner and she asks for all the most

expensive things and gives the waiters a florin each

for a tip.

(VARYA GOES TO ANYA AND HUGS HER.)

WIDEN TO A

TWO-SHOT.   VARYA

I know.

ANYA

(SUDDENLY CHEERFUL) Come, tell me about

everything. Has the interest on the mortgage been

paid?

VARYA

How could it be?

ANYA

Oh, dear!

VARYA

(GESTURING WITH HER ARM) This place will be

sold in August.

ANYA

Oh, dear!

VARYA

(CHANGING HER TONE AND LOOKING AT A

BROOCH ANYA IS WEARING) You've got on a brooch

that looks like a bee.

ANYA

(SADLY) Mama bought it for me.

(ANYA DANCES AROUND THE ROOM.)

ANYA

(GAILY) When I was in Paris I went up in a balloon.

VARYA

Oh, I'm so glad you're back, my pretty one.

(VARYA EMBRACES ANYA.)

VARYA

I trudge about all day, looking after things and I think
and think. What are we to do? If we could only marry
you off to some rich man, it would be a load off my
mind. I would go into a retreat and then to Kiev, to
Moscow; I would tramp about from one holy place to
another, always tramping and tramping. What bliss!

ANYA

(LOOKING AWAY) The birds are singing in the gar-
den. What time is it now?

VARYA

It's past three. Time to go to bed.

WIDEN SHOT TO   (FIRS ENTERS WITH COFFEE, FOLLOWED BY
TAKE IN WHOLE   DUNYASHA.)
ROOM.
                     ANYA

(LOOKING TOWARD DOOR) But first we'll have our
coffee.

(FIRS AND DUNYASHA PUT COFFEE AND CUPS ON
TABLE WITH AN AIR OF CEREMONY.)

CLOSE IN ON FIRS

AS HE ARRANGES

THE CUPS, ETC.

FIRS

(MUMBLING TO HIMSELF AND CRYING) My

mistress has come home. Now I'm ready to die.

(HE LOOKS TOWARD THE DOOR THROUGH WHICH

MADAM RANEVSKY, LOPAKHIN, LEONID, AND

PISHTCHIK ENTER THE ROOM FOR COFFEE.

LEONID IS MAKING GESTURES AS IF PLAYING

BILLIARDS.)

MADAM RANEVSKY

What is the expression? Let me see. . ."I'll put the

red in the corner pocket, double into the middle. . ."

LEONID

(TO MADAM RANEVSKY) And I'll ship the red into

the right hand pocket.

(THEY SIT DOWN WHILE FIRS SERVES THEM

COFFEE.)

LEONID

Once upon a time, Lyuba, when we were children, we

used to sleep here, side by side in two little cots.

And now I'm 51, and I can't believe it.

LOPAKHIN

Yes, time flies.

LEONID

What's that, Lopakhin?

LOPAKHIN

Time flies, I say.

LEONID

(DISDAINFULLY) There's a smell of patchouli.

(ANYA, FINISHING HER COFFEE, GOES TO HER

MOTHER AND KISSES HER.)

ANYA

I'm going to bed. Good night Mama.

(ANYA CIRCLES THE ROOM KISSING EVERYBODY

GOODNIGHT AND LEAVES.)

VARYA

(RISING) Well, gentlemen, time you were off.

MADAM RANEVSKY

(LAUGHING) You haven't changed a bit, Varya.

(VARYA KISSES MADAM RANEVSKY AND LEAVES.)

CLOSE IN ON TWO-
SHOT OF MADAM
RANEVSKY AND   (FIRS IS PUTTING A FOOTSTOOL UNDER MADAM
FIRS.   RANEVSKY'S FEET.)

WIDEN SHOT TO   MADAM RANEVSKY
INCLUDE OTHERS.
(JOYOUS) Can it be me that's sitting here? I want to

jump and wave my arms about. Surely I must be

dreaming. I love my country; I couldn't see out of the

window from the train I was crying so hard! Thank

you, Firs, thank you. I'm so glad to find you still
alive.

FIRS

The day before yesterday.

LEONID

(TO MADAM RANEVSKY) He's hard of hearing.

(FIRS WALKS OUT OF PICTURE.)

LOPAKHIN

I have to go. (KISSING HER HAND) Dear Lady, I am
only a merchant, and Leonid here says I'm a snob, a
money-grubber. He can say what he likes. My father
was your father's serf, and your grandfather's serf
before him. But you did so much for me in the old
days that I've forgotten everything, and I love you. . .
like a sister, more than a sister.

(LOPAKHIN SITS DOWN AGAIN. MADAM RANEVSKY,
PAYING NO ATTENTION TO HIM, JUMPS UP, GOES
TO THE CUPBOARD AND KISSES THE CUPBOARD.)

CAMERA FOL-

LOWS HER.

MADAM RANEVSKY

My darling old cupboard!

(SHE GOES BACK TO THE GROUP.)

PISHTCHIK

Dear Madam, I must go. Could you loan me 25 pounds
for the interest on the mortgage on my estate?

MADAM RANEVSKY

(GRACIOUSLY) It's really a fact. . .I haven't any
money, Pishtchik.

PISHTCHIK

(ACCEPTING IT) I'll find it somewhere. I never lose
hope. Good night, my dear.

(PISHTCHIK LEAVES.)

CLOSES IN ON A
THREE-SHOT OF
MADAM RANEVSKY,
LOPAKHIN, AND
LEONID.

LEONID

(NOT MOVING) And I must go too.

LOPAKHIN

I long to say something charming and delightful to
you, but there's no time to talk. Well, yes, I'll put it
in two or three words. You know that your cherry
orchard is going to be sold to pay the mortgage. The
sale is fixed for the 22nd of August.

REACTION SHOTS
OF MADAM
RANEVSKY AND
LEONID AS
LOPAKHIN TALKS.

LOPAKHIN

But don't be uneasy, my dear lady, I have a plan.
Listen to me carefully! Your property is only 15

miles from the town. The railway runs close beside
it. And if only you will cut up the cherry orchard,
and the land along the river into building lots, you'll
get at least 2,500 pounds a year out of it.

LEONID

(TO LOPAKHIN) Come, come, what rubbish you're
talking!

MADAM RANEVSKY

(TO LOPAKHIN) I don't understand what you mean.

CHANGE ANGLE
FOR ONE-SHOT
OF LOPAKHIN

(LOPAKHIN RISES AND ADDRESSES THEM LIKE A
SALESMAN.)

LOPAKHIN

In two words, I congratulate you! You are saved.
You'll have to clear the ground, pull down all the old
buildings. . .this house for instance, which is no
longer fit for anything, and cut down the cherry
orchard.

THREE-SHOT.

MADAM RANEVSKY

(RISING, INDIGNANT) Cut down the cherry orchard!
If there's one thing that's interesting in this whole
province, it's our cherry orchard!

LOPAKHIN

There's nothing remarkable about the orchard,
except that it's a very big one.

LEONID

(RISING, ARROGANT) Our cherry orchard is mentioned in Andreyevsky's Encyclopedia!

LOPAKHIN

(SHRUGGING) If you don't make up your mind, or think of any other way, on the 22nd of August the cherry orchard and the whole property will be sold at auction!

WIDEN SHOT.

LEONID

(RISING AND GOING TO THE CUPBOARD) What gibberish! (TOUCHING THE CUPBOARD AND LOOKING TOWARD MADAM RANEVSKY) Do you know how old this cupboard is, Lyuba? A hundred years old. It's a wonderful thing.

CLOSE IN ON
LEONID AT THE
CUPBOARD.

LEONID

Beloved and venerable cupboard; honor and glory to your existence, which for more than a hundred years has been directed to the noble ideals of justice and virtue. Your silent summons to profitable labor has never weakened in all these hundred years. (BEGINS TO WEEP) You have upheld the courage of succeeding generations of our humankind; you have upheld faith in a better future, and cherished ideals in us of goodness and social consciousness.

(LOPAKHIN AND MADAM RANEVSKY ARE SILENT.)

HOLD ON LEONID
WEEPING AT THE
CUPBOARD. THEN
WIDEN TO INCLUDE
OTHERS.

LOPAKHIN

Yes.

MADAM RANEVSKY

The coffee's finished. Let's go to bed.

LOPAKHIN

If you make up your mind about selling the orchard,

let me know. Good night.

(HE KISSES MADAM RANEVSKY'S HAND AND EXITS.)

MADAM RANEVSKY

Good night.

(LEONID AND MADAM RANEVSKY GO TO THE

WINDOW.)

CLOSE IN ON
THEM AT
WINDOW.

MADAM RANEVSKY

It really is true. . .I don't have any money.

LEONID

(OPENING THE WINDOW) The orchard is all white.

Remember, Lyuba, how it goes on and on, shining like

silver on moonlit nights? Do you remember?

MADAM RANEVSKY

(LOOKING OUT) Oh, my childhood, my pure and

happy childhood! The orchard was just the same then

as it is now; nothing has changed. It's all white, all
white. Now the sun is coming up and looks at the
white blossoms against the sky.

PULL BACK TO
SHOW FIRS COM-
ING INTO THE
ROOM.

(FIRS ENTERS AND STARTS PICKING UP COFFEE
CUPS. MADAM RANEVSKY AND LEONID GO TO
HIM.)

FIRS

(LOOKING TOWARD THE WINDOW) In the old days,
forty or fifty years ago, they used to dry the cherries
and soak them and pickle them and make jam of
them. . . .

MADAM RANEVSKY

Whatever are you talking about, Firs?

LEONID

He mumbles.

FIRS

The dried cherries used to be sent in wagons to
Moscow. . .a heap of money.

MADAM RANEVSKY

Good night, Leonid. I'm going to bed. Good night,
Firs. Come on Leonid.

(MADAM RANEVSKY AND LEONID LEAVE WHILE
FIRS IS STILL PILING THE CUPS AND SAUCERS
ON A TRAY.)

CLOSE SHOT OF

FIRS.

                                        FIRS

                    (MUMBLING TO HIMSELF) There was some way

                    they used to do it in the old days. . . .

CLOSING TITLES

AND CREDITS.

FADE TO BLACK.

A Doll's House Ibsen

IN MANY RESPECTS Ibsen's *A Doll's House* represents the kind of popular drama concerning personal relationships which, at its lowest level, is called soap opera. Torvald Helmer's wife, Nora, once forged her dying father's signature to a bond in order to take her sick husband to Italy where, the doctors said, he had the only chance to regain his health. Now, his health restored, Torvald has been promoted to manager of the bank where Krogstad, the man from whom Nora borrowed the money, is also working. Krogstad tries to blackmail Nora; he threatens to present the note with the forged signature to her husband in the hope of keeping—if not bettering—his uncertain position in the bank. Meanwhile, Nora's friend, a woman, who also knows Krogstad, arrives suddenly . . . and away we go in a play that reveals many human problems and weaknesses.

Although the characters involved have some problems that might not be relevant today, each character has genuine and universal personality conflicts. For example, Nora has been playing the little girl—helpless, sweet, and lovely—first for her father, then for her husband. Basically weak, Torvald plays the role of the strong man in his home. Krogstad, the moneylender, is trying to achieve respectability. Mrs. Linde, Nora's old friend, wants a little fun before she dies.

If you can develop these basic human conflicts, you will give the drama stature. You may wish to present the entire story of *A Doll's House,* but in this condensed version of Act I you have the challenge of revealing the essential character and motivation of the principals on which the whole play depends.

Because *A Doll's House* is an example of so-called realistic drama, many of the props and most of the setting are essential to the action. An imaginative director undoubtedly could stage it with drapes or abstract scenery; but for an acting and directing exercise, probably the best technique would be to use a simple, realistic set.

Scene from A Doll's House*

HENRIK IBSEN

Adapted by Rome Cowgill

CAST

TORVALD HELMER
NORA—his wife
DR. RANK
MRS. LINDE—Nora's old school friend
NILS KROGSTAD
HELEN—a maid
A PORTER

SET

INTERIOR, DAY: *A comfortably-furnished living room. An entrance door at the back, another door to the left which leads to Torvald's study, and an archway to a hall. Easy chairs, and a rocking chair, and a stove. An atmosphere of middle class comfort. It is winter.*

VIDEO

(TITLES OVER A
MINIATURE DOLL'S
HOUSE SITTING
UNDER A CHRIST-
MAS TREE. AT
CLOSE OF TITLES,
DOLLY IN TO
FRONT DOOR OF
DOLL'S HOUSE.

AUDIO

---

* Adapted from *The Best Known Works of Ibsen* (New York: Blue Ribbon Books, 1928), by permission of Walter J. Black, Inc.

DOOR OPENS AND WE CUT TO A LIVING ROOM SET.	(A MAID IS OPENING THE ENTRANCE DOOR. NORA COMES IN WITH HER ARMS LOADED WITH PARCELS, FOLLOWED BY A PORTER WITH A CHRISTMAS TREE. NORA TELLS THE MAID TO TAKE THE TREE AND PUTS THE PACKAGES ON A TABLE.)

NORA

Put the Christmas tree over there in the

corner, Helen. (TO THE PORTER, TAKING OUT HER

PURSE) How much?

PORTER

Sixpence.

NORA

(GIVING HIM MONEY) Here's a shilling. No, no, no,

keep the change.

PORTER

Thank you, ma'm.

(PORTER GOES OUT THROUGH THE ENTRANCE

DOOR. NORA, LAUGHING, GOES TO THE TREE

WHICH THE MAID IS SETTING UP. FROM HER

COAT POCKET SHE TAKES OUT A PACKAGE OF

MACAROONS AND OFFERS ONE TO THE MAID.)

HELEN

Thank you, mum. It's a beautiful tree.

NORA

Be sure the children don't see it. Is my husband in?

HELEN

Yes, mum. (GESTURES TOWARD STUDY DOOR.)

In his study. I'll go see to the children now.

(HELEN EXITS THROUGH THE ARCHWAY. NORA

STANDS BACK TO ADMIRE THE TREE, DOING A

LITTLE DANCE OF JOY. SHE STOPS ABRUPTLY

WHEN SHE HEARS TORVALD.)

TORVALD (V.O.)

Is that my little lark twittering out there?

(NORA GOES TO THE CHRISTMAS TREE, PUTTING

SOME OF THE PARCELS UNDER IT, UNWRAPPING

ONE, A DOLL.)

NORA

Yes, Torvald, it is.

TORVALD (V.O.)

Is that my little squirrel bustling about?

NORA

(CRAMMING A MACAROON INTO HER MOUTH)

Um-hum. (NORA PUTS THE MACAROONS BACK

INTO HER COAT POCKET AS TORVALD COMES

TORVALD

When did my squirrel come home?

NORA

Just now. Come here, Torvald, and see what I've

bought the children.

(NORA STARTS TO OPEN THE PACKAGES.)

MOVE IN TO TWO-
SHOT OF NORA
AND TORVALD BY
THE TREE.

                                    TORVALD

All this? Has my little spendthrift been wasting

money again?

(NORA, WITH A PACKAGE IN HER HAND, STOPS

UNWRAPPING IT AND DROPS IT.)

                                     NORA

But Torvald, this year we can really let ourselves go

a little. You're going to have a big salary and earn

lots and lots of money.

                                    TORVALD

Yes, after the new year.

                                     NORA

Oh, we can borrow till then.

                                    TORVALD

(TAKING HER PLAYFULLY BY THE EAR) The same

little featherhead! Suppose I borrowed 50 pounds

today and then on New Year's Eve I was killed . . . .

                                     NORA

(PUTTING HER HANDS OVER HER MOUTH) Don't

say such horrid things.

TORVALD

But suppose it happened . . . what then?

NORA

I wouldn't care whether I owed money or not.

TORVALD

Just like a woman. But, seriously, Nora, you know what I think about that. No debt, no borrowing.

WIDEN ANGLE AS
NORA MOVES
AWAY.

NORA

(MOVING AWAY FROM HIM) As you please, Torvald.

TORVALD

(FOLLOWING HER) Come, Come! My little skylark must not droop her wings. Is my little squirrel out of temper? (TAKING OUT HIS WALLET) What do you think I have here?

NORA

(TURNING QUICKLY TO HIM) Money!

TORVALD

(TAKING SOME BILLS FROM HIS WALLET) Do you think I don't know what a lot of money is needed at Christmas?

NORA

Thank you, thank you, Torvald! That will keep me going for a long time.

REVERSE ANGLE.   (NORA PUTS THE BILLS IN HER COAT POCKET

AND, SUDDENLY JOYOUS AGAIN, GOES TO THE

TREE. TORVALD FOLLOWS HER.)

NORA

Come, let me show you what I've bought . . . and all

so cheap. A new suit for Ivar, and a sword! A horse

and a trumpet for Bob; a doll and a bed for Emmy . . .

they're very plain but she'll soon break them up any-

way.

TORVALD

(POINTING TO UNOPENED BOX) What's this?

NORA

No, no, you can't see that till evening.

TORVALD

(AMUSED) Very well. But tell me, you extravagant

little person, what would you like for yourself?

NORA

Money.

TORVALD

(PUTTING HIS ARM AROUND HER) It's a sweet little

spendthrift . . . but she uses up a deal of money.

NORA

I really save all I can.

TORVALD

(LAUGHING) That's very true . . . all you can. But

you can't save anything.

WIDEN ANGLE AS

NORA MOVES

AWAY.

NORA

(MOVING AWAY) You haven't any idea how many

expenses we skylarks and squirrels have.

TORVALD

And I wouldn't want you to be anything but just what

you are, my sweet little skylark. But do you know, it

strikes me that you're looking rather uneasy. Look

straight at me. (TORVALD WAGS HIS FINGER AT

NORA, WHO LOOKS STRAIGHT AT HIM) Hasn't Miss

Sweet-tooth been breaking rules?

NORA

(STILL LOOKING STRAIGHT AT HIM) What makes

you think that?

TORVALD

Not even taken a bite of a macaroon or two?

NORA

I wouldn't think of going against your wishes.

TORVALD

(GOING TOWARD HER) Ah, then, it's your little

Christmas secrets.

NORA

(TURNING FROM HIM) Did you remember to invite

Dr. Rank?

TORVALD

No. But I'm sure he'll come. Oh, I am looking forward
to this evening.

NORA

So am I.

TORVALD

Remember last Christmas? For a full three weeks
beforehand you shut yourself up every evening making
Christmas ornaments . . . and with precious little
result.

NORA

You shouldn't tease me about that again. It wasn't my
fault that the cat got in and tore everything to pieces.

TORVALD

Of course not, poor little girl. But it's a good thing
our hard times are over.

NORA

It's wonderfully lovely to hear you say so. I've been
thinking how we ought to arrange things, Torvald. As
soon as Christmas is over . . .

(A BELL RINGS. NORA STARTS TO PICK UP THE
WRAPPINGS. TORVALD MOVES TOWARD THE
STUDY DOOR.)

TORVALD

If it's a caller, remember, I'm not at home.

(NORA, HAVING ACCOMPLISHED VERY LITTLE IN TIDYING THE ROOM, TAKES OFF HER COAT AND GOES TO THE ENTRANCE DOOR AND OPENS IT. WE SEE MRS. LINDE STANDING TIMIDLY IN THE DOORWAY.)

CLOSE IN ON MRS. LINDE AT THE DOOR, OVER NORA'S SHOULDER.

MRS. LINDE

Nora?

NORA

(DOUBTFUL) How do you do?

MRS. LINDE

You don't recognize me, I suppose.

NORA

No . . . Yes! Christine! Is it really you?

(NORA BACKS INTO THE ROOM, CLOSING THE DOOR AFTER CHRISTINE, WHO ENTERS.)

TWO-SHOT.

To think I didn't recognize you! Oh, my poor dear Christine, do forgive me.

MRS. LINDE

What do you mean, Nora?

NORA

I'd forgotten. You're a widow.

MRS. LINDE

Yes, for two years now.

NORA

Any children?

MRS. LINDE

No. Nothing. Not even any sorrow or grief to live
upon.

NORA

But is that possible?

MRS. LINDE

It happens sometimes.

NORA

But I haven't even asked you to sit down. Here, give
me your coat.
(MRS. LINDE GIVES NORA HER COAT. NORA
THROWS IT CARELESSLY OVER A CHAIR. THE
TWO WOMEN SIT DOWN.)

NORA

I want to hear about everything. Only there's one
thing I'm so happy about I just have to tell you! My
husband has been made manager of the bank.

MRS. LINDE

What good luck!

NORA

You have no idea.

MRS. LINDE

You always were a spendthrift.

NORA

That's what Torvald says now. But I've had to work very hard. (WAGS HER FINGER AT MRS. LINDE) "Nora, Nora," (IMITATING HER HUSBAND THEN LAUGHING) I'm not so silly as you think. You know that Torvald was dreadfully ill right after we were married, and the doctors said it was necessary for him to go south.

MRS. LINDE

I remember. You spent a whole year in Italy.

NORA

Yes, and it saved Torvald's life. But it cost a tremendous lot of money. (BEAT) I ought to tell you that we got it from Papa.

MRS. LINDE

That was just about when he died, wasn't it?

NORA

Yes. While I was in Italy. I was expecting Ivar any day and I had my poor, sick Torvald to look after, so I never saw my father again. But how horrid of me . . . my husband has not had a day's illness since. And you have lost yours.

MRS. LINDE

That's all right, Nora. I came here hoping to have the good luck to get some regular work, something to keep me busy.

NORA

You look so tired. Wouldn't it be better to go away to

some resort?

PULL BACK AS   (MRS. LINDE GOES TO LOOK AT THE PRESENTS

MRS. LINDE GETS   UNDER THE TREE.)

UP. FOLLOW.)
                                    MRS. LINDE

I have no father to give me money for a trip.

TWO-SHOT.   (NORA WALKS UP TO MRS. LINDE.)

NORA

Christine, I'm sorry.

CLOSE IN ON

MRS. LINDE.
                                    MRS. LINDE

I'm the one who should be sorry. When you told me

about Torvald's promotion, I was happier for myself

than for you. Maybe Torvald could get me something

to do.

NORA

(JOYOUSLY) Of course, Christine, just leave it to me.

I'll broach the subject very cleverly.

MRS. LINDE

How kind you are, Nora. Especially because you know

so little of the troubles of life.

NORA

Do you really believe that?

MRS. LINDE

Small household cares and that sort of thing . . .

NORA

Everyone looks down upon me. Everyone thinks I am incapable of anything serious. If they only knew . . . Papa didn't give me the money for Torvald's trip . . . (TRIUMPHANTLY) I borrowed it.

MOVE IN TO CLOSE
SHOT OF NORA.

Torvald has never known, and his pride would have been hurt if he'd found out that I, silly Nora, had to get the money to save his life. (PROUDLY) And I've paid back almost all of it. Last Christmas they thought I was making ornaments but I was copying manuscripts.

(A BELL RINGS.)

MRS. LINDE

There's the bell. I'd better go.

NORA

No, don't go . . . it's sure to be for Torvald . . . it's probably Dr. Rank.

FOLLOW NORA TO
THE DOOR.

SHE OPENS DOOR CONFIDENTLY, BUT BY HER POSTURE INDICATES SHOCK.

NORA

(BREATHLESSLY) Mr. Krogstad.

PULL BACK.

(KROGSTAD FOLLOWS NORA INTO THE ROOM. SHE STOPS HIM.)

What is it? Why did you come here?

KROGSTAD

Bank business. I hear your husband is to be the
manager. I want a better job and you can get it for
me.

NORA

(GESTURING TOWARD MRS. LINDE) Shh . . .
(MRS. LINDE PICKS UP HER COAT AND WALKS
TOWARD THE DOOR.)

MRS. LINDE

Nora, this is Christmas Eve and I know you have a
lot to do. I hope you'll remember what you said, and
I'll be in touch with you tomorrow.
(KROGSTAD STANDS ASIDE AND NORA ALMOST
DESPERATELY CLUTCHES MRS. LINDE.)

NORA

Don't go.

MRS. LINDE

(OPENING THE DOOR) Goodbye, Nora. (TURNING
HER HEAD TO KROGSTAD) And goodbye, Mr.
Krogstad.
(MRS. LINDE EXITS. AS DOOR CLOSES, NORA
TURNS TO KROGSTAD, PUZZLED.)

NORA

Do you know her?

KROGSTAD

Yes. But it's no matter, I want to see your husband.

NORA

He's not at home.

KROGSTAD

Then, I'll wait for him. (ARROGANTLY MOVES INTO ROOM, REMOVING HIS OVERCOAT AND SITTING DOWN. NORA FOLLOWS.)

NORA

You're not going to tell my husband that I owe you money?

KROGSTAD

I might.

NORA

(PROUDLY) It was my joy to help my husband by borrowing the money from you, Mr. Krogstad. And sometime after it was all paid, I planned to tell him. If you tell him now, he'll pay you up and we need have nothing more to do with you.

KROGSTAD

You have a very bad memory, Mrs. Helmer. I have the bond you signed that you told me was counter-signed by your father.

NORA

(FEAR BEGINNING TO SHOW) Yes?

KROGSTAD

Do you remember the day your father died? . . . the

day of the month I mean?

(KROGSTAD TAKES THE BOND FROM HIS POCKET.)

NORA

Papa died on the 29th of September.

KROGSTAD

Your father's signature is dated the 2nd of October.

Was it your father himself who signed his name here?

NORA

(AFTER A PAUSE) If Papa had not been so ill, he

would have signed his name, Mr. Krogstad.

KROGSTAD

In a court of law it would be hard to prove.

NORA

But I've been paying you regularly.

KROGSTAD

That's not the point. Your husband has been appointed

manager of the bank, and I want you to use your in-

fluence to help me keep my job.

NORA

But I have no influence.

KROGSTAD

Then I'll have to show your husband this note.

WIDEN ANGLE.   (KROGSTAD RISES, PUTS THE NOTE IN HIS

POCKET, AND GOES TO THE ENTRANCE DOOR. HE

OPENS THE DOOR.)

(AS HE EXITS) You can let me know tomorrow, Mrs. Helmer.

CLOSE IN ON
NORA STANDING
AT THE DOOR.
FOLLOW HER.

(NORA GOES TO THE CHRISTMAS TREE AND STARTS TO ARRANGE THE CHRISTMAS PACKAGES AGAIN.)

TORVALD (V.O.)

Nora? Who was here?

(NORA JUMPS UP, BEING THE LITTLE GIRL AGAIN, HOLDING A DOLL IN HER HAND.)

NORA

Nobody was here.

(TORVALD ENTERS FROM STUDY AND GOES TO NORA.)

TORVALD

(EMBRACING HER) My little songbird must never lie to me. A songbird must have a clean beak to chirp with . . . no false notes. I saw Krogstad leave.

NORA

(CHILDISHLY) Oh, yes, he was here for a minute. I forgot.

TORVALD

If he was begging you to talk to me about his job, it

would do no good now anyway. (POMPOUSLY) The matter is settled. I will not have a man like that in my bank. My little songbird doesn't know, but Krogstad once forged another man's name. That's why my sweet little Nora must promise me not to ask anything for him. I feel physically ill when I am' in the company of such people.

                    NORA

(BEAT. SHOCKED.) All right, Torvald, all right. (FEIGNING GAIETY) Let's not talk about it tonight, please?

(NORA PICKS UP A BOX OF ORNAMENTS AND STARTS PINNING THEM TO THE TREE WHILE TORVALD SMILES AMUSEDLY.)

                    NORA

I have to trim the tree and get everything ready for the children. It's Christmas Eve and your little songbird is so happy!

CLOSING TITLES
OVER NORA PIN-
NING ORNAMENTS
MERRILY ON
TREE. FADE TO
BLACK.

15

The Molière Story Rome Cowgill

THE SO-CALLED stool technique of staging requires the ultimate finesse in acting and directing in spite of its apparent simplicity. Actors in everyday dress sit on stools or on chairs, spotlighted against an undefined background and usually referred to as limbo. However, they do not remain seated as though chained to their stools and merely speak their lines. They act with intensity and as if they were costumed and playing on a completely dressed set. Depending on the dramatic effectiveness of the scene, one or more of the actors may stand up and walk to another lighted area and give a total performance of physical action. Often hand props are used, and sometimes one scene may be staged with a minimal suggestion. Slides and other visuals add variety and emphasize dramatic points. In this type of production, a few actors play many parts. It seems to make for easy direction: small cast, no costuming, and practically no set! But these are the very factors that force actors and director to use their greatest skill and finesse.

In the following exercise three actors, one actress, and a narrator tell the story of Molière with excerpts from scenes of some of his comedies. The four actors play a total of fourteen roles and, although most of the roles are brief, each actor must give the viewer the total impact of the character. In every instance the narrator identifies the character before he appears, and in some cases hand props are suggested to further establish the character. For example, the two actors who play the theater critics share a snuff box. They also appear in other roles, but each time they play the critics the snuff box helps to identify them. It might be effective if, each time they appear, one ties on a patently false Van Dyke beard. On the other hand, the snuff box could be eliminated altogether. This, of course, is entirely up to the director.

The visuals indicated are equally subject to directorial discretion. For example, if you cannot find or reproduce a clear drawing of a tennis court theater, you can omit it and put the narrator on screen for his verbal description. The same is true of many of the graphics.

The Molière Story

ROME COWGILL

CAST	SET
ANNOUNCER	*Black cyclorama and four stools.*
NARRATOR	
THREE ACTORS	
ACTRESS	

VIDEO	AUDIO
PAN OR TILT PIC-TURE OF ANCIENT GREEK THEATER.	TYPICAL GREEK TYPE MUSIC B.G.
SUPER "FROM ATHENS..."	ANNOUNCER
	From Athens...
CUT TO STILL OF BROADWAY AT NIGHT.	
SUPER "TO BROADWAY."	BROADWAY MUSIC B.G.

REMOVE SUPER.

PAN OR TILT

BROADWAY

PICTURE.

                              ANNOUNCER

. . .to Broadway. The living theater, brought to you

through the lives of the world's greatest playwrights.

From ancient to modern. . .and tonight, the master of

comedy, Molière. We tell his story through his

friends. . .in modern dress.

NARRATOR IN

WAIST SHOT

LIGHTED AGAINST

BLACK.

                              NARRATOR

(HOLDS A CROWN. BESIDE HIM IS A GILT AND

UPHOLSTERED FRENCH CHAIR. PATS CHAIR)

The son of an upholsterer, (RAISES CROWN) the

friend of a king. . .a man of many enemies and many

loves, that was the 17th century Frenchman, Jean

Poquelin, known to us as Molière.

CUT TO PRINT OF

17th CENTURY

PARIS.   (V.O.) Paris, Molière's home, was more than just

                          home or city to him. It was his first love.

CUT TO PRINT OF

SEVENTEENTH

CENTURY FRENCH

THEATER.

CUT BACK TO

NARRATOR.

The theater was Molière's second love. . .

and gave him much trouble. But it was not faithless women so much as faithful enemies that brought Molière his greatest troubles. He reversed the usual procedure. . .his plays were popular successes and critical failures. The critics, like these two gentlemen here, (NOD OR GESTURE O.S.) were his enemies.

CUT TO TWO MEN

LIGHTED AGAINST

BLACK.

(MEN SEATED EITHER ON STOOLS OR, PREFERABLY, BAROQUE FRENCH CHAIRS. ONE TAKES SNUFF FROM TIME TO TIME.)

SUPERCILIOUS

Molière is cheap! Vulgar! He breaks all the rules of drama. . .centuries of French tradition!

STUDIOUS

He even laughs at France herself! And at Frenchmen!

SUPERCILIOUS

And steals most of his materials from the Italians!

STUDIOUS

I know! (SUDDENLY SNICKERING) But it's funny, all the same. (REACTION OF HORROR AT WHAT HE'S JUST SAID.)

SUPERCILIOUS

(EVEN MORE HORRIFIED) Not you, too! Mon Dieu! What is happening to France!

CUT TO NAR-
RATOR, LIGHTED
AGAINST BLACK.

NARRATOR

Why did most critics hate Molière so much! There were many reasons. First, they were accustomed to drama like this. . .from Racine's Andromache.

CUT TO MALE
AND FEMALE
LIGHTED AGAINST
BLACK.

(ACTOR AND ACTRESS USE EXTRAVAGANT GES-TURES. THEY DO NOT ADDRESS EACH OTHER. BUT DECLAIM STOICALLY TO THE AUDIENCE.)

ACTOR ORESTES

(TO US) You have wished me here?

ACTRESS HERMIONE

(TO US) Yes!

ACTOR ORESTES

(TO US) But can it be that you are saying this? These happy words to me? Open your eyes and let them see Orestes on whose presence they frowned so long!

ACTRESS HERMIONE

(STILL TO US) Yes! You, who taught them first their

power, whose love from them grew stronger with their charms, whose worth could not help but value highly, who would have had my fondest sighs and whom I truly wish to love!

PULL BACK.   VOICES FADE AND NARRATOR WALKS INTO FOREGROUND.

AS HE SPEAKS,

BLACK OUT   NARRATOR

ACTORS.   Molière wrote a different kind of play than this. . .
(GESTURING TO ACTORS). In his plays, people spoke like people and acted like people. . .not always filled with the noblest of thoughts. As in this scene from The Doctor in Spite of Himself, where a husband and wife are in the midst of a. . .discussion?

CUT TO TWO

ACTORS LIGHTED   (PLAY FOR REALISTIC COMEDY.)

AGAINST BLACK.   ACTOR SGANARELLE

No, I tell you, I will do nothing of the kind. It is for me to speak and to be the master.

ACTRESS MARTINE

And I tell you that I will have you live as I please, I didn't marry you to put up with your nonsensical goings-on!

ACTOR SGANARELLE

Oh! What an awful trouble it is to have a wife!

ACTRESS MARTINE

Cursed be the day and hour when I took it into my
head to go and say "Yes!"

ACTOR SGANARELLE

Cursed be the old idiot who made me sign my ruin!

ACTRESS MARTINE

You ought to thank heaven every moment of your life
for having me as a wife!

ACTOR SGANARELLE

True, indeed! You honored me too much, and I had
cause to be satisfied on our wedding-day. Do not force
me to speak of it, or I may say certain things. . . .

ACTRESS MARTINE

Well! What is it you'd say?

ACTOR SGANARELLE

Enough of that. It is sufficient that I know what I know,
and that you were very lucky to have me.

ACTRESS MARTINE

What do you mean by my being lucky to have you? A
man who reduces me to beggary; who eats up all I
possess.

ACTOR SGANARELLE

That's a lie; I drink part of it.

ACTRESS MARTINE

Who sells bit by bit, all that we have in the house.

ACTOR SGANARELLE

That is what is called living on one's means.

ACTRESS MARTINE

Who even sold the bed from under me.

ACTOR SGANARELLE

You'll get up all the earlier.

ACTRESS MARTINE

In short, who does not leave a single stick of furniture in the house. . .

ACTOR SGANARELLE

We shall move all the more easily.

ACTRESS MARTINE

And who does nothing from morning to night but drink and gamble.

ACTOR SGANARELLE

That's for fear of the dumps.

ACTRESS MARTINE

And do you think, drunkard, that things can always go on so?

ACTOR SGANARELLE

Now, my wife, gentle, if you please.

ACTRESS MARTINE

That I must endure forever your insolence and excesses?

ACTOR SGANARELLE

Do not get into a passion, my dear wife.

ACTRESS MARTINE

And that I shall not find the means of bringing you to

a sense of your duty?

ACTOR SGANARELLE

My dear wife, you know that I am not very patient,

and that I have a good strong arm.

ACTRESS MARTINE

I don't care for your threats.

ACTOR SGANARELLE

My little wife, my darling, your back itches as usual.

ACTRESS MARTINE

I will show you that I don't fear you at all.

ACTOR SGANARELLE

My dear, dear better-half, you intend to put me in

your debt.

ACTRESS MARTINE

Do you think that what you say can frighten me?

ACTOR SGANARELLE

Tender object of my desires, I'll box your ears.

ACTRESS MARTINE

Drunkard!

ACTOR SGANARELLE

I'll beat you.

ACTRESS MARTINE

Wine-barrel!

ACTOR SGANARELLE

I'll thrash you!

ACTRESS MARTINE

Wretch!

ACTOR SGANARELLE

I'll give you a dressing.

ACTRESS MARTINE

(SCREAMING) Oh! oh! oh! oh!

ACTOR SGANARELLE

This is the way to make you hold your tongue.

CUT TO

NARRATOR.

NARRATOR

This play, like many of Molière's, would probably have been banned in Boston. Many of his plays were banned in Paris. Why? They weren't obscene, but they mocked hypocrisy. Phonies. As he once said, in a play we'll see part of later, "I'll fling my gauntlet in the face of the whole human race!" And he did it with laughter. But Molière didn't set out to be a one-man revolution. Like many a young man today, he wanted to be an actor. It was not a respectable profession then. . .no father would boast, "My son, the actor!" and. . .(GESTURING O.S.) Molière's father felt even worse. . . .

CUT TO FATHER.

FATHER

(STANDING BESIDE ONE OF THOSE FRENCH CHAIRS. ADDRESSING US MISERABLY) I sent him through college. Maybe that was the mistake. He saw plays there and met high-society people. I (PATTING THE UPHOLSTERY ON THE CHAIR) meant for him to take over the business in time. Upholstering isn't a bad business, and it's steady. But it wasn't good enough for him. We had a terrible fight about it and he left home. I said, "At least, change your name," and he did. Thank heavens. He's already been in debtor's prison here in Paris with that first company of his. . .somebody helped get him out. But now?. Somewhere in the provinces.

CUT TO SERIES
OF PIX OF VARI-
OUS FRENCH
PROVINCES, VAN
GOGH, MANET,
ETC. PAN AND
TILT EACH.

                    NARRATOR

(V.O.) The provinces of France (NAMES ACCORDING)
. . .that was where Molière took his theater troupe
after it failed in Paris. And that was where he began
to write.

CUT TO "THE
GLEANERS". CUT
TO MOLIERE IN
COSTUME AS
SGANARELLE,

AND OTHER

COMIC ROLES.

BUILD FOR

COMIC EFFECT.   Little pieces to entertain the country folk. Comedies,

because after a day in the fields, country folk like to

laugh. Molière made them laugh, as an actor as well

as a writer. . .and a manager and director. He and

his troupe worked hard. After a day of traveling over

bumpy roads in carts, they set up stage on a tennis

court.

CUT TO PICTURE

OF TENNIS COURT

STAGE. PAN.   Tennis court theaters were common in those times,

particularly in the provinces. Tennis courts were

roofed and walled with balconies on the sides. Set up

a platform at one end, fill the floor with benches. . .

and you have a theater. . .of sorts. Heavy curtains

near the rear of the platform made a backstage area

for changing costumes and storing props. It was

theater in the raw. Particularly backstage. . .

CUT TO WIDE AN-   (ONE ACTOR WEARS A RUFF, ONE A SHAWL, ONE

GLE SHOT OF OUR   A HELMET. ONE IS STRUGGLING TO FASTEN A

ACTORS IN FRONT   SWORD BELT.

OF HEAVY DRA-   ON A ROUGH TABLE, A COUPLE OF HAND PROPS.

PERIES.   NEAR IT, A LARGE WOODEN BOX. THERE IS A

GENERAL SENSE OF MAD CONFUSION THROUGH-

OUT THIS SCENE.

ACTOR 1

Mon Dieu! This belt!

ACTOR 2

(RUMMAGING AT THE TABLE) Where is the crown?
The crown! For my big scene with Molière! The
crown. . . .

(ACTOR 2 DARTS TOWARD BOX, STEPPING ON
END OF SHAWL ACTRESS IS ADJUSTING.)

ACTRESS

You fool! Pig!

ACTOR 3

Shush! They'll hear you!

(BIG SOUND OF LAUGHTER AND APPLAUSE.)

ACTOR 2

(RUMMAGING THROUGH BOX) Listen! Scene one is
over. I'm on. And I can't find. . . .Oh, mon Dieu!
Here it is!

(ACTOR 2 TAKES CROWN FROM BOX AND PUTS IT
ON HIS HEAD, THEN WITH REGAL BEARING
PUSHES HIS WAY THROUGH THE CURTAIN. THE
APPLAUSE AND LAUGHTER HAVE DIED DOWN.
THE THREE ACTORS WATCH ACTOR 2 SILENTLY.)

ACTOR 3

Molière will be furious.

ACTOR 1

And why not? Pierre should have looked for his
crown a half-hour ago.

ACTOR 3

While he was setting up the stage?

ACTOR 1

Why not? (PATTING HIS SWORD BELT) I got myself
ready. Oh, mon Dieu! My sword! Where is my
sword!

CUT TO   (ACTOR 1 DASHES TOWARD PROP BOX.)

NARRATOR.   NARRATOR

Molière tired of the provinces and decided to bring
the troupe back to Paris. Paris was ready for him
now. The new, young King was a lively sort. He'd
heard about Molière's troup and wanted them to play
for him in the palace. And the king was absolutely
delighted. He set Molière up in a real theater. . .the
Petit Bourbon. Molière was on his way. . .to trouble,
as always, especially from the critics.

CUT TO CRITICS.   SUPERCILIOUS

Vulgar!

STUDIOUS

Anti-France!

SUPERCILIOUS

And his last play was a failure.

STUDIOUS

He's through. If it weren't for the King. . .

SUPERCILIOUS

Not even the King will stand for everything.

STUDIOUS

You mean. . .les femmes?

CUT TO SERIES
OF PIX OF
BEAUTIFUL
YOUNG WOMEN
OF THE PERIOD.

NARRATOR

(V.O.) But it was not women who caused Molière
trouble, and it was not the King who made him great.
Molière had developed from a writer of farce to a
writer of social comedy.

CUT TO PICTURE
OF MOLIERE.
SERIES OF STILLS
FROM VARIOUS
PLAYS, OBVIOUSLY
SATIRICAL.

He mocked pomposity and hypocrisy wherever he
found it.

CUT TO
NARRATOR.

Some people say that was why his theater, the Petit
Bourbon, was torn down without his knowledge. It was
certainly not the King's doing. The King promptly
gave him another theater. . .the Palais Royal. And
there Molière continued his merciless mocking.
These lines from The Misanthrope could be Molière's
declaration of his personal independence.

CUT TO ACTOR

IN LIMBO.

ACTOR ALCESTE

I have seen and suffered too much. Court and city

alike provoke me to fury. It fills me with depression

and reduces me to utter despair to see men living as

they do. I see nothing but base flattery, injustice,

selfishness, treachery, hypocrisy, villainy every-

where. I can bear it no longer. It infuriates me. I

intend to fling my gauntlet in the face of the whole

human race!

CUT TO

NARRATOR.

NARRATOR

Molière's challenge. . .his gauntlet in the face of the

whole human race. . .

STILL OF

VOLTAIRE, DOUR.

with laughs, In his play, Tartuffe, Molière dared to

laugh at religious hypocrites. The play was banned.

But the King did not abandon Molière. And Molière

did not abandon the theater. He continued to provoke

laughter from the foibles and fables of ordinary men.

He wrote a play about a hypochondriac. . .The

Imaginary Invalid, mocking doctors and patients

alike. Here we see the imaginary invalid, Argan. . .

CUT TO ACTOR

ARGAN.

(ARGAN ON ONE OF THOSE FRENCH CHAIRS WITH

A FOOT STOOL, WIPING HIS BROW AND FEELING

HIS OWN PULSE.)

CUT TO
TOINETTE.

(TOINETTE IN LIMBO CARRYING A NUMBER OF THINGS OVER HER ARM. AS NARRATOR SPEAKS, SHE GLUES A BEARD ON HER CHIN, PUTS A TOP HAT ON HER HEAD, AND THROWS A CAPE OVER HER SHOULDERS.)

And Argan's maid servant, Toinette, dressing herself up to pretend to be a doctor. Completely dressed, Toinette walks in to see her imaginary invalid.

CUT TO ARGAN.

(ARGAN AS BEFORE, STILL TAKING HIS PULSE, ETC. TOINETTE, WITH BEARD, HAT AND CAPE, WALKS INTO THE PICTURE.)

TOINETTE

I hope you will forgive my impertinence in calling thus. But your reputation as an illustrious patient led me to come to see you.

ARGAN

You do me great honor, sir.

TOINETTE

You are studying me intently, sir. How old do you think I am?

ARGAN

Oh, I should say, twenty-six, or at the most, twenty-seven.

TOINETTE

(LAUGHING) Oh, no. I am ninety.

ARGAN

Ninety!

TOINETTE

Yes. You see, the secret of long life and youth is not unknown to me.

ARGAN

It's unbelievable. (AMAZED)

TOINETTE

(STEPPING TOWARD HIM) I travel from village to village, empire to empire, all over the world to find patients worthy of my care. Patients with important maladies—complicated cases, are the ones that interest me, though I do wish, sir, that you had been given up as hopeless by all your doctors, that I might more completely show you the excellence of my craft.

ARGAN

I thank you, sir, for your good wishes.

TOINETTE

(TO HIM) Give me your pulse. No, no, beat properly! (PAUSE) Well, I shall attend to that. Who has attended you?

ARGAN

Dr. Purjon.

TOINETTE

(TAKING VERY LARGE BOOK FROM TOP OF PILE SHE WAS CARRYING, AND FLIPPING THROUGH IT)

He is not listed among the important doctors.

(CLOSES BOOK WITH A BANG)

What does he say is wrong with you?

ARGAN

My liver, but other doctors say it is my spleen.

TOINETTE

Blockheads! It is your lungs!

ARGAN

My lungs?

TOINETTE

(TAKING A LARGE BOOK AND PENCIL) Precisely.

What are your symptoms?

ARGAN

Well, sometimes I have headaches—

TOINETTE

(WRITING IN BOOK. EACH TIME, SHE WRITES THE

SYMPTOM, AND THEN LOOKS UP FOR MORE) The

lungs.

ARGAN

And my eyes get hazy—

TOINETTE

(WRITING) The lungs.

ARGAN

My heart aches—

TOINETTE

(WRITING) The lungs.

ARGAN

My arms and legs ache—

TOINETTE

(WRITING) The lungs.

ARGAN

My stomach aches—

TOINETTE

(WRITING) The lungs. Do you eat a lot?

ARGAN

Yes, sir.

TOINETTE

(WRITING) The lungs. Do you drink?

ARGAN

Yes, sir.

TOINETTE

(WRITING) The lungs. Are you always sleepy after meals?

ARGAN

Yes, sir. (QUESTIONINGLY) The lungs?

TOINETTE

(WRITING AND NODDING) The lungs. Do you know what is your great ailment?

ARGAN

No, sir.

TOINETTE

(CLOSING BOOK WITH A BANG. DROPS IT ON FLOOR, NEARLY HITTING ARGAN'S FOOT AND HE JUMPS) The lungs. What does your doctor order you to eat?

ARGAN

Strained soup.

TOINETTE

He's ignorant!

ARGAN

Lean fowl.

TOINETTE

Ignorant.

ARGAN

Lean veal.

TOINETTE

Ignorant.

ARGAN

Fresh eggs.

TOINETTE

Ignorant.

ARGAN

Diluted wine.

TOINETTE

Ignorantus, ignoranta, ignorantum. (TAKING UP A

THIRD BOOK) Your blood's too thin. (READS FROM

BOOK) Drink your wine undiluted. (LOOKS AT HIM)

Your constitution is too thin. (CONSULTS BOOK) Eat

fat beef, pork, cheese, rice pudding, and bread.

(CLOSING BOOK WITH A BANG, DROPS IT ON

FLOOR) Your doctor's a fool. I'll send you another,

and (PUTTING ALL THREE BOOKS BACK IN A PILE)

come myself while I'm in Paris.

ARGAN

(RISING) That's very kind of you.

TOINETTE

(STEPS UP TO HIM AND TAKES HIS LEFT ARM)

Look at this arm. (THEY BOTH INSPECT IT CLOSE-

LY) What do you do with it?

ARGAN

(UNCERTAIN) Why, I, I . .

TOINETTE

(THROWING ARM DOWN IN DISGUST) I'd amputate

it at once, if I were you.

ARGAN

But why?

TOINETTE

It absorbs all the nourishment from this side of the

body and prevents it from developing properly.

ARGAN

But I need my arm.

                    TOINETTE

And that right eye — (POINTING TO IT) cut it out

immediately.

                    ARGAN

Cut out my eye?

                    TOINETTE

. Certainly. It interferes with the other. Truly, sir, if

you cut it out, the left will be much better. I can't

understand how your doctors could have neglected

you in this way!

                    ARGAN

Well, there's no great hurry about all this.

                    TOINETTE

I must go. (PICKING UP HER BOOKS) I'm sorry to

leave so soon but I must hurry to attend an urgent

consultation about a man who died yesterday.

                    ARGAN

Died yesterday?

                    TOINETTE

Yes. We must decide what should have been done to

have cured him. (BOWS) Your servant. (EXITS

QUICKLY. ARGAN LOOKS AFTER HER, SPEECH-

DRAW BACK ON   LESS.)

ARGAN'S ACTION.

NARRATOR

(NARRATOR WALKS INTO FOREGROUND.) <u>The</u> <u>Imaginary Invalid</u> was Molière's last performance on stage. A few hours after the final curtain, he collapsed and died. If Molière had written his own death scene, he could not have done better. He was one of the great playwrights on the high road from Athens to Broadway.

CLOSING TITLES.

FADE TO BLACK.

16

The Beggar's Opera John Gay

THE SMASH HIT not only of the year but of the century—according to some scholars—was John Gay's *The Beggar's Opera* when it opened in London in 1728. Basically, this play is a burlesque, poking fun at pretentious opera and overdone sentimentality. In addition, in its time it satirized certain social and judicial customs which, although not prevalent today, still delight audiences who enjoy seeing any kind of graft or corruption exposed.

For you, as actor or director, the important thing to remember is that *The Beggar's Opera* is boisterous fun and offers a challenge to many contemporary musicals. One of the director's first problems will be casting. For example, although the music does not call for operatic talent, you may have to decide whether to choose an actor who does not sing well, or a singer who requires a great deal of direction and rehearsal to act even reasonably well. Or, should you try to work around the problem? On the other hand,

if you find an actor who can project the devilish exuberance of Macheath but cannot carry a tune, should you let him speak the words of his two songs in rhythm—or try a lip sync with his songs prerecorded?

Another decision you will have to make is how much choreography, if any, should be used in scenes such as the Lucy and Polly duet. We have indicated only that they are facing each other after cornering Macheath, but their song gives them opportunity for enough movement and gesture to become a dance. Obviously your decision will depend not only on your personal preference, but also on the time and talent available to you. Because the social satire relates to a definite period and place, set and costumes should probably be identifiable with their time. It will be up to you to make the choice between strict and suggested realism.

Music for the songs in *The Beggar's Opera* is included in the Appendix.

Scene from The Beggar's Opera*

JOHN GAY

Adapted by Rome Cowgill

CAST	SET
POLLY	INTERIOR, DAY: *Old Newgate Prison in London.*
LUCY	
MACHEATH	
PEACHUM	

VIDEO	AUDIO
TITLES SUPERED OVER SHEET MUSIC OF "GREENSLEEVES." CUT TO SINGLE SHOT OF MAC- HEATH IN THE NEWGATE PRISON. HE IS DRINKING FROM A FLAGON AND SINGING.	(MUSIC: ORCHESTRAL "GREENSLEEVES" UNDER.

---

* Adapted from *Twelve Famous Plays of The Restora- tion and Eighteenth Century* (The Modern Library, 1933), with the permission of Random House, Inc.

MACHEATH

AIR #1: "GREENSLEEVES"

Since laws were made for every degree,

To curb vice in others as well as me,

I wonder we han't better company,

Upon Tyburn Tree!

But gold from law can take out the sting;

And if rich men like us were to swing,

'Twould thin the land, such numbers to string

Upon Tyburn Tree!

(MACHEATH TAKES ANOTHER SWIG FROM THE

FLAGON AND LOOKS UP STARTLED AS WE

HEAR. . .)

LUCY (V.O.)

Macheath!

(LUCY RUNS INTO THE PICTURE AND UP TO

MACHEATH AND EMBRACES HIM.)

LUCY

The warden was out of the way, today, and I took the

first opportunity to come and see you, my dearest

dear. I am in the utmost despair.

WIDEN ANGLE.	MACHEATH

(MACHEATH PUTS DOWN HIS FLAGON AND BACKS

AWAY.) But your father is the jailer!

(LUCY STEPS TOWARD HIM BUT HE STILL MOVES

BACK.)

LUCY

(DRAMATICALLY) My father's hard heart is not to be softened. You are going to hang, and I will be a widow.

MACHEATH

(MOVING TOWARD HER AND EMBRACING HER) If I could raise a small sum. . .maybe twenty guineas, would that move him? Your father's income from the escape of prisoners must amount to a considerable sum every year. Money well timed and properly applied will do anything.

LUCY

(CLINGING TO HIM) What love or money can do shall be done. All my comfort depends upon your safety.
(MACHEATH PUSHES HER AWAY, LOOKING OFF SCREEN AS WE HEAR. . .)

POLLY (V.O.)

Macheath!

THREE-SHOT AS
POLLY RUNS INTO
THE PICTURE
AND UP TO
MACHEATH.

(POLLY FLINGS HERSELF ON MACHEATH WHILE LUCY LOOKS ON, ENRAGED.)

POLLY

My dear husband! Was a rope ever intended for this neck! Oh, let me throw my arms about it and throttle thee with love!

(MACHEATH, MUCH EMBARRASSED, PULLS AWAY FROM HER.)

CHANGE ANGLE
TO SINGLE SHOT
(MCU) OF POLLY.

POLLY

(UPSET.) I'm Polly, your wife!

CUT TO MCU OF
MACHEATH.

MACHEATH

Was ever there such an unfortunate rascal as I am?

CUT TO MCU OF
LUCY.

LUCY

Was there ever such another villain!

CHANGE TO
THREE-SHOT.

POLLY

Oh, Macheath! I'll stay with thee till death. No force shall tear thy dear wife from thee now. Think what thy Polly suffers to see thee in this condition.

(MACHEATH TURNS TO LUCY, SHIELDING HIS MOUTH WITH HIS HAND.)

MACHEATH

She's out of her mind!

LUCY

Surely men were born to lie and women to believe them. Oh, villain! Villain!

POLLY

Am I not thy wife? Thy neglecting me too severely proves it. (MOVING TOWARD HIM) Look at me! Am

I not thy wife?

(MACHEATH MOVES AWAY AS LUCY AND POLLY
PURSUE HIM. THEY FOLLOW HIM AS HE CON-
TINUES TO BACK AWAY.)

LUCY

Perfidious wretch!

POLLY

Barbarous husband!

LUCY

Hads't thou been hanged five months ago, I'd been
happy!

POLLY

And I too.

LUCY

Art thou then married to her? Has't thou two wives,
monster?

MACHEATH

(IMPLORING) If women's tongues can cease for an
instant. . .

LUCY

I won't!

POLLY

Justice bids me speak! Sure, my dear, there ought to
be some preference shown to a wife. You must be
distracted by your misfortunes, or you could not
treat me this way.

LUCY

Oh, villain! Villain! Thou has't deceived me. I could

even inform against thee with pleasure.

(THEY HAVE BACKED MACHEATH INTO A CORNER

AND ARE FACING EACH OTHER.)

MEDIUM THREE-
SHOT.

(GIRLS SING AND MACHEATH LOOKS DESPERATE.)

LUCY & POLLY

AIR #2: "IRISH TROT"

POLLY

I'm bubbled.

LUCY

I'm bubbled.

POLLY

Oh, how I am troubled.

LUCY

Bamboozled, and bit.

POLLY

My distresses are doubled.

LUCY

When you come to the tree,

Should the hangman refuse,

These fingers, with pleasure,

Could fasten the noose.

POLLY

I'm bubbled.

                              LUCY

I'm bubbled.

                              POLLY

Oh, how I am troubled.

                              LUCY

Bamboozled, and bit.

My distresses are doubled.

WIDEN ANGLE AS   (MACHEATH BREAKS AWAY FROM THE TWO

MACHEATH   GIRLS, GOES OVER AND TAKES ANOTHER SWIG

MOVES.   FROM HIS FLAGON.)

                              MACHEATH

(TO LUCY) Rest your fears, my dear Lucy. This is

all an idea of Polly's to make me desperate with you

in case I get off. If I am hanged, she would like to be

thought of as my widow.

CHANGE ANGLE.   (LUCY AND POLLY COME UP TO MACHEATH.)

                              POLLY

Have you the heart to persist in disowning me?

                              MACHEATH

Have you the heart to persist in saying that we're

married? I have troubles enough.

                              LUCY

(WITH GREAT DIGNITY, TO POLLY) Really, Miss

Peachum, you only expose yourself. It's barbarous of

you to worry a gentleman in his circumstances.

                              POLLY

(WITH EQUAL DIGNITY) Decency, madam, might teach you to behave yourself with some reserve with the husband while his wife is present.

MACHEATH

(VERY GRAVE) Seriously, Polly, this is carrying the joke a little too far.

LUCY

(TO POLLY) If you are determined, madam, to cause a disturbance in the prison, I shall be forced to send for the warden to show you the door. I'm sorry you oblige me to be so ill-bred.

POLLY

Give me leave to tell you, madam, these forward airs don't become you in the least, madam, and my duty, madam, obliges me to stay with my husband, madam.

WIDEN ANGLE TO SHOW PEACHUM.

(PEACHUM CHARGES IN, IN A RAGE, TOWARD POLLY.)

PEACHUM

Where's my daughter? Ah, there you are, you hussy! Come you home, and when your fellow is hanged, hang yourself.

(POLLY CLINGS TO MACHEATH AS HER FATHER GRABS HER BY ONE ARM.)

POLLY

Dear father, do not tear me from him. I must say more to him.

PEACHUM

(PULLING POLLY AWAY FROM MACHEATH) Women
are all alike.

FOLLOW
PEACHUM.

(PEACHUM PULLING POLLY, WHO HOLDS HER
ARMS OUT IMPLORINGLY TO MACHEATH.)

POLLY

AIR #3: "IRISH HOWL"

Now power on earth can ere divide,

The knot that sacred love hath tied.

When parents draw against our mind

The true-love's knot they faster bind.

Oh, oh, re, oh, amborah,

Oh, oh, re, oh, amborah.

(AT THE END OF THE SONG HER FATHER PULLS
HER OUT OF THE PICTURE.)

CUT TO MAC-
HEATH GOING UP
TO LUCY.

MACHEATH

(GOING UP TO LUCY) I am naturally compassionate,
dear Lucy, so I couldn't treat that girl as she de-
served. That's what made you suspect there was
something in what she said.

LUCY

Indeed, my dear, I was strangely puzzled.

MACHEATH

And you think your father could help me escape?

LUCY

I know my father is gone. If I can find the keys, I'll

let you out.

(MACHEATH EMBRACES HER.)

MACHEATH

Make haste!

(LUCY MOVES OUT OF THE PICTURE)

MOVE IN ON

MACHEATH, TO

A MEDIUM CU.

MACHEATH

AIR #4: "WOULD YOU HAVE A YOUNG VIRGIN"

If the heart of a man is depressed with cares,

The mist is dispelled when a woman appears;

Like the notes of a fiddle, she sweetly, sweetly

Raises the spirits and charms our ears.

Roses and lilies her cheeks disclose,

But her ripe lips are more sweet than those.

Press her,

Caress her

With blisses,

Her kisses

CLOSING CREDITS   Dissolve us in pleasure, and soft repose.

AND END TITLES,

WITH ORCHESTRAL

VERSION OF AIR

NO. 4 UNDER.

FADE TO BLACK.

17

Interrogation Christopher Knopf

Interrogation WAS CHOSEN as the outstanding half-hour anthology television drama of 1959–1960 in the Television-Radio Writers Annual Awards presented by the Writers Guild of America. The script was originally produced on the Dick Powell-Zane Grey Theater.

In directing *Interrogation* you will be working with television at its best; not only in terms of the quality of the script but also in the script's use of the medium, developing the basic conflicts of the drama with scenes which can be most effectively shown in close or medium-close shots. The drama begins with the conflict of opposing military forces. This is a large scale, but the drama quickly moves to personal conflict between two military leaders, and the inner conflicts of an apparent coward and a real one.

As director or actor, your job is to increase the intensity of the suspense involved in the battle of wits, and give the audience the emotional impact of the self-realization that man achieves—sometimes tragically.

Because *Interrogation* was produced as a television film, the script format is one commonly used for motion pictures. However, with minor adjustment and imaginative use of studio scenery the production can easily be done live. Here again you can test your creativity.

Interrogation*

CHRISTOPHER KNOPF

Cast	Sets

CAST

Captain William Krag
Corporal Henry Durbin
del Armija
Cota
Gonzales
Palza

SETS

EXTERIOR:
    Small clearing.
    Bushy area.
    Dry wash.
    Mexican tent.
INTERIOR:
    Small enclosure.
    Tent.

FADE IN:

1. EXT. SMALL CLEARING. NIGHT.

(LOCATED IN JAGGED, BRUSH-COVERED MEXICAN HILL COUNTRY. FOUR MEXICAN SOLDIERS, CARE-LESSLY DRESSED IN THEIR GAUDY UNIFORMS-- CIRCA 1847, MEXICAN-AMERICAN WAR--HUDDLE ABOUT A CAMPFIRE, WARMING BEANS AND TOR-TILLAS, CHATTERING AWAY IN UNINTELLIGIBLE SPANISH, THEIR LONG, SINGLE SHOT RIFLES ACROSS THEIR LAPS OR CLOSE AT HAND.

SCENE OPENS TO A BURST OF LAUGHTER

* Reprinted by special permission of Christopher Knopf.

FROM THE GROUP, OBVIOUS REWARD FOR A
GOOD DIRTY JOKE. AS THE LAUGHTER SUBSIDES
A SOLDIER RISES, MOVES TOWARD CAMERA. PAN
HIM TO ONE OF SEVERAL HORSES TETHERED TO
SHRUBBERY AT THE END OF THE CLEARING.
DIGGING INTO A SADDLE BAG, HE PULLS OUT A
FLASK. THE THREE BY THE FIRE RESPOND,
RAUCOUSLY CALL THE OTHER BACK TO THEM.)

AS THE SOLDIER TURNS TOWARD THE FIRE,
HOLD TILL HE IS OUT OF SCENE, THEN MOVE
THROUGH THE HORSES TO THE EDGE OF THE
CLEARING AND COME ON A FACE PEERING IN
FROM THE THICKET.)

2. CLOSE ON THE FACE OF CAPTAIN WILLIAM
   KRAG.

(BY HIS DRESS AN OFFICER IN THE UNITED
STATES ARMY, IN HIS MIDDLE THIRTIES, KRAG
IS A LARGE MAN, MASSIVE AND PHYSICAL, HIS
TOUGH, BLUNT FACE, THE OVERTIGHT EXPRES-
SION AROUND THE CORNERS OF HIS MOUTH,
CONVEYING A KIND OF COMPULSIVE COURAGE
AND STRENGTH. AS HE LIES IN THE DUST AT
THE EDGE OF THE CLEARING, HIS UNIFORM
POWERED WHITE WITH PUMICE, HIS EYES, QUICK
AND ALERT, TAKE IN HIS SURROUNDINGS. THEN
HE WITHDRAWS.)

3. EXT. BRUSH LEADING AWAY FROM CLEARING.
 NIGHT.

(ON KRAG, "CRABBING" HIS WAY ON ELBOWS,
STOMACH AND KNEES, DOWNHILL AWAY FROM
THE CLEARING. REACHING THE LIP OF A DRY
WASH, KRAG THROWS HIMSELF OVER THE EM-
BANKMENT.)

4. EXT. DRY WASH. NIGHT.

(AS KRAG TUMBLES DOWN THE EMBANKMENT TO
THE BED BELOW WHERE CORPORAL HENRY
DURBIN HOVERS OVER TWO CANVAS-COVERED
PACKS, HIS BACK TO CAMERA AND KRAG. DUR-
BIN, WHEN WE SEE HIM, IS A MEDIUM-SIZED MAN,
IN HIS LATE THIRTIES, WITH A ROUND, BLOND,
OVERLY-SENSITIVE FACE. THOUGH HIS INSTINCTS
ARE DECENT AND LOYAL, IN ALMOST EVERY
OTHER WAY HE DIFFERS FROM KRAG: UNSURE,
SELF-DOUBTING, WHERE KRAG APPEARS CONFI-
DENT; NONDESCRIPT, A FACE IN THE CROWD,
WHERE KRAG STANDS OUT; A FOLLOWER, WHERE
KRAG SEEMS A NATURAL, GIFTED LEADER OF
MEN.)

                    KRAG

(BREATHLESSLY—HIS VOICE KEPT LOW) There're
four of them. This wash'll take us just past their
camp. From there it's a run, a hundred yards to a

thicket. . .(HE STOPS, STARES AT DURBIN'S BACK.)

KRAG

Durbin. . .? (NO ANSWER) Durbin! (HE SCRAMBLES
OVER TO THE CORPORAL, GRABS HIS SHOULDER,
TWISTS HIM AROUND. DURBIN TRIES TO AVOID
KRAG'S EYES, BUT THE FEAR IN HIS FACE BE-
TRAYS HIM.)

KRAG

What's the matter with you?

DURBIN

Nothing, sir.

KRAG

You're sick?

DURBIN

We'd better get moving. . . (HE STARTS TO MAKE A
MOVE TOWARD THE PACKS, BUT KRAG PULLS
HIM BACK.)

KRAG

Look at me!

(DURBIN TRIES TO FIGHT BACK, BUT HE CAN'T.
HIS SHOULDERS SAG.)

DURBIN

(PAINFULLY) I'm afraid.

KRAG

We'll be through their lines in five minutes. . .!

DURBIN

I don't want to be afraid. I prayed to God I wouldn't

be. . .that I'd be like you. But I'm not like you. I'm

not a brave man.

KRAG

(ASTOUNDED) You volunteered. In the name of

heaven, why'd you come, you didn't have to. . .

DURBIN

Because I wanted to prove. . .

KRAG

What?

DURBIN

(DESPERATELY) I've never killed a man in my life.

What happens if I have to kill a man?

KRAG

You'll kill him! Anyone who tries to stop us. . .

DURBIN

(HE WANTS TO BELIEVE IT) Yes, sir. . .

KRAG

Nobody ever blew a mission on me. By God, not yet!

DURBIN

(MORE RESIGNED THAN CONVINCED) Yes, sir.

(KRAG STUDIES DURBIN, CLEARLY WORRIED.)

KRAG

(NODS TOWARD THE PACKS) Get your pack on.

Whatever happens, stay close to me.

(DURBIN STARES AT KRAG A MOMENT MORE.

DRAWING COMFORT FROM THE CAPTAIN'S RE-

ASSURANCE AND STRENGTH, HE TURNS TO REACH

FOR HIS PACK. AS HE DOES, A SHADOW FALLS
OVER IT. WHIRLING, DURBIN LOOKS UP, AT THE
TOP OF THE BANK ABOVE THE WASH. A LOOK
OF HORROR COMES TO HIS FACE. A HALF-CHOKED
CRY ESCAPES HIS THROAT.

5. ON KRAG.

STARTLED BY THE CRY, KRAG TURNS FROM HIS
OWN PACK, LOOKS UP AT THE BANK. INSTANTLY,
HIS HAND GOES FOR HIS GUN, BUT BEFORE HE
CAN REACH IT, THERE'S AN EXPLOSION! REEL-
ING FROM A BULLET THAT SLAMS INTO HIS
SHOULDER, KRAG SPINS BACK AGAINST THE OP-
POSITE BANK AS:)

6. ON THE FOUR MEXICAN SOLDIERS.

(THE SOLDIERS, RIFLES TRAINED ON KRAG AND
DURBIN, SLIP DOWN THE EMBANKMENT AND IN-
TO THE WASH.)

FADE OUT.

FADE IN:

7. INT. A SMALL ENCLOSURE. NIGHT.

(THREE SIDES FORMED BY ROUGH, BLEACHED
BOARDS, THE ROOF BY OTHER BOARDS LYING
FLAT ACROSS THE TOP. THE FOURTH SIDE
OPENS OUT INTO THE NIGHT, A HEAVY, RUSTING
IRON GATE ACROSS THE OPENING BARRING EXIT.

OPEN ON KRAG. STRIPPED OF WEAPONS, CAN-

TEENS, AND EXCESSIVE PARAPHERNALIA, HIS
HANDS LASHED SECURELY BEFORE HIM, HE
STALKS ABOUT THE ENCLOSURE, GLANCING AT
THE CEILING, CHECKING THE WALLS. A LARGE
SPLOTCH OF RED SHOWS ON HIS SHIRT, RIMMING
THE AREA WHERE THE BULLET ENTERED HIS
SHOULDER, THE WOUND ITSELF UNBANDAGED,
UNATTENDED. ON THE FLOOR OF THE ENCLO-
SURE, HUDDLED AGAINST THE FAR WALL, HIS
HANDS ALSO LASHED BEFORE HIM, SITS DURBIN,
FRIGHTENED, DESPERATELY TRYING TO CON-
CEAL HIS MOUNTING FEAR. OUTSIDE THE EN-
CLOSURE TWO MEXICAN GUARDS, COTA AND
PALZA, EACH EQUIPPED WITH A BAYONETTED
RIFLE, SQUAT ON THEIR HAUNCHES, WATCHING
KRAG WITH INTENSE CURIOSITY. HOLD FOR A
BEAT, THEN:)

COTA

(CALLING IN TO KRAG) Hey, man. . .

(AS KRAG TURNS:)

COTA

Maybe you got whiskey, heh?

(IGNORING THE TAUNT, KRAG PLACES HIS HANDS
ON THE GATE, DRAMATICALLY TESTS IT FOR
STRENGTH. THE MOMENT HE TOUCHES THE
IRON, PALZA BRINGS HIS BAYONET DOWN, A

SLASHING GESTURE AIMED AT SLICING OFF

KRAG'S FINGERS. PULLING HIS HANDS AWAY

FAST, KRAG GLARES OUT AT THE GUARD, COLD

SWEAT FORMING ON HIS FACE.)

COTA

(STILL TO KRAG) I let him kill you quick for

whiskey.

(TURNING HIS BACK ON THE GUARDS, KRAG

MOVES BACK INTO THE ENCLOSURE.)

8. KRAG AND DURBIN.

(AS KRAG CONTINUES HIS PACING:)

DURBIN

They're. . .they're going to question us, aren't they?

That's what he means?

KRAG

You don't know a thing.

DURBIN

They'll come and take us away and. . .

KRAG

Whatever happens, that's all you give them. You

didn't even know where you were going when you left

with me. I was the only one, I never told you. . . .

DURBIN

(DESPERATELY--EYES CLOSED IN PRAYER) God

give me courage. . . .

KRAG

Now, listen! What I mean, you listen! Four thousand

men are back in our camp. You know what

happens to them if you tell what it was

we came to do?

                    DURBIN

Even if we didn't say anything. . .getting captured

before we could. . .

                    KRAG

They've still got a chance. Not as much as if we'd

done what we came for. Only tell what it was. . . .

                    DURBIN

Once I. . .I heard about a man they captured. He

wouldn't tell what they wanted to know. . . .

                    KRAG

Durbin. . .

                    DURBIN

(CONTINUING) . . .so they put a red hot poker up to

his eyes. . .

                    KRAG

You're working things up in your mind. . .!

                    DURBIN

(CONTINUING). . .and when they were done they

turned him loose on the desert. . . .

                    KRAG

Nothing worse than they've done in combat. You must

know that.

                    DURBIN

Yes, sir, I've heard. . . .

KRAG

(STOPPED) What do you mean, heard?

(DURBIN LOOKS AWAY. KRAG STARES AT HIM AN

INSTANT, THEN WITH SICKENING REALIZATION:)

KRAG

You've never been in combat. . .?

DURBIN

(WEAKLY) No, sir. . . .

KRAG

(STUNNED) Durbin. . . .

DURBIN

I've never even had a gun in my hands, not in a

fight. . . .

KRAG

(APPALLED) Then what. . .?

DURBIN

I've been on building roads, sir.

KRAG

Building roads? What're you doing here?

DURBIN

(EVASIVELY) They said they needed a man, a

volunteer, who knew explosives.

KRAG

There were a dozen others who could have gone, why

you?

(DURBIN LOOKS AT KRAG, A FLEETING GLANCE,

THEN LOWERS HIS EYES.)

DURBIN

All my life, I've. . .I don't know, wondered about my-

self. It wasn't so bad when there wasn't war, but. . .

when war came. . .seeing friends, people I knew,

people like you, go into fighting, getting shot at, blown

to pieces and me. . .just sitting there back of the

lines, waiting till they was done. . .then building

roads to towns they'd taken and died in. . . (HE

BREAKS OFF)

KRAG

Go on, let's hear. . . .

DURBIN

It just. . .got to where I couldn't live with it no more.

So when I heard about this. . .that it was Captain

William Krag asking for a volunteer to go in with

him. . .I just, I don't know. . .wanted to do my part. . .

I wanted to prove I could.

(KRAG STARES AT DURBIN AN INSTANT,

THEN RISES, CAMERA PULLING BACK

AS HE MOVES TOWARD THE CENTER

OF THE ENCLOSURE.)

KRAG

(STUNNED, LITTLE SHAKE OF HIS HEAD) You

picked a time.

DURBIN

(NOT SURE HE'S HEARD) Sir. . .?

KRAG

(COVERING QUICKLY) I said. . .you'll be fine,
Durbin.

DURBIN

(UNABLE TO BELIEVE HIS EARS) You. . .you mean
that?

KRAG

(FALSE WORDS AS HE DESPERATELY TRIES TO
FIGURE WHAT TO DO NEXT) I wouldn't trade you
for anyone I could name.

DURBIN

(WANTING TO BELIEVE IT) You're. . .you're just
saying that. I mean. . .a man like you, all the things
you done. . .the fighting. . .people you killed, the
citations they give you. . .wanting a fella like me
to. . . .

(A SUDDEN RATTLING AT THE GATE. BOTH MEN
TURN.)

9. NEW ANGLE

(FEATURING KRAG AND DURBIN IN F.G., THE
GUARDS IN B.G., OPENING THE GATE TO A MEXI-
CAN OFFICER, LIEUTENANT GONZALES, A
THICKLY-MUSTACHIOED BULL OF A MAN WITH A
TWISTED STOGIE STUFFED INTO HIS MOUTH, AND
A COMFORTABLE PAUNCH DRAPED OVER HIS
BELT. STOPPING JUST INSIDE THE ENCLOSURE,
GONZALES PEERS AT THE PRISONERS. KRAG

STEALS A GLANCE AT DURBIN, THEN TURNS TO

GONZALES.)

KRAG

So?

GONZALES

(TO KRAG--IN SPANISH) Come.

(KRAG SHRUGS HIS SHOULDERS, AN INVOLUNTARY

GESTURE, THEN STARTS TOWARD GONZALES, BUT

AS KRAG REACHES GONZALES, THE MEXICAN OF-

FICER HOLDS HIS HAND OUT AGAINST KRAG'S

CHEST, STOPPING HIM.)

GONZALES

(IN SPANISH) Wait!

(FOR A MOMENT, A BRIEF ONE, GONZALES

MEASURES KRAG, THEN LOWERS HIS EYES TO

DURBIN. DURBIN SEES THIS, SO DOES KRAG.

BOTH MEN TENSE.)

KRAG

(TRYING TO PUSH PAST GONZALES) Let's get on

with this.

GONZALES

(PUSHING KRAG BACK, NODDING DOWN AT DURBIN,

IN SPANISH) That one first, I think.

(DURBIN'S MOUTH DROPS OPEN.)

KRAG

(DESPERATELY) A lousy, two-striped corporal?

You think he knows a thing. . .?

GONZALES

(EMPHATICALLY--IN SPANISH) Him.

KRAG

(INCREASING DESPERATION) I told you. . .he's

nothing. I wouldn't trust him to curry a horse. . .

(GONZALES TURNS, GESTURES ONE OF THE

GUARDS TO MOVE IN FOR DURBIN.)

KRAG

(FRANTIC NOW, THROWING HIMSELF AT

GONZALES) I'm the one you want! Me. . .!

(THE BACK OF GONZALES' HAND COMES UP

HARD, CATCHES KRAG FULL ON THE MOUTH,

SENDS HIM REELING BACK AGAINST THE WALL.

DESPERATELY, KRAG TRIES TO RISE, IS MET BY

A QUICK CHOP ON THE NECK BY GONZALES.

STRUGGLING BACK TO HIS FEET, KRAG SEES

DURBIN, ALMOST IN A STATE OF SHOCK, BEING

LED FROM THE ENCLOSURE BY COTA. KRAG

STUMBLES TOWARD THE OPENING, REACHES IT

JUST AS THE GATE IS SLAMMED CLOSED IN HIS

FACE.)

KRAG

(RAGE IN HIS FACE AS HE YELLS AFTER GON-

ZALES) Me, you yellow-livered stinking. . .

(REALIZING IT'S HOPELESS) Durbin! In the name

of Heaven, don't tell them! Don't tell them. . .!

(AS CAMERA MOVES IN ON, HOLDS ON HIS
FACE. . .)

DISSOLVE TO:

10. INT. SMALL ENCLOSURE. NIGHT.

ON KRAG, PACING THE ENCLOSURE LIKE A
CAGED PANTHER. TURNING TO THE GATE ONCE
AGAIN HE PLACES HIS HANDS ON THE BARS,
STARES OUT, HIS FACE A MASK OF TENSE ANXI-
ETY. PALZA, LEFT TO WATCH OVER HIM, LOOKS
UP AT HIM COLDLY.)

PALZA

(IN SPANISH) Get back! (AS KRAG PAYS HIM NO
HEED) Get back!

(AS HE SPEAKS THIS LAST, PALZA JABS HIS
BAYONET THROUGH THE BARS AT KRAG, A QUICK
MOVEMENT, WHICH SENDS KRAG RECOILING
BACK INTO THE SHADOWS AT THE FAR END OF
THE ENCLOSURE. PALZA WATCHES KRAG A
MOMENT, THEN HALF TURNING, HE STARES OFF
INTO THE NIGHT.)

11. CLOSE ON KRAG.

(AS HE REACHES THE REAR OF THE ENCLOSURE,
DESPERATELY TRIES TO FIND SOME WAY TO
STRUGGLE FREE FROM HIS BINDINGS. BUT HE
CAN'T. HOLDING HIS HANDS AGAINST THE
WARPED, PROTRUDING EDGE OF A BOARD, HE

TRIES TO USE THE EDGE TO CUT THROUGH THE
BINDINGS, MANAGES ONLY TO CATCH THE ROPE
ON A FISSURE IN THE WOOD. WITH AN ANGRY
GESTURE, HE YANKS HIS WRISTS FREE. AS HE
DOES, THERE'S A SLIGHT SPLITTING SOUND.
KRAG STOPS, STARES DOWN AT THE WOOD, RE-
ACTING TO WHAT HE SEES:)

12. INSERT: THE BOARD.

(THE FISSURE HAS LENGTHENED SEVERAL IN-
CHES, FORMING THE BEGINNING OF A SIZABLE
SPLINTER, FOUR INCHES WIDE AT ITS BASE.)

13. BACK TO SCENE 11.

(KRAG STUDIES THE SPLINTER, FASCINATED. A
GLANCE BACK AT THE GUARD, THEN KRAG,
EVERY MOVEMENT GEARED TO CAUSE NO
ALARM, REACHES DOWN AGAIN, GENTLY GRABS
HOLD OF THE BASE OF THE SPLINTER, CARE-
FULLY WORKS IT, LENGTHENING IT TO SIX
INCHES, EIGHT. IT COMES OFF IN HIS HANDS: A
TEN INCH "DAGGER" OF WOOD, ITS POINT AS
SHARP AND DEADLY AS A STILETTO. FOR AN IN-
STANT, KRAG STANDS THERE, HIS BACK TO THE
GATE, HIS BREATH COMING HEAVILY. THEN HE
DARES A GLANCE OVER HIS SHOULDER AT
PALZA.)

14. PALZA. AS SEEN THROUGH GATE. POV.

(SQUATTING SOME THREE OR FOUR FEET AWAY

FROM THE GATE. HIS BACK STILL HALF TURNED

TO KRAG, HIS RIFLE RESTING AGAINST HIS KNEE,

HE WORKS AT LIGHTING A STOGIE.)

15. NEW ANGLE.

(KRAG IN F.G., PALZA SEEN THROUGH THE GATE

IN B.G. HOLDING HIS HANDS DOWN, THE "DAGGER"

TURNED UP AND HIDDEN AGAINST HIS WRIST,

KRAG CROSSES TO THE GATE.)

                    KRAG

Hey.

(PALZA LOOKS UP, STARTLED, HIS HAND GOING

QUICKLY TO HIS RIFLE)

                    KRAG

(NODDING AT THE CIGAR) A smoke, okay?

(AS THE GUARD CONTINUES TO STARE AT HIM)

                    KRAG

Fumar?

(THE GUARD STUDIES KRAG FOR A MOMENT

MORE, THEN RISES. A TAUNTING LOOK ON HIS

FACE, HE EDGES A LITTLE CLOSER TO KRAG,

TAKES A LONG, DELIBERATE DRAG ON THE

STOGIE, BLOWS THE SMOKE TEMPTINGLY INTO

KRAG'S FACE. KRAG MEASURES THE DISTANCE

BETWEEN HIMSELF AND THE GUARD: TWO FEET

AT LEAST.)

KRAG

Uno fumar.

(THE GUARD CHUCKLES, HIS LIPS SPREADING
BACK TO SHOW LARGE WHITE TEETH.)

KRAG

Solamente uno fumar. Okay?

(WITH DRAMATIC, ALMOST COMIC GESTURES THE
GUARD PLACES THE STOGIE IN HIS MOUTH AGAIN,
TAKES A SECOND LONG DEEP DRAG, AGAIN BLOWS
THE SMOKE INTO KRAG'S FACE.)

KRAG

Solamente uno.

(HOLDING THE CIGAR OUT TO KRAG--HIS BODY
JUST BARELY OUT OF REACH--PALZA WAVES
THE THING BEFORE KRAG'S NOSE, AT THE SAME
TIME INCHING HALF A FOOT CLOSER. KRAG
MEASURES THE DISTANCE AGAIN, HIS HANDS
CLASPING THE "DAGGER" TILL WHITE SHOWS AT
HIS KNUCKLES. IT'LL TAKE A PERFECT THRUST,
STRAIGHT THROUGH THE BARS, AND NEVER A
SECOND CHANCE. HE DRAWS IN HIS BREATH,
HOLDS IT A BEAT--THEN SUDDENLY STARTS AT
THE SOUND OF APPROACHING FOOTSTEPS. AS
THE GUARD TURNS TO THE FOOTSTEPS KRAG
PULLS BACK INTO THE SHADOWS, LOOKS DES-
PERATELY FOR A PLACE TO HIDE THE "DAGGER."
FINDING NONE, HE DROPS IT ON THE FLOOR IN A

FAR CORNER, TURNS AT THE SOUND OF THE
GATE BEING OPENED, REACTS IN HORROR TO
WHAT HE SEES:)

16. DURBIN.

(BEING HALF-LED, HALF-DRAGGED IN BY COTA
AND GONZALES, UNABLE TO HOLD HIS LEGS
WITHOUT HELP. HE HAS BEEN THROUGH A
TERRIBLE BEATING--AS TERRIBLE AS WE ARE
PERMITTED TO SHOW--HIS SHIRT IS DRAPED
OVER HIS CHEST, BUT IT'S CLEAR THAT BENEATH
IT THERE ARE TORTUROUS WOUNDS. HIS FACE
IS BLOODIED, HIS EYES GLAZED FROM PAIN.)

17. KRAG.

(HE CONTINUES TO STARE AT DURBIN, APPALLED.
THE CORPORAL IS LED BEFORE HIM. FOR A
MOMENT, THE TWO JUST STAND THERE, KRAG'S
EYES DESPERATELY ASKING THE QUESTION.
WITH AN ANGRY SHOVE, GONZALES PUSHES DUR-
BIN TO THE GROUND. A SINGLE, SHARP CRY,
THEN DURBIN LIES THERE SILENT, BREATHING
HEAVILY THROUGH HIS PAIN. KRAG LIFTS HIS
EYES TO GONZALES.)

                    KRAG

You pig. You filthy swine.

(GONZALES GRABS HIM BY THE ARM, PULLS HIM
ROUGHLY TOWARD THE OPENING)

(AS KRAG MOVES PAST COTA:)

                              COTA

(WRY LITTLE GESTURE) I tole you man. It could

have been quick for whiskey.

(A BACKWARD GLANCE AT DURBIN STILL LYING

ON THE FLOOR, AND KRAG TURNS, FOLLOWS

GONZALES OUT INTO THE NIGHT.)

DISSOLVE TO:

18. EXT. MEXICAN CAMP. NIGHT (STOCK).

19. ANGLE BEFORE TENT.

(THICKLY POPULATED WITH TENTS AND CAIS-

SONS SILHOUETTED AGAINST THE NIGHT. KRAG,

GONZALES IN THE LEAD, COTA CLOSE AT HIS

HEELS. ARRIVING AT A LARGE TENT, LIGHT

SHINING OUT FROM WITHIN, GONZALES GESTURES

KRAG AND COTA ARE TO WAIT, THEN DUCKS IN-

SIDE. THE SOUND OF MUFFLED VOICES INSIDE

THE TENT, A SHARP, UNINTELLIGIBLE COMMAND

AND GONZALES REAPPEARS.)

                           GONZALES

(GESTURING KRAG TO ENTER--IN SPANISH) In-

side.

(KRAG HESITATES, THEN, WITH A PROD FROM

COTA, MOVES ON INSIDE THE TENT. COTA POSI-

TIONING HIMSELF OUTSIDE, GONZALES FOLLOW-

ING KRAG.)

20. INT. TENT. NIGHT.

(IT'S A LARGE TENT, A WHALE-OIL LAMP HANG-
ING FROM THE CENTER POLE GIVING LIGHT TO
THE PLACE. DIRECTLY BELOW THE LAMP IS A
SMALL TABLE, THE EQUIPMENT AND PERSONAL
EFFECTS TAKEN OFF KRAG--CANTEEN, GUNBELT,
REVOLVER MINUS SHELLS, ETC.--LYING ON TOP
OF IT. A BENCH FLANKS ONE SIDE OF THE
TABLE, A CHAIR THE OTHER. ON THE FLOOR,
BESIDE THE TABLE, ARE THE CANVAS COVERED
PACKS, NOW OPEN, THE EXPLOSIVES WITHIN
THEM CLEARLY EXPOSED. ON THE FAR WALL
OF THE TENT, OPPOSITE THE ENTRANCE, HANGS
A MEXICAN ARMY MAP OF THE MEXICAN STATE
NUEVO LEON, SHOWN TO BE DIRECTLY ADJA-
CENT TO AND SOUTH OF TEXAS. TO ONE SIDE
OF THE MAP IS A LIQUOR SIDEBOARD BEARING A
COUPLE OF BOTTLES AND GLASSES. BEFORE THE
MAP, HIS BACK TO CAMERA, STANDS A MEXICAN
OFFICER, COLONEL FRANCISCO del ARMIJA, A
TALL MAN, GRACEFUL, LITHE AND MUSCULAR,
MAGNIFICENTLY COSTUMED. AS KRAG IS
BROUGHT TO A HALT MIDWAY BETWEEN THE
ENTRANCE AND THE TABLE BY GONZALES, del
ARMIJA CONTINUES STUDYING THE WALL MAP,
HIS BACK TO CAMERA AND PRISONER. AT LENGTH
HE TURNS, REVEALING A MAN IN HIS EARLY FOR-

TIES, MORE CASTILIAN THAN MEXICAN INDIAN,
HIS STRIKING, CYNICAL FACE PLANED SMOOTH
AND HARD, ALL THE FAT BURNED OFF HIM BY
WAR AND THE CARE OF COMMAND. FOR A LONG,
UNHURRIED MOMENT HE STUDIES KRAG, HIS
PENETRATING, EMOTIONLESS EYES TAKING IN
THE MAN. BUT FOR ALL HIS COMPOSURE THERE
IS ABOUT HIM AN UNEASY RESTLESSNESS, A TEN-
SION BORN OF THE KNOWLEDGE THAT TIME IS
CLOSING IN UPON HIM. AS HE TURNS AWAY:)

del ARMIJA

(IN SURPRISINGLY POLISHED ENGLISH) Name.

KRAG

Krag.

del ARMIJA

(HE TURNS BACK, STARES AT KRAG, EYEBROWS
ARCHED IN SURPRISE) Krag? (BEAT) William
Krag?

(AS KRAG REMAINS SILENT, del ARMIJA CON-
TINUES HIS STARE, STUDYING KRAG WITH NEW
INTEREST:)

del ARMIJA

Forgive my stare. But to see you are flesh and blood.
The reports of my men have you a dragon with four
heads and forked tongues that breathe fire. (GESTUR-
ING TOWARD THE BENCH BEFORE THE TABLE)
Sit down.

(AS KRAG REMAINS STANDING:)

                    del ARMIJA

You will need attention for that wound. Gonzales. . .

                    KRAG

The wound's fine.

(del ARMIJA STUDIES KRAG AN INSTANT MORE,
THEN TURNS, BEGINS PACING THE AREA BE-
TWEEN THE TABLE AND THE MAP.)

                    del ARMIJA

Four hours ago you are captured trying to pass
through my lines. In your possession were these. . .
(HE GESTURES TOWARD THE EXPLOSIVES) two
packs of explosives, enough to blow the top off a
mountain. (FACING KRAG) What were you after?

                    KRAG

(HE STARES AT del ARMIJA, AMAZED) You don't
know?

                    del ARMIJA

What were you sent to do?

                    KRAG

(HE CAN'T BELIEVE IT) But Durbin, you mean he
didn't. . .? (KRAG STARES AT del ARMIJA, SEES IT IN
THE COLONEL'S EYES. A LOOK OF ENORMOUS
RELIEF AND A LAUGH BEGINS TO BUILD IN KRAG.)

                    KRAG

(THROUGH HIS LAUGHTER; UNABLE TO BELIEVE
IT) Durbin. . .!

(GONZALES' HAND WHIPS OUT FROM BEHIND,

CATCHES KRAG ON THE BACK OF HIS NECK. HE

DROPS.)

GONZALES

(STANDING OVER KRAG; LOW, MENACING)

Two minutes alone with him. . .

del ARMIJA

Keep your tongue and hands to yourself!

(GONZALES FALLS TO BROODING SILENCE, del

ARMIJA SWINGS HIS EYES BACK TO KRAG WHO

PULLS HIMSELF OFF THE FLOOR.)

del ARMIJA

What, Capitan? What was it you were to do?

KRAG

(AS HE COMES TO A STANDING POSITION; EYES

BLACK WITH CONTEMPT AND RAGE) You go to

hell.

del ARMIJA

Then suppose I tell you. (TURNING TO THE WALL

MAP) In a day, two days, three, your Army will move

toward one of these towns. (AS HE POINTS THEM

OUT ON THE MAP) Cerralvo to my north, Herreras

to my south. The moment your General commits him-

self, my observers will so inform me and I will move

to engage your forces. To do so, however, I must

pass through this gorge to Herreras, across this

bridge to Cerralvo. Should either be blown before I
reach it, I am cut off and your attack upon the town
succeeds without resistance.

(TURNING, HE RETURNS TO THE TABLE, LEANS
ON IT, PALMS DOWN ON THE EDGE. HIS VOICE IS
SOFT, BUT HIS EYES ARE STEEL.)

                    del ARMIJA

Which was it you were to blow, Capitan? (SILENCE)
The gorge or the bridge? (STILL SILENCE) Which
way does your Army go?

(BOTH MEN HOLD THEIR POSITION, del ARMIJA'S
FACE SHOVED OUT TOWARD KRAG'S, THE MUS-
CLES IN IT PROMINENT, TAUT. A BEAT, THEN:)

                    del ARMIJA

(PUSHING BACK FROM THE TABLE) Look behind
you, capitan.

(AS KRAG GLANCES BACK AT GONZALES:)

                    del ARMIJA

These are the men of my Army. Yaquis, for the most
part. A primitive Indian people, with a primitive
culture. . . .

                      KRAG

I saw their. . ."culture" a few minutes back.

                    del ARMIJA

But a portion of what they can invent when permitted
to tax their imaginations. Some, it is said, have un-

limbered the tongue of a mute. Fifteen hundred of

them, Capitan. Any one of which--

KRAG

(STARTLED) Fifteen hundred?

del ARMIJA

You seem surprised.

KRAG

We thought--

(AS KRAG STOPS.)

del ARMIJA

What? That I had more?

(AS KRAG REMAINS SILENT:)

del ARMIJA

Only fifteen hundred poorly armed, half-starved men

to your four thousand. Good men for the most part, as

good as yours. But men who must fight with food and

powder, not these gaudy rags. . .(HE FLICKS HIS

UNIFORM) they send us. (TURNING TO KRAG) So,

you see? Even if I were to meet you on the road to

one of those towns. . .(HE INDICATES THE MAP) I

am defeated. The only hope I have is to learn which

way you are going before you start. Only then, if I am

given time enough to occupy the town ahead of you,

time to entrench, do I have a chance.

KRAG

And you think I'm going to tell you where?

del ARMIJA

I'm counting on it.

KRAG

You couldn't get Durbin to. . .

del ARMIJA

A rare one, Durbin. A patriot. (AS KRAG STARES

AT HIM) That surprises you. But true. A man who

cares more for the lives of others than he does for

his own.

KRAG

(WRYLY) And you got a notion just maybe I don't?

del ARMIJA

I am about to find out. (TO GONZALES; IN SPANISH)

Lieutenant. . .

(AS HE SPEAKS, KRAG REACHES UP, STARTS TO

UNBUTTON HIS SHIRT. ALARMED, GONZALES

MOVES TOWARD HIM.)

21. OVER KRAG ON del ARMIJA.

(AS KRAG OPENS HIS SHIRT, EXPOSING HIS CHEST.

WE DO NOT SEE WHAT'S THERE, BUT THE LOOKS

ON GONZALES' AND del ARMIJA'S FACES ARE

ENOUGH TO TELL US.)

del ARMIJA

(OVER HIS EXPRESSION) Apaches. . .

KRAG

(NODS) I took that for three days. All I had to do to

get them to stop was tell a few odd facts they wanted

to know.

22. ON del ARMIJA, AS HE STARES.

23. ON GONZALES, AS HE, TOO, STARES WITH

      NEW RESPECT.

GONZALES

(SOFTLY) Madre de Dios!

24. ON KRAG AS HE ACCEPTS THEIR STARES,

      PROUD OF THEIR REACTION. ON HIS FACE.

(del ARMIJA HAS MOVED TO THE LIQUOR SIDE-

TABLE, WHERE, DURING THE FOLLOWING, HE

SLOWLY, METHODICALLY POURS LIQUOR. KRAG

IS BUTTONING HIS SHIRT.)

del ARMIJA

(GRAVELY) Very. . .impressive, Capitan. (HE PICKS

UP A BOTTLE, GESTURES TOWARD KRAG WITH

IT) The Apaches--they left you like that?

KRAG

Two years later they wished they hadn't. The Battle

of Iron Wells. Maybe you heard of it.

del ARMIJA

(HE LOOKS AT KRAG, SURPRISED; THEN) Yes. . .I

heard of it. Two hundred of your soldiers caught

them, men, women and children, moving their camp

across the desert. How many were there? Three

hundred? Three twenty?

KRAG

I didn't count. . .

del ARMIJA

You did not have to. (POURING FROM THE BOTTLE)
All you had to do was surround them. Cut off from
water, in two days you would have forced their surrender. Instead, you attacked.

KRAG

And wiped out two hundred savages.

del ARMIJA

Along with a hundred men of your own.

KRAG

(UNFAZED) The price of victory.

del ARMIJA

Women and children?

KRAG

Children grow into warriors.

del ARMIJA

And women?

KRAG

They bear them.

del ARMIJA

Logical thoughts, Capitan. Not ones that would bring
me sleep, but logical.

KRAG

War depends on logic, Colonel. Not sleep.

del ARMIJA

(NODS TO KRAG) My apologies. Obviously there is
more of the dragon to you than I gave you credit for.

KRAG

A basic weakness with you, underestimating my
abilities. I should think after El Palo Alto--

del ARMIJA

(AGAIN SURPRISED) That, too, was you?

KRAG

Four hundred of your men killed that day. . . .

del ARMIJA

And three hundred of yours. For a town you never
had to take at all. For a town you could have passed,
left stranded, helpless behind your lines. . .

KRAG

Four hundred armed men are never helpless, Colonel.

del ARMIJA

Low on food and water. . .

KRAG

And a pounding sun to drive them mad? Throw me
against four men with their senses, but never against
one mad one.

del ARMIJA

You were against four men at El Brazito.

KRAG

What about El Brazito?

                    del ARMIJA

Four men with their senses there on top of the hill. . .

                      KRAG

Blocking my battalion from the pass.

                    del ARMIJA

And you took them. . . .

                      KRAG

I took them.

                    del ARMIJA

You. . .alone. . .no one to help. Shot them one at a

time, there in the rocks, when a detachment of a

dozen soldiers could have gained their surrender for

the asking.

                      KRAG

There's a revelation.

                    del ARMIJA

Revelation. . .?

                      KRAG

That your men would "surrender for the asking."

Personally, I've always had a healthy respect for

their courage.

(del ARMIJA STARES AT KRAG; THEN, WITH A NOD

OF HIS HEAD, AN UNSPOKEN ACKNOWLEDGMENT

OF A POINT WELL MADE.)

                    del ARMIJA

You have a confounding way about you, Capitan. . .

KRAG

(DRYLY) The last thing I'd want to do's confound
you. . .

del ARMIJA

And, I am forced to admit, a convincing one. The
mind of the fox. . .the hide and conscience of the
boar. . .the perfect warrior. . .logical. . .coldly
vicious. . .invulnerable. . .(TURNING; HOLDING OUT
A GLASS) Cognac?

(AS KRAG STARES, SURPRISED, YET CHARY:)

del ARMIJA

A private blend, very rare.

KRAG

Curious thing about private blends. They always have
a way of loosening a man's tongue.

del ARMIJA

(A SHORT LITTLE CHUCKLE) A man who has held
his tongue three days against the Apaches is not
likely to lose it to one glass of brandy.

(KRAG HESITATES, THEN REACHES OUT, TAKES
THE GLASS, HIS MANNER STILL ALERT AND
CAUTIOUS.)

del ARMIJA

(STUDIES KRAG A MOMENT; THEN) Three days
with the Apaches. . .(A BEAT, THEN SEATING HIM-
SELF AT THE TABLE) It was during the--

(AS del ARMIJA SEARCHES FOR THE NAME:)

KRAG

Jicarilla uprising.

del ARMIJA

Ah, yes, the Jicarilla. (MOTIONING KRAG TO THE

BENCH ACROSS THE TABLE FROM HIM)

del ARMIJA

Sit down. (AS KRAG STILL REMAINS STANDING)

How did you happen to fall into their hands?

KRAG

(HE MEASURES del ARMIJA WARILY, SEARCHING

FOR THE HIDDEN REASON BEHIND THE QUESTION)

That's important to you?

del ARMIJA

(SHRUGS) Simply a fascination. After all, we have

something in common, the Apaches and I. We are the

only ones to ever capture you.

KRAG

(THOROUGHLY SUSPICIOUS) Four thousand soldiers

massing to move against you and you've got time to

take my history?

del ARMIJA

I am gracefully trying to pay tribute to you. My mo-

tives, I assure you, are entirely sincere, not Latin.

(AS KRAG STARES AT HIM:)

del ARMIJA

If the Apaches could force nothing from you in three

days. . .what chance do I have in a few short hours?

(KRAG DOESN'T KNOW WHETHER TO BELIEVE HIM
OR NOT. HE TAKES A DRINK, LOOKS DOWN AT
HIS GLASS.)

KRAG

(STUDIES THE GLASS A MOMENT MORE) I was on
a scouting patrol. Five years ago. I was just an
enlisted man then.

del ARMIJA

And not an officer? Somewhere I thought you were
always an officer.

KRAG

Not then. We were on this patrol and they hit us.
When it was done I was the only one left alive, and not
much at that.

del ARMIJA

So they took you--tortured you for three days. . .

KRAG

I'd been a soldier since a boy, ten years. I'd done my
job, what I had to do. I'd been shot at and hit and shot
others. But this. No one had told me how to. . .to do
this. But I did it. I saw it through. . .kept things from
them would have wiped out my whole battalion if
they'd known. After three days. . .the Apaches. . .
they value courage. . .either that, or they figured I
didn't have anything to tell. . .they let me go. My
people found me two days later on a trail, half-dead.

                    del ARMIJA

An act of supreme heroism. How did they reward

you?

(KRAG GLANCES QUICKLY AT del ARMIJA--A

STRANGE, IMMEDIATE TENSENESS ON HIS FACE.

THEN, AS HE LOOKS AWAY:)

                    KRAG

I got a commission.

                    del ARMIJA

That was all?

                    KRAG

A commission. A citation, a Presidential commenda-

tion. (HE CONTINUES, AN UNACCOUNTABLE BIT-

TERNESS VERY GRADUALLY COMING INTO HIS

VOICE) A trip to Washington. Washington! My name

and picture on recruiting posters. . .in papers. A

parade for me. Even that. Generals, Senators shak-

ing my hand and me, wherever I went, never able to

buy a drink, not even a meal.

                    del ARMIJA

(AS THOUGH OBVIOUS) You were a hero. . . .

                    KRAG

I was a soldier. . .who'd done his job, no more!

(BEAT) only--

                    del ARMIJA

What?

KRAG

They made me into something more. Something special. A super hero.

del ARMIJA

(EYES NARROWING SLIGHTLY) Why do you suppose they would want to do a thing like that?

KRAG

They needed a hook to hand their recruiting drive on. I don't know, something....(HE DOWNS HIS DRINK WITH TREMBLING HANDS)

KRAG

It had never been like that before. Before....I was just a soldier...

del ARMIJA

But not any more?

KRAG

Now it's everyone watching me.

del ARMIJA

Waiting to see what you will do the next time?

KRAG

And the next, and the one after that.

del ARMIJA

But if you're a hero...?

KRAG

It isn't enough to be a hero, you've got to live it, prove it again and again! They make you keep proving it!

(del ARMIJA STUDIES KRAG, THEN RISES, CAMERA
FAVORING HIS FACE AS HE TURNS HIS BACK ON
KRAG, MOVES TO THE LIQUOR SIDE TABLE. HIS
MOVEMENTS ARE SLOW, DELIBERATE AS HE
CAREFULLY REFILLS HIS GLASS, BUT THE LOOK
ON HIS FACE SHOWS EXCITEMENT. MORE THAN
EXCITEMENT, EXULTATION. HOLDING THE
GLASS TO THE LIGHT, HE STUDIES THE LIQUOR
WITHIN IT.)

del ARMIJA

(ALMOST CASUALLY) So that is why?

(KRAG LOOKS AT del ARMIJA, INSTANTLY ON
GUARD AGAIN.)

KRAG

What do you mean, "why"?

del ARMIJA

(STILL STUDYING THE LIQUOR AGAINST THE
LIGHT) The color to a French cognac. Magnificent.

KRAG

Why what?

del ARMIJA

(BEGINNING SLOWLY, SOFTLY, BUILDING TO THE
ATTACK) Why you throw yourself into one hell after
another--forcing a hell when none was needed. . . .

KRAG

What're you talking about?

del ARMIJA

The Apaches at Iron Wells. . .

                    KRAG

I explained. . .

                    del ARMIJA

El Palo Alto. . .

                    KRAG

There were four hundred armed men. . . .

                    del ARMIJA

(CONTINUING; OVER KRAG) Again at El Brazito.
Always, whatever you do, done for fear of losing your
reputation as a hero. Even now, the way you stand
there, refusing a bandage for your wound! Look at
you, glorying in the blood that flows from your chest,
wearing it like a badge of proof for all to see. . .!

                    KRAG

That's not true. . .!

                    del ARMIJA

Not true? Not true? (SHOVES HIS FACE AT KRAG)
Is it so painfully true that a thousand, two thousand
men have uselessly died to feed your fear!
(KRAG STARES AT del ARMIJA, THE VEINS BUL-
GING ON HIS TEMPLES, WET STREAMING DOWN
HIS FACE. HE TRIES TO SPEAK. A COUPLE OF
TRIES, THEN:)

                    KRAG

I'm afraid of nothing!

del ARMIJA

Then you are no man, but a dragon with two heads
that breathe fire!

KRAG

(A NOD AT GONZALES) Whatever he's got in that
jackal mind of his, nothing makes me tell you what
you want to know.

del ARMIJA

Nothing, Capitan? Not a single thing?

KRAG

No!

del ARMIJA

Suppose I tell you that at dawn, you and your corporal
will be put on horses. Your corporal dead, across the
saddle, you untouched. An escort takes you under a
flag of truce through my lines, returns you to your
people.

KRAG

I don't follow what. . .

del ARMIJA

Your officers, when they see you. The corporal's
body, tortured, lifeless, you unmarred but for that
bullet wound. What do you suppose they'll make of
that?

KRAG

Noth. . .nothing. What should they?

del ARMIJA

That perhaps you paid a price for your life. A price

the corporal was not willing to pay.

KRAG

(APPALLED) You think they'd ever. . .

del ARMIJA

What?

KRAG

Believe I'd tell!? Tell you a thing? They'd never!

del ARMIJA

No?

KRAG

You couldn't send me back. Not after what you've

told me. Only fifteen hundred men here. I know about

that. . . .

del ARMIJA

You think they would trust a thing you had to say?

KRAG

You. . .you couldn't take the chance. . . .

del ARMIJA

You overestimate my position, Capitan. Whether or

not they believe you, outnumbered as I am, I would

still have one chance either way, the same as I had

before you came. . .

(AS KRAG STARES AT HIM:)

del ARMIJA

The moment you are back to your lines, I move my

Army into one town or the other. Which one, you will

not know until they get there. A guess on my part,

nothing more. But if I guess right. . .if, Capitan. . .

and your Army finds me there ahead of it. . .I do not

know about your people. Mine would tear you to pieces.

(AS KRAG'S EYES WIDEN:)

del ARMIJA

Fifty-fifty, Capitan. Even odds. For me. For you.

(KRAG STARES AT del ARMIJA, TRYING TO HOLD

THE COLONEL'S GAZE. BUT HIS STRENGTH IS NO

MATCH FOR THE COLONEL'S, NOT ANY LONGER.

DROPPING HIS EYES, HE LOOKS AWAY--THE

FIRST TOUCH OF FEAR CROWDING INTO HIS FACE.

FOR THE FIRST TIME HIS HAND, AN INVOLUNTARY

MOVEMENT, GOES TO HIS WOUND, MASSAGES THE

HURT.)

del ARMIJA

(KNOWING HE HAS KRAG WHERE HE WANTS HIM)

There is, of course. . .an alternative.

KRAG

(HIS STRENGTH, HIS CONVICTION RAPIDLY DE-

SERTING HIM) No'. . .

del ARMIJA

A simple word, one word. . .

KRAG

(HIS EYES DOWN NOW, UNABLE TO MEET del

ARMIJA'S) I can't. . .!

del ARMIJA

Herreras, Cerralvo. One of the two.

KRAG

I can't!

del ARMIJA

And no one to know you told me. . . .

KRAG

Torture me! In the name of God let it be that way. . .!

del ARMIJA

No one ever to know it was you. Only Durbin. He was

the one, we will say it was him. . .

KRAG

(LOOKING UP; STUNNED) Durbin. . .?

del ARMIJA

A simple thing. A message to your command when

the thing is done, telling of it, how he broke under

torture. . . .

KRAG

What about me?

del ARMIJA

You we say were never captured. Only Durbin who

surrendered out of fear. You, with resource and

courage, bravely fought to make your way back to

your lines. Regretfully, you did not make it quite in
time.

                    KRAG

But. . .but Durbin. . .he'll know. . .

                    del ARMIJA

Nothing. Not even the inscription on his gravestone.

                    KRAG

You'll kill him?

                    del ARMIJA

That shocks you?

                    KRAG

To kill him. . .

                    del ARMIJA

No different than what you've always done. . .the
wanton destruction of men to preserve your own
reputation. In this case it will be only one, not
hundreds.

                    KRAG

(THE THING TEARING AT HIM) I don't know, I. . .
I don't know. . .

                    del ARMIJA

(A WRY, KNOWING SMILE ON HIS FACE) Think
about it, Capitan. I appreciate it is a pressing decision. Take your time. Say. . .half an hour?
(A BEAT MORE del ARMIJA HOLDS HIS GAZE ON
KRAG, THEN LOOKS TOWARD GONZALES, NODS

THE OFFICER IS TO TAKE KRAG AWAY. MOVING
IN, GONZALES GRABS KRAG ROUGHLY.)

del ARMIJA

(IN SPANISH) Gently!

(GONZALES GLANCES TOWARD del ARMIJA WITH
SOME ANNOYANCE, BUT DOES AS TOLD--RELAXES
HIS GRIP ON KRAG, LEADS HIM WITH RELUCTANT
GENTLENESS FROM THE TENT, CAMERA MOVING
IN ON del ARMIJA, HOLDING ON HIS FACE, HIS
EXPRESSION CONFIDENT.)

DISSOLVE TO:

25. EXT. MEXICAN CAMP. SMALL ENCLOSURE.
NIGHT.

(PALZA ON GUARD BEFORE IT, DURBIN'S HUD-
DLED FORM SEEN THROUGH THE GATE, STILL
LYING WHERE HE WAS LEFT. OPEN ON KRAG,
HEAD DOWN, SHOULDERS BOWED AS HE'S
USHERED TOWARD THE ENCLOSURE BY GON-
ZALES AND COTA. AS THE PROCESSION NEARS
IT, PALZA SPRINGS TO HIS FEET, OPENS THE
GATE. A SHOVE BY GONZALES AND KRAG IS
SENT STUMBLING INSIDE.)

26. INT. SMALL ENCLOSURE. NIGHT.

(AS KRAG COMES HEAVILY AGAINST THE FAR
WALL, HANGS THERE A MINUTE, THEN SINKS TO
THE GROUND, STARES OFF AT THE NIGHT.)

27. CLOSE ON KRAG AND DURBIN.

(AS DURBIN PAINFULLY TRIES TO LIFT HIS HEAD:)

DURBIN

Sir. . .sir. . .?

(HIS EYES COME UP, FALL ON KRAG, UNTOUCHED,

UNHARMED. HE BLINKS THROUGH THE DARKNESS,

UNABLE TO BELIEVE HIS EYES.)

DURBIN

They didn't. . .they didn't touch you, they. .!

(HE BREAKS OFF, PULLS HIMSELF INTO A HALF-

SITTING POSITION.)

DURBIN

Why? Why didn't they touch you? (MOMENTARILY

PANICKED) You didn't. . .(THE OBVIOUS ANSWER

COMING TO HIM)

DURBIN

No. No. They knew. . .it'd be no use--whatever they

did, it'd be no use and. . .

KRAG

Stop it, Durbin.

DURBIN

What. . .?

KRAG

(TORTURED) You don't know what you're. . .(HE

BREAKS OFF) Just stop, let me think, let me think.

(DURBIN STOPS, STARES AT KRAG A LITTLE BE-

WILDERED, BUT STILL GAINING COMFORT FROM

THE CAPTAIN'S PRESENCE. HE EDGES A LITTLE

CLOSER TO KRAG.)

DURBIN

That wound, sir. Maybe if you was to let me. . .

(KRAG PULLS AWAY, SICK WITH HIMSELF, WHAT

HE IS--DURBIN'S BELIEF IN HIM MAKING THINGS

ALL THE WORSE.)

DURBIN

When they. . .when they took me in there--After the

first it wasn't as bad, you know what kept up in my

mind? You know what, sir? It kept up: if the Captain

could see me. That's what it was in my mind, sir. . .

(SMALL LITTLE CHUCKLE) Me. Taking the best

they had and giving them nothing, holding it in. It kept

going through me how I wished you could of seen that.

(APOLOGETICALLY) Not that I was up to you or

anything. . .I just wish you'd been there. I ain't never

been nothing before, sir, brave or anything. . .like

you been. . . .

KRAG

(ALMOST A CRY) Durbin. . .

DURBIN

Sir?

(KRAG STARTS TO REPLY, MAYBE TO TELL, TO

EXPLAIN, THEN SUDDENLY A STRANGE LOOK

COMES INTO HIS EYES. HE STARES AT DURBIN,

A SLOW REALIZATION COMING TO HIM.)

KRAG

Of course! Why didn't I realize it. . .!

DURBIN

Realize. . .?

KRAG

(PERSUADING HIMSELF) Sending us in here to blow the

gorge. (UP ON HIS FEET, THE THING TAKING FORM.)

KRAG

They knew we'd never get to it! Knew we'd never

even get through their lines. . .

DURBIN

I don't understand.

KRAG

Even made sure we wouldn't. (THE THING BUILDS)

That's why they sent us through at the wash. They

knew what was there, those men. They knew we'd be

captured, wanted us captured.

DURBIN

(UNABLE TO BELIEVE HIS EARS) Wanted us cap-

tured? They wouldn't. . .

KRAG

That's just what was supposed to happen.

DURBIN

It wasn't!

KRAG

And you, Durbin. You were supposed to be the one to

talk.

DURBIN

No! They didn't want that! They'd never. .!

KRAG

(RIDING OVER) They knew what you were, that you'd

break under torture. That's why they sent you. . .

DURBIN

They didn't send me, I volunteered.

KRAG

They chose you. They knew you'd be captured and

tortured and break. Don't you see, it's so clear!

That's what you were supposed to do. All along. To

tell them. Give them the information. False informa-

tion. And then. . .then the army. . .it would go the

other way. Durbin, it's a perfect, the perfect plan!

(HE TURNS TO THE GATE, SHOUTS OUT) Colonel!

DURBIN

(IN PANIC) Captain, don't!

(HE TRIES TO RISE, BUT KRAG'S ON HIM, HOLDING

HIM BY THE FRONT OF HIS SHIRT. IN B.G., THE

GUARDS, STARTLED BY KRAG'S BEHAVIOR,

SPEND AN INDECISIVE MOMENT, THEN COTA

BOLTS OFF.)

KRAG

(EYES ABLAZE, NEAR HYSTERIA) They'll come
now, Durbin. They'll take you. And you. . .what you
do is pretend. Take a little, whatever they give you.
Torture, Durbin, just a little. . .and then. . .then tell.
Tell them, Durbin, all that you know. . . .

DURBIN

Sir. . .You're sick, you're hurt. You don't know what
you're saying. . . .

KRAG

(FRANTICALLY) Tell them, Durbin, I order it!

DURBIN

No!

KRAG

(FURIOUS NOW) I'll have you in front of a court!
The rest of your life, wherever you go, you want that,
Durbin? People staring at you, knowing you killed
four thousand men. . . .

DURBIN

You're out of your mind!

(INFURIATED, KRAG SHOVES DURBIN AWAY,
BOLTS TO HIS FEET, RUNS BACK TO THE GATE.)

KRAG

(TO PALZA) The Colonel! Get him! Colonel!
Traer!

PALZA

(STARTLED BY KRAG'S FURY, HE BOLTS AWAY)

Lieutenant! Lieutenant!

28. ON DURBIN.

(AS HE FRANTICALLY FLOUNDERS IN THE DIRT,
TRYING TO GAIN HIS FEET.)

KRAG'S VOICE

(OVER, CALLING AFTER PALZA) Bring him, you
hear what I tell you!? I want him here! (OVER HIS
SHOULDER TO DURBIN) He's coming, Durbin.
They've gone to get him!

(SUDDENLY DURBIN STOPS, REACTS TO:)

29. INSERT: THE TEN INCH "DAGGER" OF WOOD
    LYING NEXT TO THE WALL WHERE KRAG
    EARLIER DROPPED IT.

KRAG'S VOICE

(CONTINUING; OVER) Look afraid, that's what to do,
make them think you're afraid. . .

30. ON DURBIN. (AS HE GRABS THE "DAGGER.")

KRAG'S VOICE

(CONTINUING; OVER) They like it when you're
afraid, they'll believe it that way. . .

31. ON KRAG'S FACE.

(CLOSE, AS SEEN THROUGH THE BARS OF THE
GATE, LOOKING IN FROM THE OUTSIDE OF THE
ENCLOSURE.)

KRAG

(EYES ABLAZE, SHOUTING OUT) Colonel!

(AGAIN OVER HIS SHOULDER) I see them. Durbin,
they're coming! Just a little more torture, that's all
you have to suffer. Just enough to make it look right,
then all you'll have to do is. . .

(HE STOPS, HIS MOUTH FROZEN ON THE WORD,
HIS EYES OPENED WIDE IN SURPRISE.)

32. EXT. SMALL ENCLOSURE. NIGHT.

(AS del ARMIJA LEADS GONZALES, COTA AND
PALZA FAST INTO SCENE. DARTING AHEAD OF
THE COLONEL, PALZA UNBOLTS THE GATE.)

33. INT. ENCLOSURE. NIGHT.

(AS del ARMIJA, FOLLOWED BY GONZALES, MOVES
IN. A STEP INSIDE AND BOTH MEN STOP, STARE
DOWN AT WHAT LIES AT THEIR FEET.)

34. NEW ANGLE.

(DURBIN IN F.G., HUDDLED ON THE GROUND,
KRAG AT HIS FEET, del ARMIJA AND GONZALES
STANDING IN B.G., JUST INSIDE THE ENCLOSURE.
A QUICK BEAT, THEN GONZALES MOVES TO KRAG,
HALF ROLLS HIM OVER, REACTING, AS DOES del
ARMIJA, TO WHAT THEY--BUT NOT THE AUDI-
ENCE--SEE THERE. RAISING HIS HAND TO KRAG'S
EYES, GONZALES LIFTS AN EYELID, THEN LOOKS
UP AT del ARMIJA.)

GONZALES

Muerto.

(FOR A MOMENT NO ONE MOVES; THEN SLOWLY,
del ARMIJA TAKES A STEP OR TWO TOWARD
KRAG, HIS COLD, EMOTIONLESS GAZE DOWN ON
THE LIFELESS FACE.)

DURBIN

(WRETCHEDLY) What did you do to him?

(del ARMIJA NODS, WEIGHING THE THOUGHT.)

del ARMIJA

Nothing I am very proud of.

(THEN TURNING, HE MOVES OUT OF THE PLACE,
CAMERA STAYING ON DURBIN AND KRAG IN F.G.,
LOOKING PAST THEM OUT AT del ARMIJA MOV-
ING STEADILY OFF INTO THE NIGHT.)

35. A LONG, DELIBERATE HOLD, OVER WHICH

WE. . .SLOWLY. . .

FADE TO: BLACK

PART
FIVE

Production Aids

A Production Kit

THE ATTACHED KIT will be helpful in standardizing the various forms commonly used in connection with workshop productions: checklist, budget, production analysis statement, casting list, crew call, studio lighting and floor plan, studio reservation, and requests for supplies, props, costumes, and technical equipment. In addition, the kit includes an example of a rehearsal and production schedule with a scene breakdown and production notes.

Production Check List

The student producer-director should check all items on the following list, filling in the appropriate form or writing a letter or memorandum to the proper person, to make sure that he has given his formal attention to each.

1. Script clearance
2. Script analysis
3. Budget
4. Purchase order requests
5. Reimbursement for petty cash (with receipts)
6. Script duplication
7. Audition notice
8. Casting list
9. Music (live or recorded)
10. Music clearance
11. Set description
12. Sketch of setting (with rear elevations)
13. Floor plan
14. Shop request
15. Prop list
16. Make-up and wigs
17. Costume list
18. Costume cleaning
19. Graphic list
20. Graphic arts shop request
21. Light plot
22. Light switchboard sheet
23. Light cue sheet
24. Lighting instrument schedule (list)
25. Camera shot cards
26. Master production schedule
27. Cast rehearsal schedule
28. Crew calls
29. Studio reservations
30. Engineering equipment request
31. Video tape request
32. Video tape playback
33. Telecine, film, slide, or Telop list
34. Still photos
35. Sound effects
36. Film stock footage or raw stock request
37. Transportation reservation
38. Production book

Production Budget

In a student television workshop many items that represent major expenses in a professional production are free. This is particularly true of so-called "above the line" or talent costs, such as script writers, cast, producer, director, musicians, and travel. Similarly, many of the "below the line" or studio and engineering costs, are provided without charge. However, even a workshop production will be difficult to do without a minimal budget, and the student producer-director should know in advance what his costs will be. Some of the standard budget items listed below may not be applicable, but if the student wishes to establish figures for each of them, he will get a sobering idea of the cost of his production if he were doing it on a professional basis.

STAGING SERVICES (Cost for overhead and depreciation not included)

SCENERY: Stock, Rentals, and Purchase

WARDROBE: Stock, Rentals, Purchase, and Cleaning

MAKE-UP: Stock, Rentals, and Purchase

GRAPHICS: Stock and Purchase

PROPS: Stock, Rentals, and Purchase

LIGHTING: Stock and Rental

TRANSPORTATION

SCRIPT DUPLICATION

PUBLICITY

ENGINEERING SERVICES (Overhead and depreciation costs on control room equipment, cameras, audio and video tape machines not included)

AUDIO TAPE

VIDEO TAPE

KINESCOPE

FILM: Raw stock and Processing

Analysis of Story or Program and Directing Approach

COURSE NUMBER: DATE OF THIS ORDER:

INSTRUCTOR: PRODUCTION DATES:

PRODUCTION TITLE: DIRECTOR:

TYPE: LENGTH:

Talent List

COURSE NUMBER: DATE OF THIS ORDER:

INSTRUCTOR: PRODUCTION DATES:

PRODUCTION TITLE: DIRECTOR:

	Student's Name	Home Tel. No.	Work Phone
ANNOUNCER:			
NARRATOR:			
VOICE OVER:			
OTHER:			
OTHER:			

Character Names

1.

2.

3.

4.

5.

Comments:

Request for Crew (Crew members please initial after names)

COURSE NUMBER: DATE OF THIS ORDER: PRODUCTION DATES:
INSTRUCTOR: TEACHING ASSISTANT:
PRODUCTION TITLE: DIRECTOR AND PHONE:

	Crew Member	Crew Member	Crew Member	Crew Member	Crew Member	Crew Member
DATE OF CALL-						
HOURS OF CALL-						
TYPE OF CALL-						
Director						
Ass't Dir.						
Fl. Mgr.						
Tech. Dir.						
Audio						
Video						
Designer						
Tape/Record.						
Sound Eff.						
Boom						
Camera 1						
Cable						
Camera 2						
Cable						
Camera 3						
Cable						
Lights						
Lights						
Props						
Carpenter						
Carpenter						
Paint						
Paint						
Graphic Art						
Gr. Handler						
Costume						
Makeup						
Other						
Other						

Studio Lighting Plot

COURSE NUMBER: DATE OF THIS ORDER:

DIRECTOR: PRODUCTION DATES:

PRODUCTION TITLE: INSTRUCTOR:

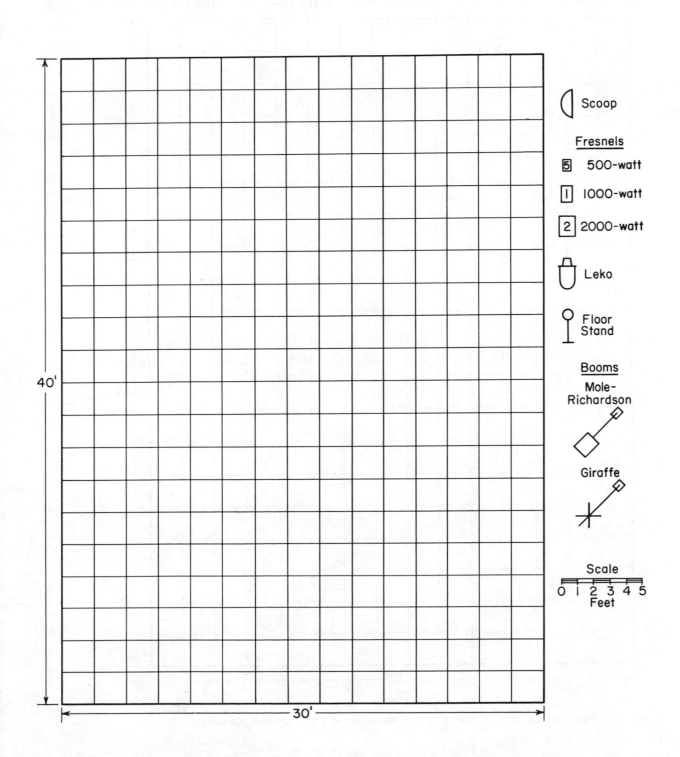

Studio Floor Plan

COURSE NUMBER: DATE OF THIS ORDER:

DIRECTOR: PRODUCTION DATES:

PRODUCTION TITLE: INSTRUCTOR:

Scale: 3/16" = 1' (Dimensions indicated by 2-foot squares)

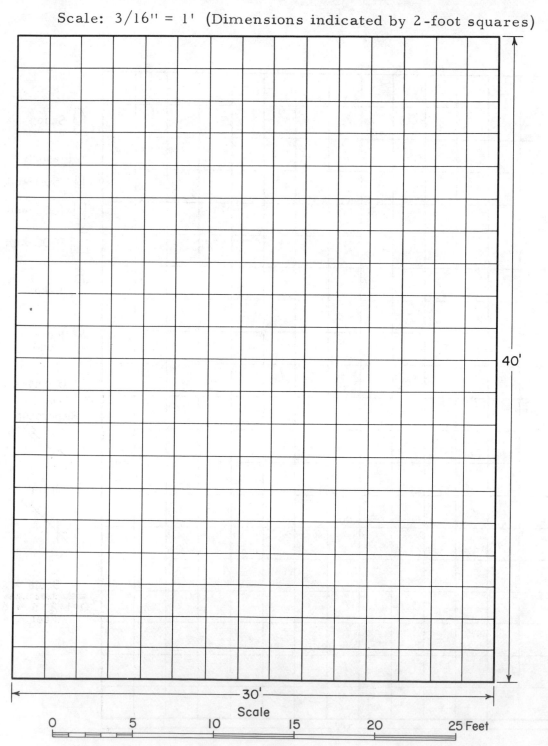

Set Description

COURSE NUMBER: DATE OF THIS ORDER:

DIRECTOR: PRODUCTION DATES:

PRODUCTION TITLE: INSTRUCTOR:

SETTING: (Cyc., flats, drapes, set pieces, doors, windows, platforms, step units, grass mats, foliage or trees, etc. Submit sketch of setting and rear elevations separately.)

FURNITURE:

HAND PROPS: (Continue list on back if necessary)

Camera and Film Request

COURSE NUMBER: DATE OF THIS ORDER:

DIRECTOR: PRODUCTION DATES:

PRODUCTION TITLE: INSTRUCTOR:

Motion Picture Film (16 mm.):

        Footage needed

        Daylight or tungsten

         A.S.A.

Still Camera Film:

         Size

         Type

         Amount   (rolls)

Motion Picture Camera:

         Silent

         Auricon S.O.F.

Still Camera:

         Polaroid Land

         Other

Video Tape or Kinescope Request

COURSE NUMBER: DATE: TIME: am
                                                        pm to

PRODUCTION TITLE OR OTHER:

RECORD: PLAYBACK:

APPROXIMATE LENGTH OF RECORDING:

TAPE NUMBER:

LENGTH OF TIME RECORDING IS TO BE HELD:

OTHER DETAILS:

                                     INSTRUCTOR:

Costume Request

COURSE NUMBER: DATE OF THIS ORDER:

DIRECTOR: PRODUCTION DATES:

PRODUCTION TITLE: INSTRUCTOR:

Quantity	Item	Condition Out	Remarks

DATE CHECKED OUT: RETURN DATE:

SIGNATURE (Student):

DATE CHECKED IN: SIGNATURE:

                                                      (Student)

Prop Request

COURSE NUMBER: DATE OF THIS ORDER:

DIRECTOR: PRODUCTION DATES:

PRODUCTION TITLE: INSTRUCTOR:

Quantity   Item   Condition Out   Remarks

DATE CHECKED OUT: RETURN DATE:

SIGNATURE (Student):

DATE CHECKED IN: SIGNATURE:

                                           (Student)

Graphic Request

COURSE NUMBER: DATE OF THIS ORDER:

DIRECTOR: PRODUCTION DATES:

PRODUCTION TITLE: INSTRUCTOR:

<u>Clearly indicate:</u> 1) Caps, lower case, or both, 2) black or grey stock, 3) color of lettering, 4) special size or type of card, and 5) whether card is to be used as super.

Equipment Request (Check each category)

COURSE NUMBER: DATE OF THIS ORDER:

INSTRUCTOR: DIRECTOR:

PRODUCTION TITLE:

CAMERA REHEARSAL DATES AND HOURS:

PRODUCTION DATE AND HOURS:

CAMERAS:	No.	Pedestal Type		Lens Complement Desired					
	1	PD7	PD10	1/2"	1"	2"	3"	6"	Zoom
	2	PD7	PD10	1/2"	1"	2"	3"	6"	Zoom
	3	PD7	PD10	1/2"	1"	2"	3"	6"	Zoom

MICROPHONES (Indicate number of each type required):

Mole Richardson boom

Century Giraffe

Lavalier

Stand

Desk

Hanging

Other

TELECINE PROJECTION (Check if needed):

Motion Picture Projector

Slide Projector

SPECIAL EFFECTS:

Script Duplication Request

COURSE NUMBER: DATE OF THIS ORDER:

INSTRUCTOR: PRODUCTION DATES:

PRODUCTION TITLE:

DIRECTOR:

<u>Amount</u>

    Ditto (Mimeo) masters required

    Ditto (Mimeo) paper required

Approved by:

(Instructor)

Reservation Request for Studios, Control Rooms, or Rehearsal Rooms

COURSE NUMBER: DATE OF THIS ORDER:

INSTRUCTOR: PRODUCTION DATES:

PRODUCTION TITLE:

Space requested:

Month: Day: From: to:

Purpose:

Requested by:

Space is available:

(Traffic Manager)

Approved by:

(Instructor)

6	7	8	9	10	11	12
1-4 PM REHEARSAL OF FULL CAST	2-3PM MARY K. STEVE 3-5PM ALL MALES		3-4:30 PM LAURIE MIKE 4-5:30 PM LINDA MIKE			1-2PM LINDA MIKE 2-3PM LINDA MIKE LAURIE 3-4PM LAURIE MIKE
13	**14**	**15**	**16**	**17**	**18**	**19**
1-4PM FULL CAST 7-8PM MARY K STEVE 8-10PM ALL MALES			1-2PM STEVE MARY K 2-4PM ALL MALES	7-10PM FULL CAST	1 PM FULL CAST	
20	**21**	**22**	**23**	**24**	**25**	**26**
COSTUMES SET CONST.	1-5 PM FULL CAST		1-5PM DRESS (3PM CAMERAMEN, A.D., T.D., AUDIO, FLOOR MANAGER, WITNESS) GRAPHICS MADE	10AM-1PM CAMERA BLOCK 2-4:30 PM RUN	10AM-12 NOON CAMERA PROBLEMS 1:30-4:30 RUN, DRESS TAPE	GRAPHICS DESIGN
27	**28**	**29**	**30**	**31**	**32**	**33**
KNXT 7-11AM BLOCK 11-12N RUN 1-2PM RUN (DRESS) 2-3:30PM TAPE						SET + LIGHT KNXT

Repertoire Workshop—*A Thing of Beauty*

K N X T (with UCLA)

Producer: William Yates
Director: Ross McCanse

Cast:

Michael Harvey .... Narrator
Linda Strawn .... Beatrice
Mary Kate Denny .... Alice
Paul Keith .... Bailey
Stephen Schwartz .... Alex
Ronald Noble .... Grey
Laurie Mock .... Dolores

Production Schedule

A. *At UCLA*

Thursday, January 24:
    9:30 am –   Crew Call
   10:00 am – 1:00 pm: Camera Blocking

   1:00 pm – 2:00 pm: Lunch
   2:00 pm – 4:30 pm: Run through

Friday, January 25:
   9:30 am –   Crew Call
 10:00 am – 11:30 am: Technical
                      problems
 11:30 am – 12:30 pm: Lunch
 12:30 pm – 1:30 pm: Run through
   1:30 pm – 2:00 pm: Make-up
   2:00 pm – 2:30 pm: Dress Rehearsal
   3:00 pm – 4:00 pm: TAPE

B. *At K N T X*

Saturday, January 26:
   Set and light Studio "B"

Sunday, January 27:
   9:00 am – 12 noon: Camera Blocking
 12:00   – 1:00 pm: Lunch
   1:00 pm – 2:00 pm: Run through
   2:00 pm – 2:30 pm: Make-up
   2:30 pm – 3:00 pm: Dress
   3:30 pm – 4:00 pm: TAPE

Scene Breakdown—*A Thing of Beauty*

SCENE	AREA	CHARACTERS	SET PIECES	PROPS
1. Poster	A	Narrator	Billboard	Paper sign
		Bailey	Bushes	Poster
		Grey	Bench	
		Alex	(Limbo)	
2. Poster	A	Narrator	Billboard	Books
		Alice	Bushes	Papers
		Beatrice	Bench	Pencils
		Dolores	(Limbo)	
3. Mirror	B	Narrator	Mirror frame	None
		Beatrice	(full length)	
		Alice	(Limbo)	
		Dolores		
4. Office	C	Narrator	File cabinet	Typewriter
		Alex	Desk & 2 chairs	Papers
		Grey	Wall frames	Small poster
		Bailey	(Black B.G.)	Pencils
5. Bench	A	Narrator	Bench	None
		Beatrice	Billboard	
		Dolores	Bushes	
			(Limbo)	
6. Pillar	D	Narrator	Pillar	Paper sign
		Grey	(Limbo)	Masking tape
				Books (or signs)

(Continued on page 258.)

Scene Breakdown—*A Thing of Beauty* (Continued)

SCENE	AREA	CHARACTERS	SET PIECES	PROPS
7. Picnic	E	Alex Alice Narrator	Bushes, grass tree limb (gray cyc.)	Picnic basket Blanket
8. Vanity #1	F	Narrator Dolores	Vanity table Oval mirror Chair (Limbo)	Lipstick Other make-up items
9. Vanity #2	F	Narrator Beatrice	Vanity table Mirror Chair (Limbo)	Snapshot Make-up items
10. Phone	D	Alice	2 chairs Table Wall Piece (Limbo)	2 telephones
11. Poster	A	Full cast	Billboard Bushes (Limbo)	Crown Mantle Scepter "Document"
12. Close	D	Narrator	None (Limbo)	None

Production Notes—*A Thing of Beauty*

A. *Notes on Set Pieces*

1. The full-length mirror frame in area B used in scene 3, is to be struck following that scene.
2. The 10-foot section of the wall frame in the office scene (scene 4, area C) is hinged. It is to be swung out of the way following scene 4. The table, chairs, and riser on which they are placed will have to be struck following scene 4.
3. The pillar in area D is to be struck following scene 6, and the chairs and table for scene 10 set in place. These will have to be removed following scene 10 in area D.
4. The two vanity tables (scenes 8 and 9 in area F) are actually one table with mirrors in the middle facing in opposite directions.

B. *Notes on Lighting*

1. As noted in the scene breakdown, all areas are to be lighted in limbo, with the exception of the picnic scene (scene 7, area E) which will be played in front of the blue-gray cyc.
2. Scene 4 (office scene, area C) will conclude with the lights coming up behind to reveal the bench in area A, and the lights will dim down on the three boys in the office. The narrator will walk from the office into scene 5 in area A.
3. Following the pillar scene (scene 6, area D) the lights will come up on the picnic scene behind the narrator, who will remain in area D for one speech.
4. The lights will be dimmed down on the picnic scene (area E scene 7) at its conclusion, leaving the narrator lighted in limbo in front of the picnic area. He will be shot from a camera located at the lip of the stage as soon as the lights dim down. Thus he will not have the picnic scene behind him.
5. In scene 11 (area A) the narrator and Beatrice will step out from the group into a pool of light, while the others become silhouetted in the background.

Audition Copy

In MANY WORKSHOPS and classes audition copy is selected from scripts scheduled for production. However, it is often helpful to hold auditions using material designed primarily to demonstrate only such things as appearance, voice quality, and general acting ability rather than suitability for a specific part. The following audition copy is planned to provide an opportunity for students to demonstrate their ability as individuals, and in relation to other actors and actresses. Included also is an audition sheet on which students can indicate essential information, and teachers record comments. These sheets can be kept in a permanent file.

Audition Copy

MAN

MEDIUM SHOT. INTERIOR. DAY.

The man is a lawyer. He WALKS INTO the camera and stops, looking quietly at a paper he holds in his hand. We assume, but cannot see, that the judge is on one side of him and the defendant on the other. We are the jury to whom the lawyer addresses most of his remarks.

LAWYER

(TO THE JUDGE) Your Honor. (TO THE JURY) Ladies and gentlemen of the jury. (INDICATING THE PAPERS) I hold here in my hand Exhibit A of this trial. . .the letter written by the defendant. You have all seen it, I believe. Am I right?

(AS THOUGH ACKNOWLEDGING NODS OF

AGREEMENT) I thought so. Now! The prosecution

has tried to persuade you that the defendant was not

in his right mind when he wrote it, and was so emo-

tionally disturbed that his request was unreasonable.

Ladies and gentlemen! I've said it before, and I'll

say it again and again! It's the prosecution that's

unreasonable in asking you to believe that the man

who wrote this letter was emotionally disturbed! It's

a deliberate attempt to distract your attention from

the actual facts of the case! And what are these facts?

Let me refresh your memory a bit. The defendant

here is accused of murder. He is accused of murder-

ing the man to whom he wrote this letter. But there

is not a shred of evidence to prove that he did.

No one saw him raise the shotgun and fire it. In

fact, no one saw him come or go from the murdered

man's house on the day of the unfortunate killing.

Further, we have brought forward witnesses to prove

that the defendant was so busy at various times of the

day in various parts of the city that he could not pos-

sibly have gone to the victim's home on that regret-

table day.

Now, we do not deny that there was ill feeling

between the two men. We do not deny that the de-

fendant wrote this letter. But, ladies and gentlemen

of the jury!—most of us, at one time or another, have

had a quarrel with someone. Some of us, surely,
have written angry letters at one time or another.
But does that mean that we are so emotionally un-
stable that we would kill? No! And yet the prosecution is basing almost its entire case on this letter. I
ask you, ladies and gentlemen, to forget the letter
and think of the facts.

Audition Copy

<u>WOMAN</u>

<u>MEDIUM SHOT. INTERIOR. DAY.</u>

The woman is an actress. She WALKS INTO the shot
holding a script which she angrily shows to two people
we cannot see, but assume are seated around her.
She addresses most of her remarks to the one who is
directly in front of her, in other words, to the camera.

ACTRESS

(INDICATING SCRIPT) Here it is! You two asked
why I think it's a lousy play, and a lousy part, and
I'm going to show you. You thought it was just sour
grapes because I hadn't been offered the part, but
here's the script that proves I was. No! Don't say
anything! I don't care about that. But I do care about
my career. So it's a play by Joel Stockton, and any-
body should be happy to have a part in it. Uh uh! Not
this play. Not this part.

Listen. I don't even come in until the second act,

and then it's not much more than a walk-on. It's the wedding reception. I enter. I look around. I try to find someone I know. I see someone I know. I go up to him and I say, "It was a lovely wedding, wasn't it?" Great dialogue, eh? Though I must admit the costume would be becoming. But, anyway, he admits that it was a lovely wedding, and I ask where the happy couple is, he tells me, and I walk off.

Can you imagine? They have to get me on then because I have more later, but what a stupid way to do it! Look, Marvin, you remember me in "Four Square"? I was the lead. I starred. I had some great reviews. And remember "Tin Hat"? Oh, that was a real play! And a real part! Oh, sure, I know, it was a few years ago, but. . .after that, I should do a walk-on in the second act, and a small scene in the third act of a play that's so lousy it won't run more than a couple of weeks anyway? No!

Remember, Marvin, in "Four Square"?—that scene where I held back the whole mob? (RE-ENACTING) "Stop! No! What do you think you're doing!"

Oh, if I could have a part like that again! And. . . if I only knew what to do about this one!

Audition Copy

MAN AND WOMAN

They are husband and wife, seated at a table; each studying a sheet of paper, and each with a pencil in hand.

MARY

You understand, Joe, these are only rough plans. The architect won't do blueprints until we're pretty sure what we want.

JOE

(PUZZLED) But I can't make head or tail of this, so how'll I know whether it's what I want or not?

MARY

Oh, Joe, that's silly! (RISING AND GOING OVER TO HIM) Look, let me show you! Here's the living room, here's the dining room, there's the kitchen, and. . .

JOE

I can read, Mary! I know that's the living room, that's the dining room, that's the kitchen, and there's the blasted family room. What I mean is, what's it all going to look like?

MARY

We've been over it and over it and over it!

JOE

I know! We want a big fireplace, sliding glass

doors to the patio, formica in the kitchen and pine panelling in the family room; but how can I tell from this whether it's going to be like that?

MARY

I told you. These are rough plans. To give us the idea of the proportions, mostly.

JOE

(RISING) O.K. So...(LOOKING AT PLAN AND THEN POINTING) in the living room, the fireplace is over there, the sliding doors are over there, the...

MARY

No! The fireplace is over there! And the doors are over there!

JOE

That doesn't make sense. Look! Now, I'm the fireplace. (STANDING VERY STILL)

MARY

All right.

JOE

(SQUINTING AT PLANS) Now, to my left, over there, are the sliding doors.

MARY

(STARTING TO MOVE) All right. I'll be the sliding doors.

JOE

What'd you say?

MARY

(STOPPING) I'll be the sliding doors.

JOE

(LAUGHING) Oh, Mary!

MARY

Well, you're the fireplace!

JOE

(STILL LAUGHING) I know. But. . .

MARY

(BEGINNING TO LAUGH) Oh, Joe! How silly!

(BOTH LAUGHING, THEY RELAX AND MOVE

TOWARD EACH OTHER TO EMBRACE.)

Audition Copy

TWO MEN

The two men are Navy officers on a ship sailing to

Alaska a couple of hundred years ago. They are

standing side by side with hands resting on a table on

which, we assume, are charts.

OFFICER 1

Sir, on this chart, Koshigin Harbor is perhaps two

days away. . .if the wind holds.

OFFICER 2

Yes?

OFFICER 1

I know how important it is to reach Kodiak before the bad weather sets in, but I suggest that we stop at Koshigin for a few days. . .to give the men a rest. . . perhaps to hunt some food. . .and certainly to find fresh water.

OFFICER 2

(POINTING) I know as well as you that these charts are scarcely accurate, but. . .why waste time in Koshigin when Kodiak is only a few hundred miles further?

OFFICER 1

We need water. We need food. And the men need a rest.

OFFICER 2

But we had enough supplies for the trip. I know we did!

OFFICER 1

You've been ill, sir. Very ill.

OFFICER 2

That has nothing to do with. . .(DOUBLE TAKE) What do you mean?

OFFICER 1

While you were sick, sir, we had many storms. We are weeks overdue. Our supplies. . .and our men. . .are almost exhausted.

OFFICER 2

(BEAT) How long was I ill?

OFFICER 1

Seven weeks, sir.

OFFICER 2

Head for Koshigin.

Audition Copy

TWO WOMEN

MEDIUM SHOT

The two women are an important business executive
and her secretary. They are seated across from
each other at a desk on which there are some papers.
The secretary is taking dictation.

EXECUTIVE

There! Give it the usual close and that'll do for
today. . .as far as dictation is concerned.

SECRETARY

(FINISHING HER SHORTHAND) Yes, Miss Wills.
(LIFTING HER HEAD) As far as dictation is concerned? Is that all?

EXECUTIVE

Not really. That's all the dictation for today. . .
or ever. You may type it up, leave it for me, and. . .
go. Your check is ready for you at the payroll office.

SECRETARY

I don't understand.

EXECUTIVE

You don't need to. I'm letting you go. . .that's all.

SECRETARY

(RISING) But Miss Wills, you should give me a

reason!

EXECUTIVE

(RISING) I don't need to give you a reason for

anything.

SECRETARY

(GATHERING SUPPLIES) In a way, I suppose not,

but. . .well, when a person is fired, a person has a

right to know why.

EXECUTIVE

You know why.

SECRETARY

I'm afraid I don't.

EXECUTIVE

I don't know whether you're stupid, or that you

think I am. You've been here for two years. For the

past year and a half, you've been trying to get my job.

SECRETARY

That's just not true.

EXECUTIVE

Mr. Harris says it is.

SECRETARY

Mr. Harris! But. . .

EXECUTIVE

Mr. Harris has been my friend much longer than he's been yours. And, just remember, in your next job, not to talk too much to people you don't know too well. Good-by, my dear, and good luck!

Audition Sheet

NAME: CLASSIFICATION:

ADDRESS: TELEPHONE NO:

HOME ADDRESS:

SPECIAL INTERESTS IN TV:

Class Schedule   Photo

	M	Tu	W	Th	F	S
8						
9						
10						
11						
1						
2						
3						
4						
5						
7-11						

(Do not fill in below)

APPEARANCE:

VOICE QUALITY:

REGIONAL CHARACTERISTICS:

GENERAL COMMENTS:

USE FOR:

RATING: 1   2   3   4   5

Auditioned by:

Rank the candidate by circling one of the numbers on the rating scale in the lower left-hand corner of the sheet. The candidate fills out the class schedule by marking an "x" at the times when he is busy.

Marking the Script

A CLEARLY MARKED SCRIPT is a blueprint of your production—a record of the many decisions you have made in your preplanning and subsequent rehearsals. If you have prepared carefully you should have your production so well in mind that you need not keep your eyes glued to the script when calling out the indicated directions. You should have time to look at the control room monitors, glancing at your script as a ready reference. When you do look down at your script you should be able to see directions that are plainly marked and easily recognized. Do not clutter your script with too many notes. Have your assistant-director write out any extended comments you wish to remember, or insert blank sheets of paper in your script folder for notation purposes.

One of the best ways to indicate a key shot is to draw a simple sketch, either on your shooting script or on a sheet insert. Also, by numbering your shots, you can quickly identify them for the cameraman to check with his *shot card*. If in your script the writer has already typed out camera directions or actions, simply circle them instead of repeating them in the conventional penciled abbreviations.

The following is a list of the most commonly used symbols for indicating script directions in a television production, together with an example of a marked script.

Symbols for Television Script Marking

DIRECTIONS FOR CONTROL AND FILM PROJECTION ROOMS

SYMBOL	MEANING
①	**Take camera 1.** The specific word on which the director
②	wishes to *take* is usually marked with an x or something
①	similar, or if the shot is taken on an action (e.g., an actor (rising), the action is circled.
Fade in or FI or ◁①	**Fade in** camera 1. The point at which the director wishes to begin his fade is indicated with an x
Fade out or FO or ▷	**Fade out** camera 1. The reverse of *fade in*. Signal is usually given as "Fade to black."
Diss or ⊗ ②	**Dissolve to** camera 2.
roll film	**Roll Film.** Start film projector.
Slide or SL	**Take slide** or *change slide*.
Hit music or Sneak or Fade in	**Begin music** with sharp attack (or **fade it in** gradually).

DIRECTIONS FOR CAMERAMEN

Pan R **Pan right** (or left).

Dolly in or DI **Dolly in.**

Dolly back or DB or PB **Dolly back** or **pull back.**

Tr R **Truck right** (or left).

Zoom in **Zoom in.** Not usually abbreviated.

Opposite is **zoom out.**

Release ① **Release camera 1.** Advises cameraman that he is free to set up his next shot.

CAMERA SHOTS

All of these are general descriptions.

LS **Long shots** (wide angle).

MS **Medium shots** (medium angle).

CU **Close-ups** (narrow angle):

When referring to a shot of a person on the screen it is usually clearer to describe it as a:

HS **Head shot,** a

SS **Shoulder shot,**

ChS **Chest shot,**

WS **Waist shot,**

TS **Thigh shot,**

KS **Knee shot,** or

FS **Full shot.**

Tight **Tight shot** (with picture filling the frame). Not abbreviated.

Loose Opposite is **loose shot.**

1 Shot Shot with **one person** in the frame.

2 Shot Shot with **two persons** in the frame.

3 Shot Shot with **three persons** in the frame.

Gr Shot **Group shot.**

O/S **Over-shoulder shot.** (Taken over the shoulder of the person in the foreground of the picture, looking into the face of the person in the background.)

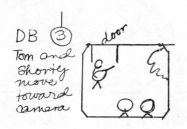

DB ③
Tom and Shorty move toward camera

1. (JIM GOES UP THE STEPS BUT STOPS AS TOM COMES UP TO SHORTY. WE SEE JIM IN BACK-GROUND HOLDING THE GUITAR AND OBVIOUSLY LISTENING.)

TOM (URGENTLY TO SHORTY)

② 2 Shot
Tom + Shorty

2. Don't ride tonight, Shorty!

SHORTY (BRISTLING):

Why not?

TOM:

I'm tryin' to be a good friend, Shorty.

③

3. Don't ride alone tonight.

(BEHIND THEM, JIM PUTS THE GUITAR DOWN ON THE PORCH. HE STARTS MOVING SLOWLY TOWARD THEM.)

SHORTY (COLDLY FIERCE):

o/s
CU
① Tom

4. When I can't ride alone, when my boss don't trust me and a good friend suspicions me. .,.

TOM (PAUSE, THEN GENTLY):

③ 3 Shot

5. It ain't that way at all, Shorty.

JIM (EAGERLY): (coming down stairs)

② o/s CU Shorty

6. I'll ride with you, Mr. Shorty. I'd be glad to.

③ 3 Shot

7. (SHORTY LOOKS BEWILDERED.)

TOM (SPEAKING TO JIM BUT LOOKING AT SHORTY):

No, Kid. . .there's times when a man don't want nothin' nearer to him than his horse and the

8. stars. Better turn in.

② CU
Shorty   9.

① Diss

jim [tree]

Fade in ③
3 Shot

Music

(INTERIOR. NIGHT. A MAN IS LEANING AGAINST
A TREE IN THE MOONLIGHT. HE IS EXAMINING
A GUN, APPARENTLY WAITING FOR SOMEONE.)
(SHORTY, TOM, AND JIM SIT DOWN ON STEPS OF
THE BUNKHOUSE. SHORTY STARTS TO PLAY
MINOR CHORDS ON HIS GUITAR.)

① CU

                SHORTY (TALKS TO GUITAR):

I may be only acting foreman, but I been doin' my

job as best I can, and I can still tell a mouthy kid

to hold his tongue. And the day I know that Mr.

② CU Tom

Cantry's hired spies to check on me, I quit.

                        TOM:

What makes you think it's you? Besides, it don't

do no good to talk about a man behind his back. Go

③ 3 Shot

to him in the morning. . .have it out. Meanwhile. . .

let's have a song, or a yarn. . .it'll clear the air.

                JIM (ENTHUSIASTICALLY):

Yeah!

                SHORTY (GLUM):

Yeah. (TRYING TO BRIGHTEN) There was that

time I worked for another crazy feller. . .man who

② CU Jim

hired a bareback rider from the circus. (JIM GRINS)

③ 3 Shot   Ready
            for rise

She rode standing up, which was a great advantage,

Music out

③ 3 Shot
(Cont'd)

on account of she could see farther. (STOPS STRUM-

MING AND GIVES UP) It's no good. (RISES) I'm

gonna ride. Here, kid. Put this in the bunkhouse for

me, will you?

JIM:

Sure!

Timing the Program

BASICALLY, all that is involved in timing a television program is the ability to use a stop watch and add the minutes and seconds. You will find that it is much easier to time the various parts of a program rather than rely on the running time of the production as a whole, because a slight change in tempo over a period of half an hour can result in an over-all difference of two or three minutes. It is standard procedure to keep two sets of time: 1) running time from the top of the program to the close; and 2) a time for each segment of the program. By timing the segments in rehearsal you can simply add them up to determine approximately how close you are to the desired total time of a production, and then make any necessary adjustments. During dress rehearsal you will get a fairly accurate running time that can be indicated at intervals in small figures on the margin throughout your script. When the program is on the air, compare these figures with the running broadcast time to find out whether the program is running short or long.

As another example, suppose you have a news program that begins at 4:00 P.M. and runs to 4:14:30. It is made up of the following segments:

Segment	Segment Time	Running Time 4:00:00 P.M.
1. Headlines	:30	4:00:30
2. Opening commercial	1:00	4:01:30
3. News	11:00	4:12:30
4. Feature	1:00	4:13:30
5. Closing commercial	:45	4:14:15
6. Closing routine	:15	4:14:30
	13:90=14:30	

BACK TIMING

Back timing is a standard method of insuring that a live broadcast will end on time; it tells the performer how many minutes remain at given points toward the end of the program. The director usually signals the performer at 3 minutes, 2 minutes, 1 minute, 30 seconds, and 15 seconds before the close. In the case of the above news program, the timing would be 4:11:30, 4:12:30, 4:13:30, 4:14 and 4:14:15. However, in this particular program the significant signal cannot come later than two minutes before the close (4:12:30), because the closing commercial (segment 5) and closing routine (segment 6) are fairly inflexible. If the time was running long at one minute before the end of the program, it would already be too late to correct it. Any necessary adjustment must take place before the performer reaches segments 5 and 6.

Let us suppose that the last news story in segment 3 is timed for 30 seconds. But as the newscaster concludes the preceding story he gets the director's signal that only two minutes remain. He must then either skip the last story and go on to the feature (segment 4) or, if he wishes to read the story, cut the feature in order to end at the required 4:13:30. Segments 5 and 6 will then automatically carry the program to 4:14:30.

Because these decisions must be made in a second, without letting the audience become aware of the problem, it is extremely important to time the segments as accurately as possible.

Hand Signals for Television Floor Managers

his cue to begin. The red tally lights on the camera also help him to know when he is on the air. In a sequence involving a camera change, the floor manager should point to the live camera to remind the performer which camera to address.

1. **"Stand by!"** usually accompanies the 30-second "stand-by" cue before the program begins. It also serves to "ready" the performer just before he receives his cue to start.

2. **Like this:** "Cue!" is given in response to the director's signal "Cue talent!" Cue the performer from a position near the camera so that when he receives his cue he will be facing the "taking" lens. Often, when the performer addresses the viewer directly, the director gives his "cue talent" signal first and then "takes" the shot. The performer draws a natural breath and begins just as the camera cuts or dissolves to his picture. This forestalls the momentary frozen look of the performer while he waits for his cue. Another way of achieving this is to have the performer occupied with appropriate "business" (that is, a newscaster looking at his copy) when he receives

3. **Not like this:** In cueing the performer the floor manager should not stand too far away from the camera, obliging the performer to turn his head to receive his cue. The floor manager should also remember that, in a sense, he is introducing the performer. A cue given with a scowl or a frantic look is not likely to help the performer off to a good start.

4. **"One minute!"** alerts the performer to the fact that he has *one minute* to go. The floor manager should give the cue from a position in the performer's direct line of vision so that he does not have to turn his head to observe the signal.

5. **"Half minute!"** cautions the performer to start his concluding remarks, if he hasn't already done so.

6. **"Fifteen seconds!"** Some directors prefer to use a large circular motion of the arm overhead indicating "Wrap it up!"

7. **"Cut!"** means five seconds. Finish your sentence immediately and stop!

8. **"Speed it up!"** is given when the program is running long, and pace must be stepped up to come out on time. Again, when delivering this signal the floor manager should be in the performer's direct line of sight.

9. **"Slow down!"** tells the performer that he is going too fast, or that the program is running short, and he should retard to make up time.

Preparing Title Cards

EACH EXERCISE in this text should be produced as an individual program complete with beginning, middle, and end. In most cases, identifying titles and possibly a workshop insignia are required, with simulated television station call letters. This involves the use of printed or illustrated title cards.

In preparing title cards you are faced with certain limitations in the area on the card available for actual copy. To begin with, there is the 3 by 4 aspect ratio of the television picture. You are further limited by the fact that, because of less than ideal conditions of transmission and reception, the television picture framed on the studio camera (the *scanned area*) is slightly cropped around the border by the time it is viewed on the home receiver. You must take this loss into account when you prepare your title card, confining your lettering and illustrations to what is known as the *safe* or *copy area*.

How is this *copy area* determined? There are several formulas, each slightly different from the others; but they are similar in that they result in generous margins on the title card to insure that the information will come through on the home receiver. The Society of Motion Picture and Television Engineers recommends a simple method, with slight modifications, described as follows:

1. Establish a rectangle with a 3 by 4 aspect ratio in the center of the card. If you use an 11 by 14–inch card,[1] you can do this by marking off an inch of dead space around the entire card and leaving an area of 9 by 12 inches. This is the *scanned area* of your card.

2. Mark off one tenth of the height of the

scanned area with a horizontal line on the top, and another tenth with a horizontal line on the bottom.

3. Mark off one tenth of the length of the *scanned area* with a vertical line on the left side, and another tenth with a vertical line on the right side.

4. This will leave a rectangle centered in the *scanned area* measuring 7.2 by 9.6 inches. If you are using a conventional ruler, the figure can be rounded out to $7\frac{1}{4}$ by $9\frac{1}{2}$ inches. This is your *copy area*.

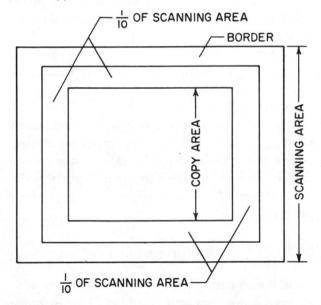

If you wish to make 2 by 2–inch photographic slides to use for film projection on your program, there is detailed information on how to prepare slides in the *Data Book on Slides* of the Eastman Kodak Company. Essentially, slides are made by photographing a title card with a 35–millimeter camera and mounting the film between cover glasses or holders called "ready mounts." The *copy area* on a 2 by 2–inch slide is $\frac{5}{8}$ by $\frac{7}{8}$ inches. For a $3\frac{1}{4}$ by 4–inch slide it is $1\frac{3}{4}$ by $2\frac{3}{8}$ inches.

---

[1] Other standard card sizes are 14 by 17 inches, 14 by 22 inches, and 16 by 20 inches.

Sets for the Beggar's Opera

WHEN YOU PLAN or design a set for television, you face several problems. First, it must include areas for the necessary action. Second, it must provide mobility for cameras, mikes, and crews. Third, it must reflect your interpretation of the mood and style of the drama. Is it complete realism? Is it one of the varieties of selective realism? Is it completely nonobjective? Or is it stylized? Probably your decision on style and mood will come first, after a long study of the script—a study which will also acquaint you with the physical requirements of your set.

It is quite possible that if and when you direct this scene from *The Beggar's Opera* you will use an entirely different set. Our purpose is to show how, in roughly the same area and with the same physical requirements, you can achieve different styles and moods and explain how your style of direction will vary with each.

The scene is a prison cell in an Eighteenth Century London jail. Its basic physical requirements are a sitting area for Macheath; an entrance; an area for a chase, and depth for the composition of pictures with as many as four people.

REALISTIC SET

In the realistic set (p. 283) the set is constructed from flats and columns. The entrance is an arch, open to show the realistic effect of heavy walls. Through the arch we see steps, giving depth to the scene. Behind the window seat is a barred window with a backing flat behind it. The area for Macheath is against one column backed by a "wild" wall.[1] The foreground col-

umn gives perspective and depth to the set from the angle seen in the illustration. However, it is on casters and can be easily moved. This makes it possible for camera and crew to shoot from that position or from a position which the column would otherwise block. With the castered column, wild wall, and angled flats there is not only mobility but, in spite of the relatively small area, also ample opportunity for depth staging and interesting angle shots as well as long shots of entrance and chase.

MODIFIED REALISTIC

The modified realistic set is constructed of realistic set pieces placed against a black duvetyn cyc. There are columns, a door, a window seat, bench and table. The foreground column, again, is castered, and there is a third column in the background to give perspective. The playing areas are essentially the same, but the mood is entirely different. In the first place, lighting is extremely important. The lighting that comes through the window and is seen on the floor gives a sense of tiles because of the barred window. In directing, you can ignore the floor when necessary; but for an opening shot you might wish to use it. The lighting here is also concentrated on the columns and the door and, in itself, outlines the playing areas. In other words, in spite of the castered foreground column, this set provides less mobility of action. In directing on this set you would tend to shoot close, concentrating on shoulder shots and working your depth shots against the barred window or the door.

THE STYLIZED CAMEO SET

The stylized set is built of flats, distorted in size and shape, and set against a cyc that is

---

[1] A "wild" wall is a wall that can be easily and quickly removed to permit camera and crew to shoot from that angle.

Realistic set

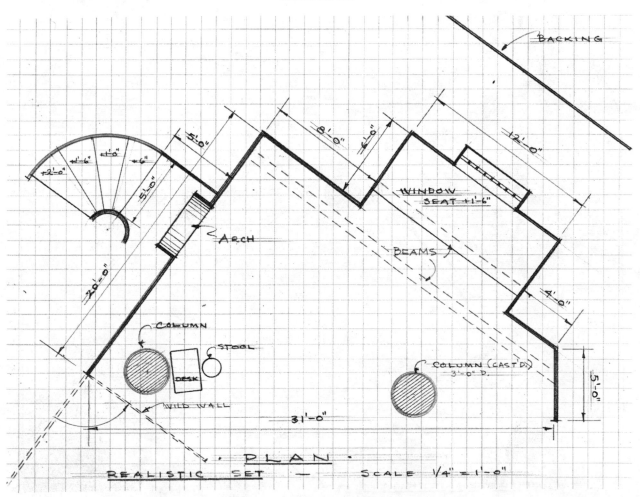

BACKING

WINDOW SEAT +1'-6"

ARCH

BEAMS

COLUMN

STOOL

DESK

WILD WALL

COLUMN (CAST D.)
3'-0" D.

5'-0"

8'-0"

6'-0"

12'-0"

4'-0"

5'-0"

20'-0"

5'-0"

2'-0"

1'-6"

1'-0"

6"

31'-0"

· P L A N ·

REALISTIC SET — SCALE 1/4" = 1'-0"

Modified realistic set

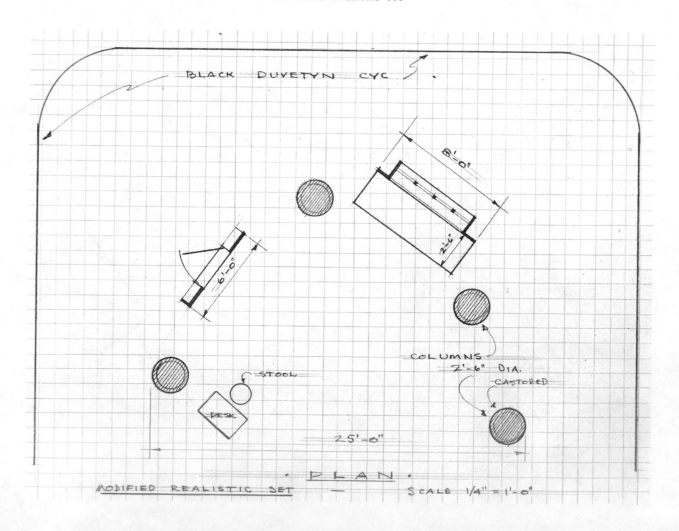

BLACK DUVETYN CYC

COLUMNS
2'-6" DIA.
CASTORED

STOOL

DESK

25'-0"

8'-0"

6'-0"

MODIFIED REALISTIC SET — PLAN. SCALE 1/4" = 1'-0"

Stylized set

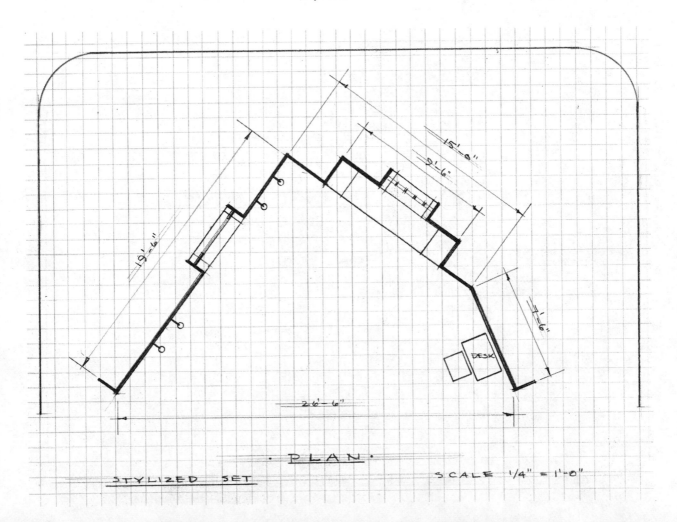

· P L A N ·

Cameo set with light projection

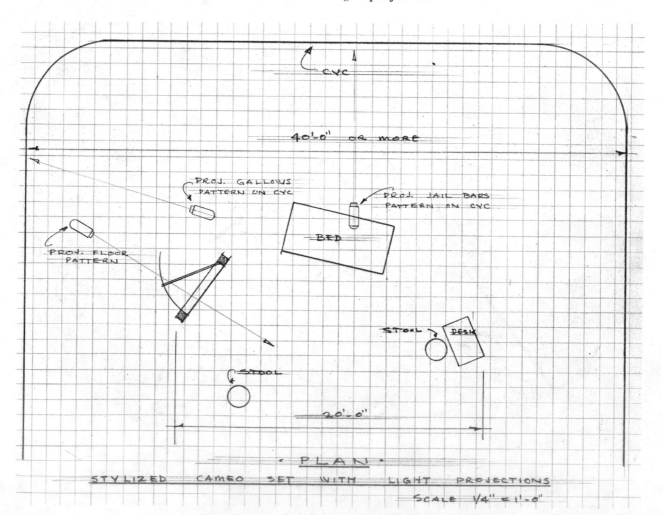

CYC

40'-0" OR MORE

PROJ. GALLOWS
PATTERN ON CYC

PROJ. JAIL BARS
PATTERN ON CYC

BED

PROJ. FLOOR
PATTERN

STOOL ← DESK

STOOL

20'-0"

· P L A N ·

STYLIZED CAMEO SET WITH LIGHT PROJECTIONS

SCALE 1/4" = 1'-0"

equally important for the viewer to see. In the modified realistic set the cyc was an undefined background; here it is essential, because it serves to remind us that this is make-believe. The cameo set is a minimum background for the action, but the essential playing areas are much the same as in the realistic and in the modified realistic sets. There is the stool and the table for Macheath; there is a door for the entrances of Polly, Lucy, and Peachum; there is the barred window and window seat or bed, but there are no columns. In this set columns are not needed; we are not trying to give an illusion of reality, but only a highly stylized suggestion of the area in which the scene is played.

If you choose this type of set, it will be because you wish to emphasize the broader comedy elements of the scene. Bright total lighting will make the cyc clearly visible, and you can stage the chase through the door and around the flat into which the door is built. You may even stage the chase around the entire cameo set, and use the bed or window seat as a change of elevation for your actors. Your cameras will have almost complete mobility here, and your staging in depth will require you to take complete advantage of your cyc.

LIGHT-PROJECTION SET

In the light-projection set, cutouts fitted over ellipsoidal lamps and projected against a black cyc provide the expressionistic suggestion of the prison cell. The only set piece is the door. The light-projected gallows behind the door not only indicate that this is a prison cell, but also provide a back light to silhouette and give the set perspective. This back light helps to establish a nonrealistic style.

In this set, the acting areas are defined by light. Wherever you can put a light on an actor, and focus a camera on him, you have an acting area. If that light temporarily washes out one of the scene projections, do not worry; your actors will simply be in limbo, lighted against black.

Because the set is nonrealistic, your style of direction can exaggerate the comedy of the scene to the point of farce, if you wish. You can take great liberties with your camera for comedy effects, but should avoid unnecessary tricky shots.

Music for the Beggar's Opera

AIR NO. 1

(Macheath)

GREENSLEEVES

Since laws were made for ev— ery de— gree, To

curb vice in oth—ers as well as me, I won—der we han't

bet — ter com—pa— ny, Up— on Ty—burn Tree!— Since

Tree!— But gold from law can take out the sting; And

if rich men like us were to swing, 'Twould

thin the land, such num—bers to string Up—on Ty—burn Tree! But Tree!

288

AIR NO. 2

(Polly and Lucy)   IRISH TROT

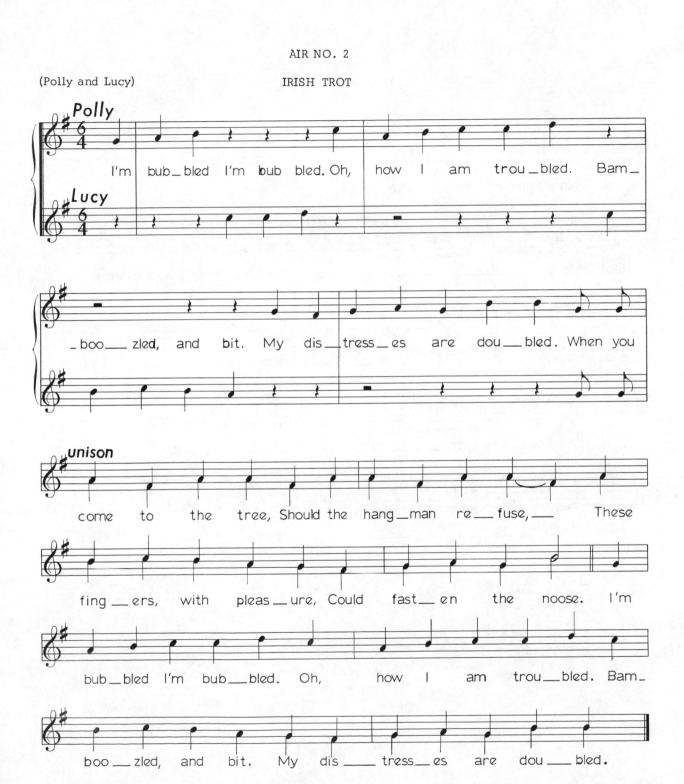

AIR NO. 3

(Polly)   IRISH HOWL

No power on earth can ere di __ vide, The

knot that sa_____ cred love hath tied. When par_ents draw a_

_gainst our mind The true __ love's knot they fast__er bind.

Oh, oh, re, oh, am_bo_rah, Oh, re, oh, am_bo_rah, oh, am_bo_

rah. The knot that sa_____ cred love___ hath___ tied.

AIR NO. 4

(Macheath)

WOULD YOU HAVE A YOUNG VIRGIN

If the heart of a man is de __ pressed with cares, The

mist is dis __ pelled when a wo __ man ap __ pears; Like the

notes of a fid __ dle, she sweet __ ly, sweet __ ly

Rais __ es the spir __ its and charms our ears.

Ros __ es and lil __ ies her cheeks dis __ close,

But her ripe lips are more sweet than those.

Press her ca __ ress her With bliss __ es, Her kiss __ es, Dis __

solve us in pleas __ ure and soft re __ pose.

GLOSSARY

Academy Leader Film numbered in descending order, foot by foot, from 11 to 3 and used for cueing up the attached film in the projector.

A.D. Assistant Director.

Ad Lib Unscripted lines or movement.

Arc Slightly curved dolly in or out.

Aspect Ratio The 4 by 3 ratio of the television picture.

Audio Sound portion of a program.

Audio Engineer Engineer responsible for the sound portion of a program.

Audition A reading or tryout to select performers for a program.

Backlight Lighting placed behind the subject, opposite the camera.

BCU Big close-up; same as ECU and XCU.

BG Abbreviation for background, referring either to sound or picture.

Backing Any form of scenery placed behind a door or window to create the illusion of an adjacent room or of the outside.

Backtiming Timing the length of a program from its end to one or more key points as a means of checking whether the program is running on time; when these points are reached the director can make necessary adjustments if the program is running long or short.

Balance Picture composition that presents a pleasing arrangement of objects. In sound, a satisfying relationship of voices, music, and sound effects.

Barn Doors Hinged flaps, which open like barn doors, attached to spotlights to regulate the light beam.

Base Light General studio illumination.

Blocking Planning the action and movement of performers.

Boom An extension arm for either mike or camera.

Camera Chain Television camera, power supply, and sync generator.

Camera Light A small spotlight mounted on the front of the camera, often called an "inky."

Cheat To move a performer toward an object or another performer that might be at an angle which would not be normal, but which looks natural on the screen.

Close-Up A shot showing an object at very close range.

Composition The harmonious and pleasing arrangement of objects in the picture.

Control Room The room that is the center of control for sound and picture.

Cover Shot A wide angle shot covering a large area of the set.

Crawl A drum which moves titles and graphics in such a way that they seem to be moving slowly up the screen; sometimes used to describe the closing credits.

Credits A listing, usually at the end of the program, giving credit to those who helped to create the program.

CU Close-up.

Cue A cue to start action, usually given by hand.

Cut A direction to stop action; also the deletion of material from a script, and term used to describe a transition from one scene to another by the instantaneous switch from one camera to another.

Cyc Cyclorama; a curved background for a set, sometimes cloth, sometimes painted canvas.

Depth Staging Positioning objects and performers in foreground, middle, and background rather than horizontally.

Dimmer A device to control the brightness of a light.

Dissolve A transition in which the image from one camera momentarily overlaps the image from another, with one gradually disappearing as the other appears.

Distortion In video, an exaggeration of perspective, height, or width; in audio, of the balance of sound.

Dolly A moveable support or platform on which a camera is mounted; also the direction for moving a camera toward an object (dolly in) or away from an object (dolly back).

Downstage   Toward the camera.

Dress   A final rehearsal; also arranging the minor properties which "dress" the set.

Drop   A curtain or hanging dropped from above.

Dry Run   A rehearsal without cameras.

Dubbing   Transferring recorded sound from one medium to another.

Dutchman   A strip of cloth or paper pasted between, or over the crack between two flats.

ECU   Extreme close-up; same as BCU and XCU.

Editing   Selecting and sometimes rearranging portions of a program to achieve the most interesting effect.

Elevation   A true to scale drawing of a set.

Ellipsoidal Spot   A spotlight with an intense directional beam that can be trimmed and shaped by shutters, or fitted with cutouts for light projection effects.

Establishing Shot   A shot, usually a long shot, that establishes the location of a scene by showing all of its essential elements.

Fade   In audio, to change the volume of sound, as *fade up* (gradually increasing volume) and *fade out* (gradually decreasing sound until it is no longer heard). In video, to reduce or increase signal strength, as *fade in* (gradually increasing the brilliance of the image) and *fade out* (gradually reducing the brilliance of the image until it disappears). *Fade to Black* and *Go to Black* are conventional terms for describing the disappearance of the picture at the end of a scene.

Fill Light   A light which fills in or adds additional light to an area of the set which would otherwise be in shadow.

Film Clip   Prerecorded film inserted into a television production.

Flat   In reference to sets, the canvas or cloth covered frames used to represent walls of rooms or other backgrounds. In lighting, an even illumination.

Flip Cards   Title cards changed by rapid flipping off an easel.

Floodlight   A nondirectional and diffused light used to illuminate a set.

Floor   The studio or the studio floor.

Floor Manager   The person in charge of the activities in the studio, taking directions from the director in the control room and relaying them to actors, cameramen, and others on the set.

Floor Men   The crew in charge of physical setup, set dressing; sometimes called stagehands.

Floor Plan   A diagram showing positions of set and set pieces in a studio.

Fluorescent Light   A light produced by mercury vapor electron tubes. To adjust a camera lens for the maximum clarity and sharpness of a picture.

Footage   A length of film; normal speed for 35mm film is 90 feet per minute, for 16mm 36 feet per minute.

Footcandle   A light measurement based on the amount of light thrown by one candle on an object one foot away.

Frame   The area of each individual picture.

Frame-Up   A direction to cameraman to center the picture or position it within the normal area of the screen.

Friction Head   A mounting head on a camera that counterbalances it by a strong spring.

f-Stop   The ratio between the focal length of a lens and the diameter of its iris or diaphragm opening; the larger the marked f-stop, the smaller the opening, and the smaller the f-stop, the larger the opening.

Go to Black   A direction to fade the picture to total blackness.

Graphics   Cards with printed information and/or illustrations; usually used for titles.

Grey Scale   The degrees of shades between white and black which can be reproduced by television cameras.

Group Shot   A shot framed to show a group of people.

Headroom   The space between a performer's head and the top of the set. Also the space seen on the screen between the top of the performer's head and the top of the screen.

High Key   A brilliantly lighted set with few shadows.

Hold   A direction to a cameraman to hold his position as it is.

Hot   A camera or microphone that is turned on; also an object too brilliantly lighted.

Hot Spot   A portion of the picture in which there is too much light.

Idiot Sheet   A sheet or card lettered with lines or cues and placed out of camera range, but within easy view of performer.

Image   The picture transmitted by the camera.

Image Orthicon An extremely sensitive television camera, often referred to as an IO.

Incandescent Light A very brilliant light produced by filaments.

Key The lighting treatment of a set in terms of brightness.

Key Light The main source of illumination on any area of a set.

Kine Abbreviation for kinescope, and often used to refer to a recording filmed from a kinescope.

Kinescope The cathode ray television tube.

Lead-In An introduction to any scene or segment of a program.

Lens The eye of the camera that picks up rays of light from a scene and projects them as an image.

Lens Turret The revolving mount on the front of a camera, holding up to four lenses which can be rotated into position for shots.

Level The volume or intensity of sounds or voices; also the intensity of light on a set.

Lighting The illumination of a set.

Light Level Intensity of illumination expressed in footcandles.

Light Plan A sheet indicating sources of lights and direction of beams.

Limbo An undefined background, often a dark cyc, against which actors and props are lighted.

Lip Sync Synchronization of lip movements of an actor with spoken lines that have been recorded separately.

Live In sound, a satisfying amount of reverberation, neither too brilliant (too live) nor too dull (dead). In production, a program broadcast at the time it is performed.

Loosen A direction to a cameraman to get a broader picture, either by moving the camera or by changing the lens.

Low Key Illumination of low intensity with a predominance of dark areas.

Modeling Light A light usually placed to the front and side of an object or performer to accentuate contours and increase the illusion of depth.

Monitor An instrument for receiving the television picture in the control room during rehearsals and broadcast to check quality of broadcast and picture composition. Sometimes used as a verb, meaning the act of checking.

MS Medium shot, a relative term meaning a shot somewhere between close and long.

Off-Camera A performer is heard but not seen on the screen; sometimes referred to as Off-Screen but most often as VO (Voice Over).

One-Shot A shot which shows only one person.

Over-Shoulder Shot A shot from behind and over the shouder of a performer.

Pan Abbreviation for panoramic. To move the camera horizontally across the scene.

Pedestal A wheeled camera mount with a hydraulically operated lift to raise or lower the camera.

Perspective In sound, the apparent distance from which a voice or sound is heard as related to the action on the screen. In picture, the illusion of depth, sometimes created by painted flats, sometimes by camera angles.

POV Abbreviation for point of view, referring to the position in the scene from which the camera shows a given character's view of it.

Producer The person in charge of organization, administration, and usually of the finances of a program or series.

Props Abbreviation for properties, the furniture and decorations for sets, and the small articles carried and used by performers, usually referred to as Hand Props.

Provisional Cut A tentative cut marked near the end of a script for use if a show runs long.

Rear Screen Projection A previously photographed slide or motion picture background projected from the rear on a translucent screen. The television camera photographs actors performing in front of the screen, giving the illusion that they are in the projected background.

Rim Light The same as back light.

RP Abbreviation for Rear Screen Projection.

Riser A movable platform used to raise the positions of actors or props in relation to the camera, for more satisfying picture composition.

Running Time The time from the beginning of a show to any particular point noted while the production is in progress.

Run-Through A rehearsal.

Scanning The movement of the electron beam as it scans each line of the picture from left to right.

Scanning Area The area of a picture that is picked up by camera and monitors; it is larger than the area of the picture seen on the home television screen.

Scenery The flats, walls, curtains, drops, cyc, or

rear screen projection which create a setting for a scene.

Scoop   A floodlight.

Set   The playing area and scenery for one program or scene.

Shading   The control of black and white levels of the picture.

Signal   Picture or sound transmitted electronically.

Signature   A picture, usually accompanied by music or sound which identifies a series or commercial.

Slide   A transparency projected by transmitted light through a special projector and picked up by the television camera.

Sound Effects   The live or recorded sounds that give the effect of occurring at the time of the accompanying action.

Spotlight   A light that focuses a sharp beam on a specific object or spot.

Stand By   A verbal cue to be ready to go on the air within seconds.

Stock Shot   A film of some easily recognizable place (the Empire State building) or activity (a plane taking off) previously photographed to help establish a locale.

Story Board   A series of sketches with minimal dialogue to indicate the high or key points of a program.

Stretch   A direction to performers to slow down.

Strike   To take down a set.

Strip Lights   Lights attached in a row of six to eight in a housing equipped with a reflector. Usually used to light a cyc, but can be used either suspended or on the floor for special effects.

Super   An abbreviation for superimposition.

Superimposition   Two pictures seen simultaneously on the same screen.

Switcher   The panel controlling the instantaneous electronic cutting from one panel to another. Occasionally used to identify the individual who punches the buttons that operate the panel.

Sync   Abbreviation for synchronization.

Take   To televise a scene which, when completed is called a "take." Also a direction to switch on a camera, "Take one!" or "Take it down!" Commonly used to call for a break in a rehearsal, "Take five!"

Talent   Actors and all other performers.

Talkback   A noun describing the speaker in the control room through which the director can talk back to the performers in the studio during rehearsal.

Tally Light   A small red light on the front of the camera; when it is lit, the camera is on the air.

T.D.   Technical Director. The individual responsible for all the engineering aspects of the program.

Telescene Room   The studio equipped to project motion pictures or stills for a broadcast.

Teleprompter   An electrically operated piece of equipment placed on or near cameras, which unrolls a performer's lines in oversized type.

Three-Shot   A shot showing three people in a scene.

Tilt   To move the camera up or down.

Title Drum   A device, usually in the shape of a cylinder, to rotate title smoothly.

Transition   The means used to go from one sequence to another, such as fade or wipe.

Traveler   A curtain placed in position by being moved across the stage rather than dropped from above.

Trimming   Adjusting a light.

Truck   To move the camera parallel to the action or scene rather than toward it or away from it.

Two-Shot   A shot showing two people in a scene.

Upstage   Away from the camera.

Video   Picture portion of a program.

Video Engineer   Engineer responsible for picture portion of the program.

Video Tape Recorder   An electronic machine for recording with magnetic tape.

Vidicon   A small camera tube, less sensitive to light than the Image Orthicon, frequently used for closed circuit broadcasts in colleges and, increasingly, for special broadcasts in the industry.

View-Finder   A small television receiver mounted on the camera to permit the cameraman to see the picture he is shooting.

Visuals   All forms of graphics and all other illustrative materials.

VO   Voice over; the performer's voice is heard but he is not seen on the screen.

VTR   Video tape recording.

Wipe   A transition that gives the effect of one picture pushing the other off the screen.

XCU   Extreme close-up; same as BCU and ECU.

Zoom   The effect achieved by a special lens, making it seem as though the camera is moving very swiftly to or away from an object.

Zoomar   Name of the most widely used zoom lens.

Index

Above-the-line costs, 63, 243
Academy leader, 49
Acoustics, 3
Acting, 72–84
Allen, Steve, 36
Angle supports, 4
Arc, 10
Aspect ratio, 19, 281
Assistant director, 6, 70
Audience testing, 11
Audio assistant, 6
Audio console, 6
Audio engineer, 6
Audio monitor, 6
Audition copy, 259–268
Auditions, 65, 259
Background, 15
Back light, 21
Back timing, 36, 276
Balance, 14
Base light (see General light), 21
Basic floor plan, 4, 248
BCU, 10, 14
Beam Parabolic Spotlight, 22
Beggar's Opera, The, 177
Below-the-line costs, 63, 243
Benny, Jack, 12
Big close-up, 10, 14
Blocking, 15, 69
"Blue plate special" make-up, 24
Boom dolly, 7
Boom microphone, 67
Budget, 63, 243–244
Camera, 7–11, 271–272
Camera control unit, 5
Camera lenses, 8–9
Camerman, 11
Camera monitors, 5
Camera mount, 7
Camera movement, 10, 11
Camera position, 9–10, 12
Canted shot, 17
Casting, 65
"C" clamps, 4
"Cheat," 15
Cherry Orchard, The, 117
Choral program, 53–60
Close-up, 9–13
Close-up lens, 8

Composition, 13–19, 66–67
Control room, 5–6
"Cover" shot, 11
Cradle head, 8
Creme-Puff, 24
Cueing procedures, 271–272
Cues, 12, 30, 49
Cut, 6, 12
Cutter, 11
Cyclorama, 4, 282, 287
Depth of field, 9
Depth staging, 15, 66, 72–73
Director, 6, 47–49, 53–54, 63–73
Dissolve, 6, 12–13
Doll's House, A, 134
Dolly, 10, 11
Dolly-in, 11
Dolly-out, 11
Door flat, 4
Drama, 86
Dress rehearsal, 70
Editing, 11–13
Ellipsoidal floodlight, 23
Ellipsoidal spotlight, 20, 22
"Establishing" shot, 8
"Eye light," 23
Fades, 6, 12–13
Field of view, 7
Fill light, 21
Film production, compared to TV, 11
Flats, 4
Floodlight, 20
Floor manager, 64
Floor plan, 4, 64, 248, 283–286
Fluorescent light, 20
Focus, 9
Follow shot, 10
Footage, 11
Footcandle, 21
Foreground, 15
Frame, 9, 13, 69–70
"Fresnel," 20, 22
Friction head, 8
Frogs, The, 87
F-stop, 9
Full shot, 10
General light (see also Base light), 21
Graphics, 47–48, 253, 281, 291
Gray scale, 4, 21

Group shot, 15
Hand signals, 277–281
High key lighting, 21
IATSE, 20
Image inverter, 16
Image Orthicon (IO), 7, 8
Incandescent light, 20
Incident light meter, 21
Intercom, 6
Interrogation, 188
Interview techniques, 35–36
"Kleig" spotlight (see "Leko"), 20
Knee shot, 10
Lead with camera, 10, 66
Leko spotlight (see "Kleig"), 20
Lenses, 7–9
Lens turret, 8
Light
  in composition, 15
  in make-up, 23–24
  in set design, 282–287
Light readings, 21
Lighting, 20–23, 282–287
Lighting control board, 6
Long shot, 8–10
"Loose" shot, 14
Make-up, 23–25
Make-up list, 25
Matched dissolve, 13
Mattes, 20
Medium shot, 9
Middle ground, 15
Mock-up camera, 7
Molière Story, The, 153
Monitor
  audio, 6
  film and camera, 5
Multiplexer, 5
Music (also see newscast), 67
Newscast techniques, 47–52
Off-screen, 14
One-shot, 10, 14
"On-the-air," 6
Opaque projector, 5
Overhead shot, 17
Over-shoulder shot, 15
Pace, 10
Pan, 10
Panel discussion techniques, 41
PAR64 lamp, 21
Perspective, 7
Preplanning, 11–12, 19
Production check list, 243
Production schedule, 256–258
Projection room, 5
Quartz light, 20, 21

Reaction shot, 12
Rear projection screen, 3
Rear projector, 4–5
Rehearsals, 29–30, 60–71
Remote pick-up, 7
Repetition rate, 5
Running time, 16, 276
Scale models, 4
Scan, 10
Scanning area, 17, 281
Scoop, 20
Script form, 29
Script marking, 271–275
Segment time, 276
Set design, 15, 249, 282–287
Sets, 4–5
Shot sequence, 10
Shoulder shot, 10
Shutters, 20
Slide projector, 5
Slides, 5, 281
Sound effects, 6, 67
Sound proofing, 3
Space, in studio, 3
  in composition, 17–18
  in control room, 6
Special effects, 4
Spiral pan, 9
Spotlight, 20
Step transformer, 21
Striplights, 23
Studio, 3–5
"Super," 13
Supercomposition, 9, 12–13
Switching unit, 5
"Talk back" microphone, 6
Taming of the Shrew, The, 101
Tape recorder, 6
Technical director, 6
Three-inch lens, 8
"Tight" shot, 10, 13
Timing, 36, 276
Title cards, 281
Truck, 10
Turntables, 6
T 24 lamp, 21
Two-shot, 10, 15
"Unmask," 25
Video control engineer, 6
Video tape, 5, 12
Vidicon camera, 7–8
Waist shot, 9–10
Wide angle shot, 9
"Wild" wall, 282
Zoom lens, 8–9